# Theban Ostraca

Edited from the originals, now mainly in the Royal Ontario museum of archaeology, Toronto, and the Bodleian library, Oxford

Alan H. Gardiner, Herbert Thompson
J. G. Milne

Alpha Editions

This edition published in 2019

ISBN : 9789353952297

Design and Setting By
**Alpha Editions**
email - alphaedis@gmail.com

University of Toronto Studies

# THEBAN OSTRACA

EDITED FROM THE ORIGINALS, NOW MAINLY IN THE ROYAL ONTARIO MUSEUM OF ARCHAEOLOGY, TORONTO, AND THE BODLEIAN LIBRARY, OXFORD


PART I. HIERATIC TEXTS: BY ALAN H. GARDINER

PART II. DEMOTIC TEXTS: BY HERBERT THOMPSON

PART III. GREEK TEXTS: BY J. G. MILNE

PART IV. COPTIC TEXTS: BY HERBERT THOMPSON



UNIVERSITY OF TORONTO LIBRARY

London: Humphrey Milford

Oxford University Press

1913

# PREFATORY NOTE

THE ostraca which are published in this volume have been selected from a large collection obtained in 1906 by Mr. J. G. Milne and myself in the neighbourhood of Thebes. As we practically bought up the whole stocks of one or two native excavators, in addition to making more discriminating purchases from other dealers, a good many of the pieces are of little interest. But, after all deductions of fragmentary, illegible, and unimportant examples, there remains a considerable proportion of the collection which offers material of permanent value for students of the history or language of Egypt. After the preliminary sorting of the potsherds, we secured the assistance of Dr. Alan Gardiner and Sir Herbert Thompson for the work of editing the texts in the native language; and the University of Toronto undertook to publish the volume.

The collection has now been divided, and about half the texts included in this volume will be found in the Royal Ontario Museum of Archaeology at Toronto, while most of the remainder will, I understand, be deposited in the Bodleian Library at Oxford.

C. T. CURRELLY.

# I

# HIERATIC TEXTS

| NOS. | |
|---|---|
| A. 1–10. | LITERARY TEXTS. |
| B. 1–18. | BUSINESS DOCUMENTS. |
| C. 1–2. | RELIGIOUS TEXTS. |
| D. 1. | ROMAN PERIOD. |

# INTRODUCTION

Among the ostraca acquired in Egypt by Messrs. Currelly and Milne but few are inscribed in hieratic characters, and these are without great importance. Nevertheless in their subject-matter they are a fairly representative collection, the epistolary being the only common class of text of which there is no specimen. Among the literary ostraca (A) there are fragments of two Egyptian books which for their popularity in the Rameside period deserve to be considered classics, namely the *Satire on the Professions* and the *Instruction of King Amenemmes I to his son.* Of the business documents (B) most are fragments of journals and accounts; dry as isolated texts of this kind may seem, in bulk they afford us a comprehensive picture of the daily practical concerns of the population that dwelt in the Theban Necropolis. The religious texts (C) consist of a fine magical spell, the most valuable accession to our knowledge contained in the series; and a fragment naming several places where Thoth was worshipped. All these texts are of Ramesside date; there is also a tiny potsherd (D 1) with part of a hymn dating from the Roman period.

# A. LITERARY TEXTS

**A 1.** Fragment of an Earthenware Pot, height 15–16 cm., greatest breadth 15 cm. The text, about thirteen lines in a good Ramesside hand, is very much rubbed, the following words being all that is legible :—

1. . . . . . . 

2. . . . 

3. . . . . . . . . . . . . . . . .  . . . . . . . . .

Probably an extract from an unknown literary text, to the subject of which there is no clear clue.

**A 2.** Limestone Fragment, height 15·5 cm., greatest breadth 11 cm. Inscribed on both sides in the same large, careless, Ramesside hand; the *recto* has preserved only the beginnings, the *verso* only the ends, of the lines. Red verse-points.

*Recto.*

1. 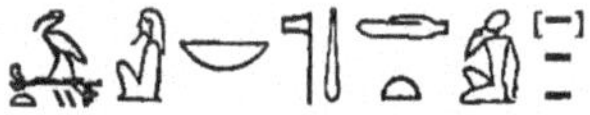 blank

2.  . . . . . .

3.  . . . . . . . . . . . . . . . . .

4.  . . . . . . . . . . . . . . .

*Verso.*

(Rest blank.)

Perhaps the beginning of a lost book of didactic nature. Why the scribe wrote the words 'Thoth, master of the hieroglyphs' in *recto* 1 is not clear. Lines 2–3 give the normal beginning of a book of this kind:—'Beginning of the instruction which a man made for [his] son. . . . [Give] thy heart to that which I say to thee; act according to. . . .' The remaining lines of the *recto* are too fragmentary to be intelligible. Note the rare word *snm* 'grief' in 7, as also above in A **1**. 2. The *verso* is no less obscure than the *recto*; we appear to have the ends of the lines complete. In 4 there is the trace of a date ('. . . day 13'), being the usual memorandum of the scribe as to when the following words were written. Then follows a sentence of proverbial (?) nature, 'He who is free from changes is a lord of wealth'; at this point the text comes abruptly to an end.

**A 3.** LIMESTONE, inscribed on one side only in a large Ramesside literary hand. Red verse-points. Height 16 cm., breadth 16 cm.

*x* lines lost.

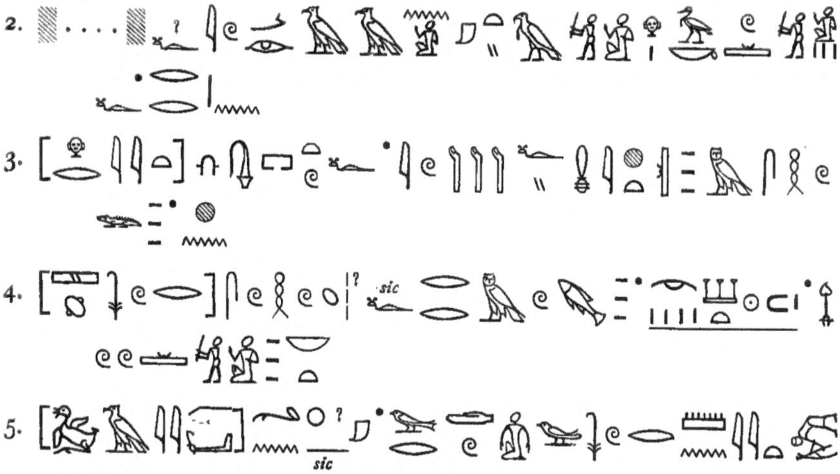

6.  Remainder of stone blank.

We have here an excerpt from the *Satire on the Professions*, of all Egyptian writings perhaps the most popular in the Ramesside schools. The text, which is fairly good, corresponds to *Sallier II*, 4, 6–9. In line 4 is a date of the kind mentioned in the notes on A 2.

**A 4.** POTSHERD, 7·5 cm. high and 12·5 cm. broad, inscribed on one side in a literary hand of the New Kingdom. Red verse-points. Incomplete in every direction.

An enumeration of minerals, obviously taken from a literary exercise of the kind known from the *Papyrus Koller* or *Anastasi IV*. This particular text appears to be unknown, and *ʾi-r-ḫ* in line 2 is a ἅπαξ λεγόμενον.

**A 5.** Fragment (8 cm. high, 10 cm. broad) of a limestone tablet that was flat on each side and rounded at the edges. Complete at top only. Literary hand of the New Kingdom, with red verse-points.

*Recto.*

*x* lines lost.

*Verso.*

*x* lines lost.

Taken from a lost didactic or gnomic work. In lines 3 and 5 of the *recto* are traces of dates. Note the following expressions and sentences:—*recto* 2, 'the ears are deaf,' read *'id* (?); 3, 'thou art rich, thou art . . . (*mʿ* is probably corrupt), thou passest thy life in . . .'; 4, 'he who is without a name shall find honour,' lit. 'he who is void of his name (shall be) for a revered one'; 5, 'hale (*wd*) of limbs is he who . . .'; *verso* 2, 'do not relax thy heart (i. e. attention), long be thy silence (?)'; 3, 'according to his deserts.'

**A 6.** Limestone, with rough surface, much worn; height 9·5 cm., breadth 12·5 cm. Large uncial Ramesside hand. The text, which might be derived from a hymn, is very fragmentary and void of all interest. The word  in line 4 is perhaps worth noting.

**A 7.** Potsherd, 5·5 cm. × 9·5 cm., with the following words in large cursive hieroglyphs:—

'I [came?], I carried off Cret[ans] . . .'

**A 8.** Irregular Red Potsherd, with some words in a big literary hand of the nineteenth dynasty; 9 × 9·5 cm. Line 1 . . . .   . . . 'like Min the son of . . .'; line 2, . . .   . . . . . 'child of'; line 3, undecipherable.

**A 9.** Limestone Fragment (12·5 × 6 cm.), with the ends of seven lines in a Ramesside literary hand; in no line are there more than three words left. Duplicate of *Millingen* 2, 5–2, 9 (the instruction of king Amenemhet I to his son) without any variants of interest.

**A 10.** Small Limestone Flake, with a few signs, written vertically, in cursive hieroglyphs of uncertain date. Line 1, . . . 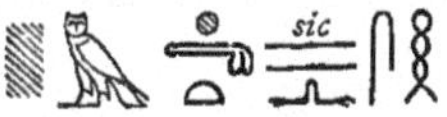  . . .; line 2, . . .  . . .

## B. BUSINESS DOCUMENTS

**B 1.** Small Fragment of Limestone (6 × 4 cm.), inscribed in hieratic of the New Kingdom (possibly Dyn. 18) on one side only. Broken on the left side.

'Amount of dates of the first month of winter, sacks . . . . Made into . . . . . (?), $\frac{3}{4}$ of a sack. Expended, second month of winter [. . . . sacks]. Day 17, 4 sacks. Total . . . . .'

Memoranda for a journal recording receipts and consumption of dates.

**B 2.** Limestone (9 × 6 cm.). A few half-illegible words of uncertain meaning.

**B 3.** Fragment of Smooth Pot (Canopus?), with the isolated word  in hieratic.

**B 4.** Limestone Fragment (6·5 × 13 cm.), with a few Ramesside hieratic signs. Accounts, without interest.

**B 5.** Upper Portion of Cream-coloured Oil-jar, inscribed in good hieratic characters with the following words:—

'Year 26, oil of the garden [of . . . . (?) king] Rameses II . . . .'

**B 6.** LIMESTONE (6 × 7 cm.), with fragments of accounts (of beer delivered ?):—

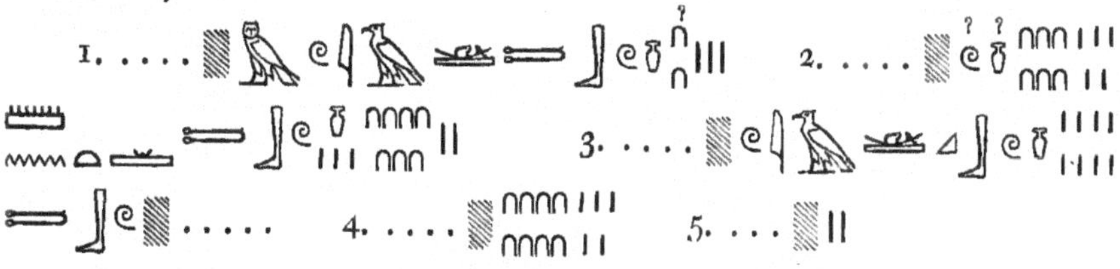

'[Day . . . ., by the hand of Amen]emuia, *ṯb*-jars, 23. . . . . 65, remaining, *ṯb*-jars, 72. . . . . [Amenem]uia, *ḳb*-jars 8, *ṯb*-jars . . . . . . . . 85. . . . . 2.'

The combination '*ḳb*-jars, *ṯb*-jars' is found elsewhere, e.g. the *Papyrus Chabas-Lieblein* at Turin.

**B 6** *bis.* LIMESTONE SLAB (17·5 × 14 cm.), inscribed on both sides in a XXth Dyn. business hand; much rubbed and to a great extent illegible. *Recto*, journal entries from day 27 to day 6 of the next month; in line 1  shows that the figures in the following lines refer to '*Šʿy*-cakes'; note that 'last day' (of the month) is written  (*sic*). A second shorter column appears to give the month's totals:—

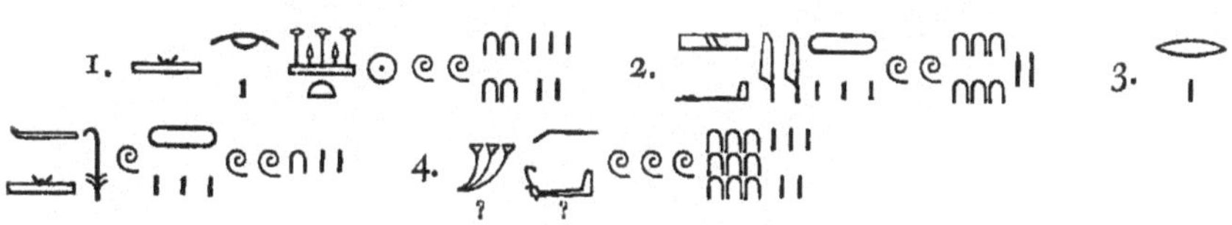

'Total, first month of Inundation, 245. *Šʿy*-cakes, 262. *R-ḥ-s*-cakes, 212. Vegetables, bundles 395.'

The *verso* consists of similar accounts, almost wholly undecipherable.

**B 7.** BROKEN POTSHERD (7 × 5·5 cm.), with parts of several lines in a legible Ramesside business hand.

. . . . *x* lines lost.

'. . . . the workman . . . ., left over, 20 bundles. Right hand. . . . Total of all the supplies (?), total, bundles. . . . Left hand, head workman of the workmen . . . . . . -mose . . . . . .'

From the accounts of the gangs of workmen belonging to the Theban Necropolis. The word 'bundles' (*ḥrš*) makes it probable that 'vegetables' (*sm*) are the commodity here in question. The words *wnmy* and *smḥy* are an as yet unsolved puzzle; they refer in some way to a twofold division of the workmen, but it is not easy to suggest an exact meaning for 'right hand' and 'left hand' here; so too in the Turin papyri, *passim*. *H̱ȝw nb* in line 4 is a not quite common expression.

**B 7** *bis*. LIMESTONE CHIP (6·5 × 4 cm.), inscribed in a Ramesside hand.

Perhaps the fragment of a letter. The name of a fish *ḳiꜣ* in line 4 seems legible enough, but the word is unknown.

**B 8.** LIMESTONE (10 × 9 cm.), incomplete. Ramesside accounts recording the deliveries of fish by various scribes. Of the seven lines preserved in part, line 6 is the most complete and may be restored as

follows: [hieroglyphs]
'Received from the Scribe Pentwer, fish 400 *dbn.*' The first five lines
follow the same scheme, but lines 1 (?), 2, 3, and 4 replace the scribe
Pentwer by [hieroglyphs] '[the scribe] Amenōne';
line 7 is an incomplete total of the fishes delivered. On the *verso* are
faint traces of similar accounts; the words [hieroglyphs]
show that the word for 'fish' is to be read *rm* throughout.

**B 9.** A THICK SLAB OF LIMESTONE, 15 cm. high by 10 cm. broad,
inscribed in uncial Ramesside characters; broken at the top, and chipped
on the right-hand side:—

1. [hieroglyphs]   2. [hieroglyphs]
[hieroglyphs]   3. [hieroglyphs] *space*   4. [hieroglyphs]
5. [hieroglyphs]

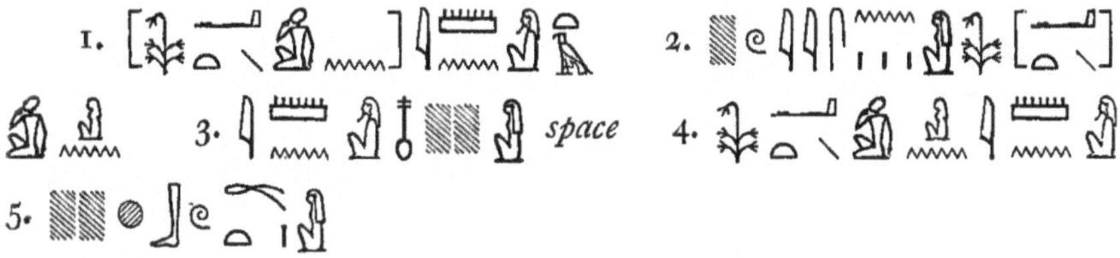

These lines contained the names of three 'chantresses of Amon', all of them
now partly illegible. The *verso* has faint traces of a similar text.

**B 10.** AN INCOMPLETE FRAGMENT OF LIMESTONE (9 × 9 cm.)
inscribed in a business hand of the Ramesside period.

*Recto.* 1. [hieroglyphs]
2. [hieroglyphs] 3. [hieroglyphs]
[hieroglyphs] (perhaps no other line is lost). *Verso.* 1. [hieroglyphs]
[hieroglyphs] *blank* 2. [hieroglyphs] *space* [hieroglyphs]
[hieroglyphs] *blank* 3. [hieroglyphs]

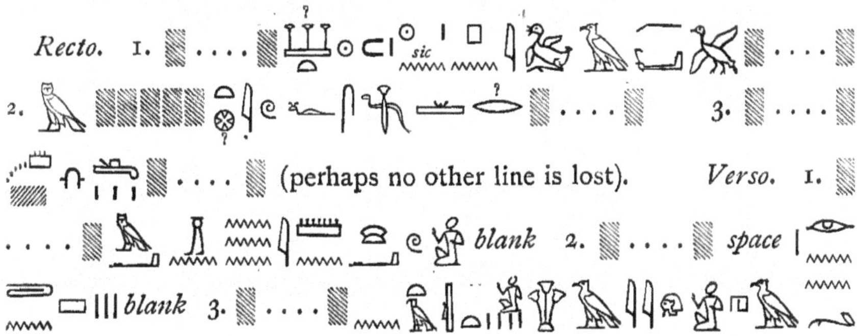

 *blank*

(Probably this was the end.)

This fragmentary text clearly refers to a bargain or dispute about the loan of an ass; several ostraca of a similar kind are known. The parties concerned are the choachyte Amenkhow and the workman Hay.

**B 11.** A Greyish-brown Potsherd, 11·5 × 10 cm., inscribed in a XXth Dyn. hand. The beginnings of nine lines seem to be journal entries of the ordinary type, not worth recording *in extenso*. The name  occurs twice.

**B 12.** A Worthless Grey-brown Potsherd with some undecipherable words in a Ramesside hand.

**B 13.** A Fragment of Limestone with rough convex surface, 12 × 10 cm. The text consists of two columns of proper names in a small and difficult cursive writing dating from perhaps the XXIst or XXIInd Dynasty. Among the legible names are the following:—(1, 10) 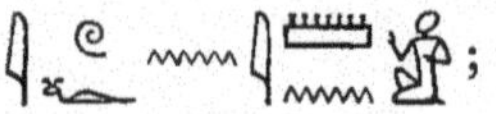; (1, 11) ; (2, 2)  

**B 14.** Limestone, measuring 23 × 15 cm. Badly-damaged accounts of the XIXth or XXth Dynasty. The text does not merit reproduction as a whole, but the following items deserve notice: (l. 5) ....  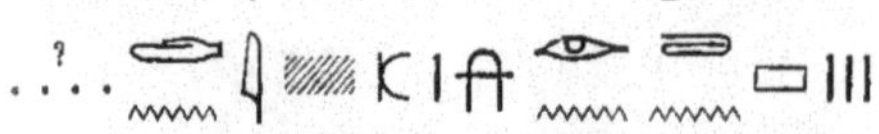 '.... a basket, value 3 *dbn*'; (l. 7 and l. 12) 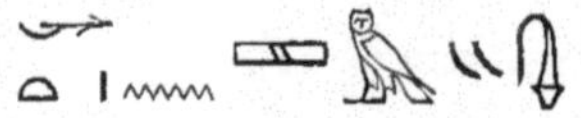 'wood for burning'; (l. 11 and l. 13) 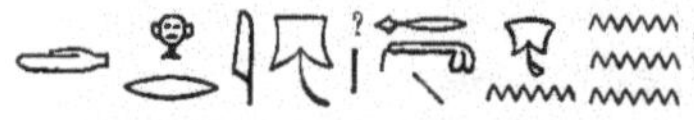 'one donkey-skin for water'.

**B 15.** A Worthless Yellow Potsherd with a few words from a business (?) text. N. K.

**B 16.** A SMALL POTSHERD with the words ‘its deficit on the last day of the month’.

**B 17.** A SMALL LIMESTONE FLAKE with some rather obscure fragments of temple accounts; the word *smd-t* seems here to have the exceptional spelling

**B 18.** A ROUGH-SURFACED RED-BROWN POTSHERD (9 × 8 cm.); the hieratic words upon it probably belong to the label of a jar for wine or oil; the only legible signs are:—1. . . . . . . . . . . . 2. . . . . . . . .

## C. RELIGIOUS TEXTS.

**C 1.** A VALUABLE LIMESTONE OSTRACON, complete at top and on the right; the other sides are damaged. Inscribed on one side only in an uncial Ramesside hand; the surface available for writing measures 21 × 11 cm.

[1] might possibly be , and an *n*.

[2] These signs look more like , but *ʿwy* must surely be the right reading; at its first occurrence the word is of still more doubtful reading, the surface being very rough.

..... *x* lines lost.

'Get thee back, thou enemy, thou dead man or woman (and so forth) who dost cause pain to N the son of M .... his flesh. Thou dost not fall upon him, thou dost not establish thyself in him. Thy head has no power over his head. Thy arms have no power over

[1] So more probably than .

[2] *Mnd* a little doubtful.

[3] (apparently so) added above line; this can only mean that should be read in place of .

[his] arms, [thy legs?] have no power [over his legs?]. No limbs of thine have power over any limbs of his. Thou fallest not upon him, so that suffering befall him. Thou hast no power over his toes, so that there be. . . . Thou weighest not ⟨upon⟩ his flesh, so that there be aught wherewith his limbs are burdened. Thou pressest not upon his breast, so that there be blood (?). Thou enterest not into [his . . ., so that there be . . . .] in it. Thou dost not take up thy position on his back, so that there is injury to his spine. Thou dost not cleave to his buttocks, so that there is *sḥsḥy*[*t*?]. [Thou dost not . . .] his legs, so that there is retreat. Thou dost not enter into his phallus, so that it grows limp. Thou dost not cast seed into [his] anus (?) . . . Thou hast no power over his toes, so that thou impedest him (?). Thou dost not press upon [his] fingers . . ., thou dost not [blind] his eyes, thou dost not deafen his ears, [thou] hast no power . . .

This is a singularly clear and simple spell for the prevention of disease. The demon is directly invoked and bidden to be gone; various possibilities of attack are then enumerated in turn, it being denied in each case that the demon is able to force an entrance by this channel. Of special interest are the statements 'thy head has no power over his head' and the following, as they contain a somewhat novel application of the magical adage that like influences like. The text is not quite free from mistakes; in line 4  must be inserted after *dns-k*, and for 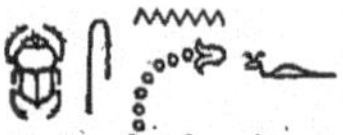 we should probably emend 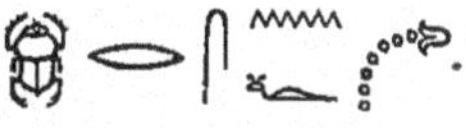. In line 6 *ḥnḥn* lacks its usual determinative , and the suffix *f* ought to be supplied after *ḥnn*. In line 7 the final *ḥ* of *sꜣḥ* has dropped out. The only unknown word is *sḥsḥy*[*t*] in line 5.

**C 2.** LIMESTONE (8·5 × 13 cm.), inscribed on both sides with large uncial writing of the New Kingdom. Complete only on the right side and at bottom.

*Recto.* Column 1. *x* lines lost.

1. 

2. 

3. 

4. 

5. 

6. 

Column 2 (separated from col. 1 by a thick curved line). *x* lines lost.

1.  ....

2. 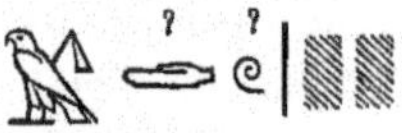 ....

3.  ....

*Verso.* Very obscure signs written in red.

The *recto* enumerates (for what purpose is not clear) a number of towns in which offerings were made to Thoth. The formula throughout is 'Offerings (*wdnw*) to Thoth in . . .' (name of town). The places mentioned are Schmun (?), Cusae, Bubastis, Meir, *'Inbw* and *Ḥ;t-k;-k;*-[*k* ?]. What town is meant by *'Inbw* is uncertain; the place-name *Ḥ;t-k;-k;*-[*k* ?] occurs in the Golenischeff Vocabulary somewhere between Ptolemais and Aphroditopolis; in the Medinet Habu list it occurs is a similar position, the local deity being 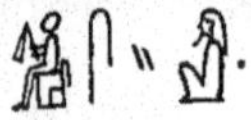. Of col. 2 of the *recto*, and of the signs on the *verso* I can make no sense.

## D. ROMAN PERIOD.

**D 1.** A POTSHERD OF RED WARE with fragments of five lines in hieratic of the Roman period, giving parts of a hymn. Without interest.

[1] It is doubtful whether  was ever written.

# APPENDIX

At the last moment it has been found possible to include in our volume a record of one of the largest and best-preserved hieratic ostraca in existence. This stone belongs to the Toronto Museum, and became available for study in England only in September, 1912, when the earlier portions of the book were already printed off.

**A 11.** Slab of Limestone, height 54 cm., greatest breadth 28 cm. Incomplete at the top of *recto* = bottom of *verso*. Inscribed on both sides in a practised but careless literary hand, the signs varying considerably as to both size and thickness in different parts of the text. The writing is of Ramesside date, and closely resembles that of an ostracon in Berlin (P 12337 = *Hierat. Pap.* III. 31). Red verse-points, and a rubric at the conclusion of the *recto*. In front of the twelfth and following lines of the *verso* there are written a few epistolary phrases. These in some cases join up so closely with the text proper of the *verso* as to appear continuous with it.

The subject-matter is a collection of four model letters, such as are familiar to us in the Anastasi, Sallier, and other papyri; such 'Complete Letter-writers' are among the commonest varieties of text found on hieratic ostraca. The spelling and the readings are here throughout extremely corrupt, and it is not always possible to discern the intended meaning. In order to facilitate the study of the ostracon, critical notes giving what I believe to be the true readings are added to the notes on the hieratic.

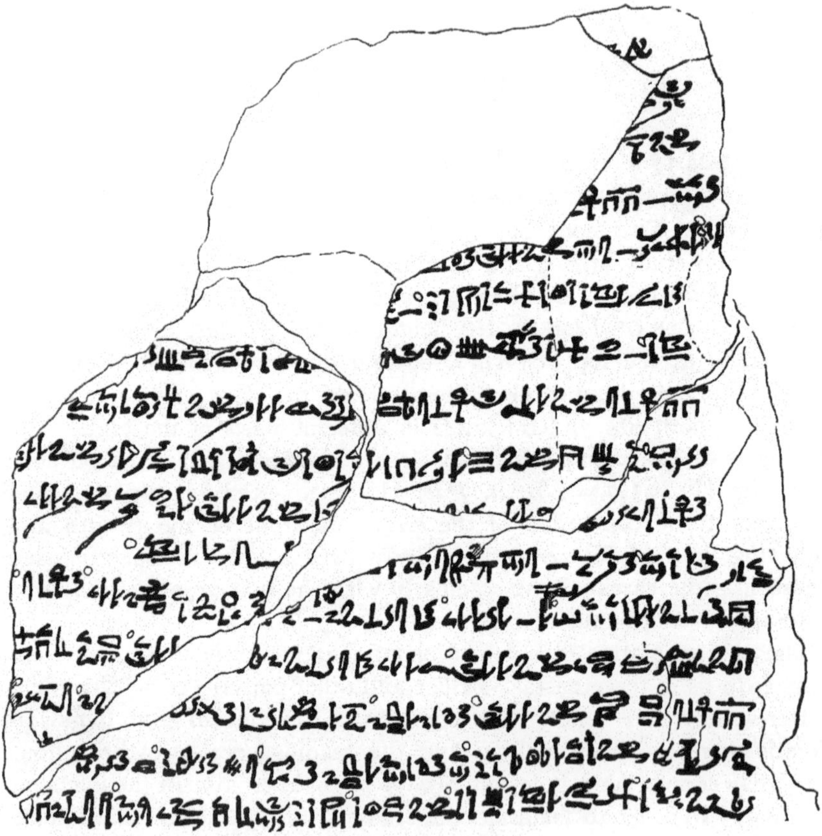

RECTO: lines 1–16.

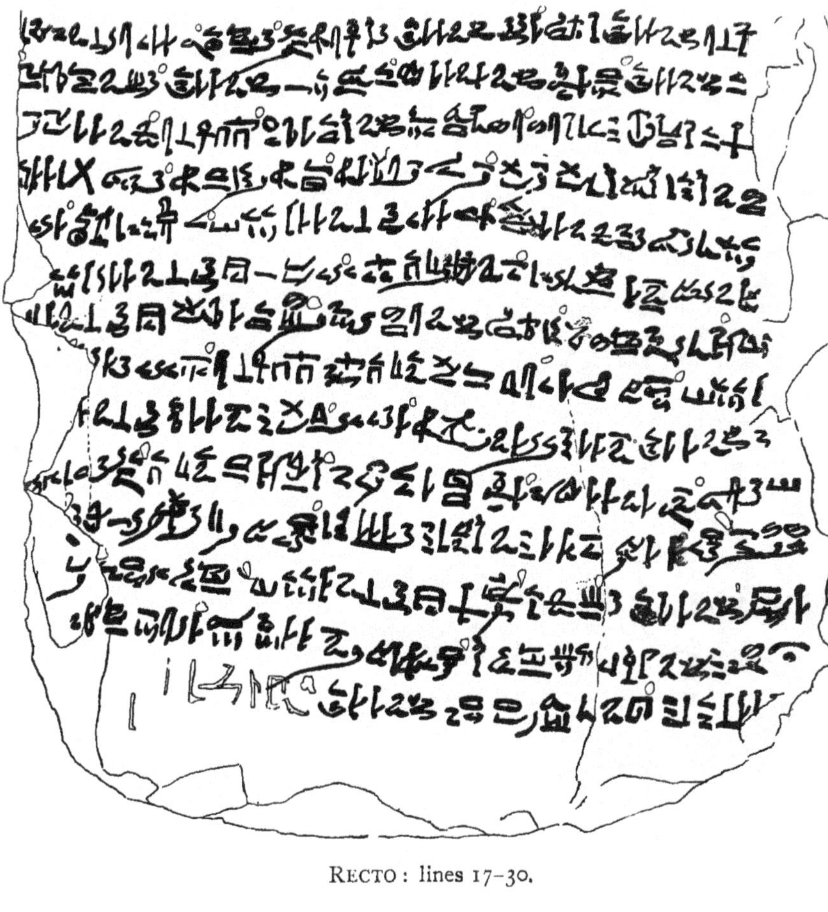

RECTO: lines 17–30.

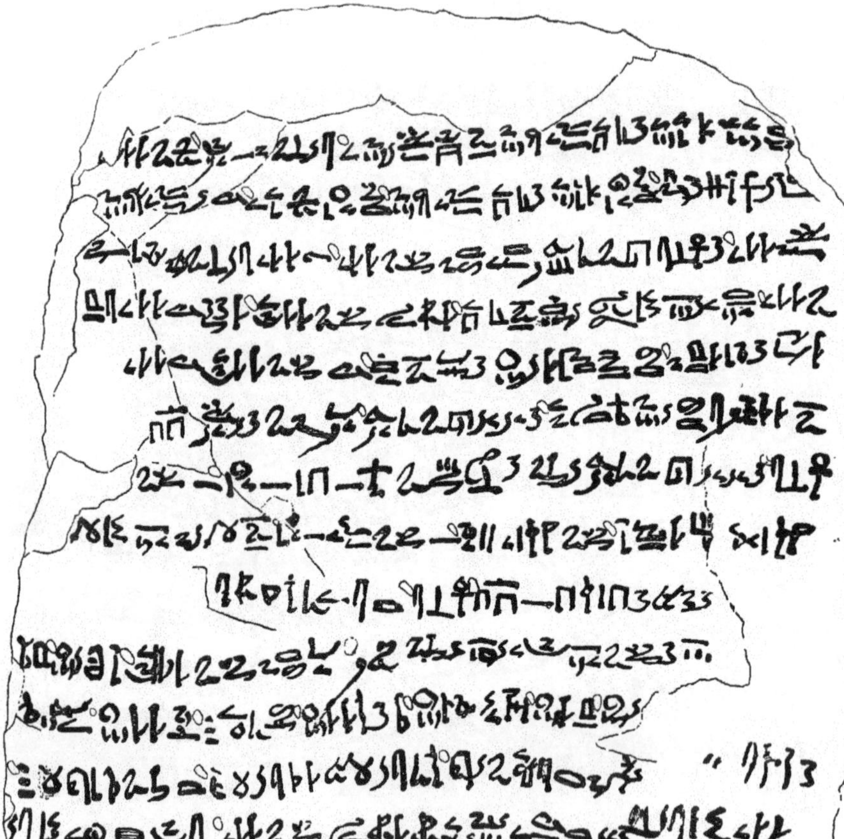

VERSO: lines 1–13.

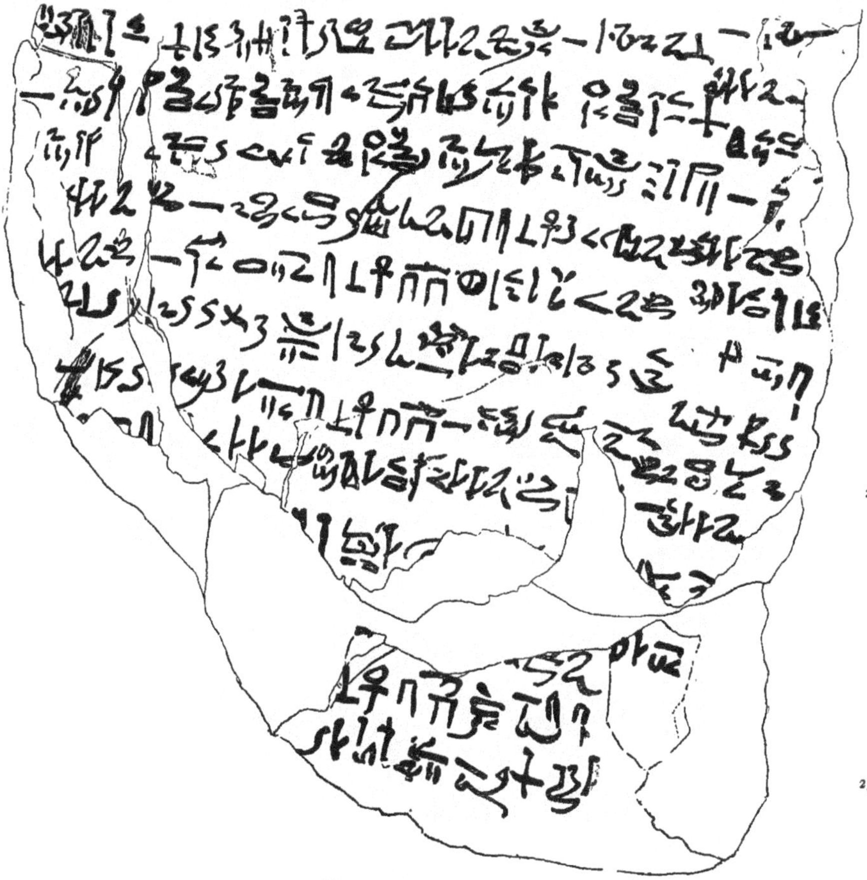

VERSO: lines 14–25.

## LETTER I (*recto* 1–11).

1. very large lacuna  2. *a* very large

lacuna  3. very large lacuna  4.

very large lacuna  5.

 more than ½ line  6. *b*

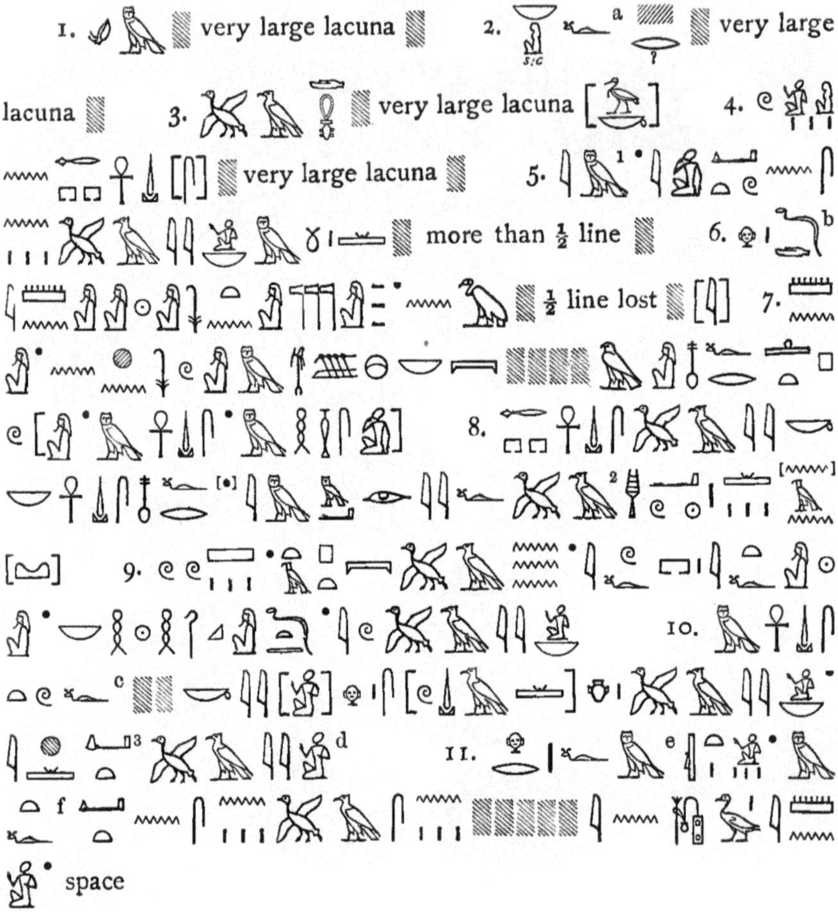


**Notes on the hieratic.** [1] Followed by two small undecipherable signs. [2] Over a deleted [sign]. [3] Corrected from [signs].

**Critical notes.** [a] Read [signs]; then probably followed *ỉmy-rꜣ n-t*, *ṯꜣ-t*, &c. [b] Emend [*tw-ỉ*] *ḥr ḏd* ⟨*n*⟩ *ʾImn*. [c] For *snb-twf* (sic), cf. below 14. [d] Emend *pꜣy-ỉ nb*. [e] Emend *n tꜣ*; for *m*? [f] Read [signs].

The servant . . . . . . . . . . . . . [salutes] his lord . . . . . . . . . . . . . .
The town [of Pharaoh (?), which is under the control of my lord, is in
good condition . . . . . . . . . . The servants] of Pharaoh [who are in it]
. . . . . . . . . . . . . . . . . . . . . . . which my lord gives to them, in due order.
[I] say to Amon-Rasontēr, to Mut . . . . . . . . Amon, to Khons in Thebes,
who receives the new-moon (?), lord of heaven . . . . . . . Neferhōtp. In
life, prosperity, health! In the praise of Pharaoh, thy good lord! May
he have the duration of the mountains, the sky and the water, being in
the house of his father Re, the lord of eternity, prince of everlasting,
my lord being in life, prosperity, and health! Again, salutations to my
lord! May my lord turn his face towards the work-people, and give to
them their [rations] . . . . .
(Written) by the scribe Si-Amon.

The first letter was not improbably addressed to the Vizier Khay, like the second
and third. Some hints as to how the defective portions should be restored may
be got from the fourth letter. The salutations occupy the best part of ten lines,
while the actual subject of the letter—a request for the work-people's wages—is
dismissed in a couple of sentences. The epithet *šsp psḏ*, here given to Khons, is
unknown to me elsewhere. For *ʿḥʿw nʾ dww*, cf. *Leipzig Ostracon* 5.

LETTER II (*recto* 12–30).

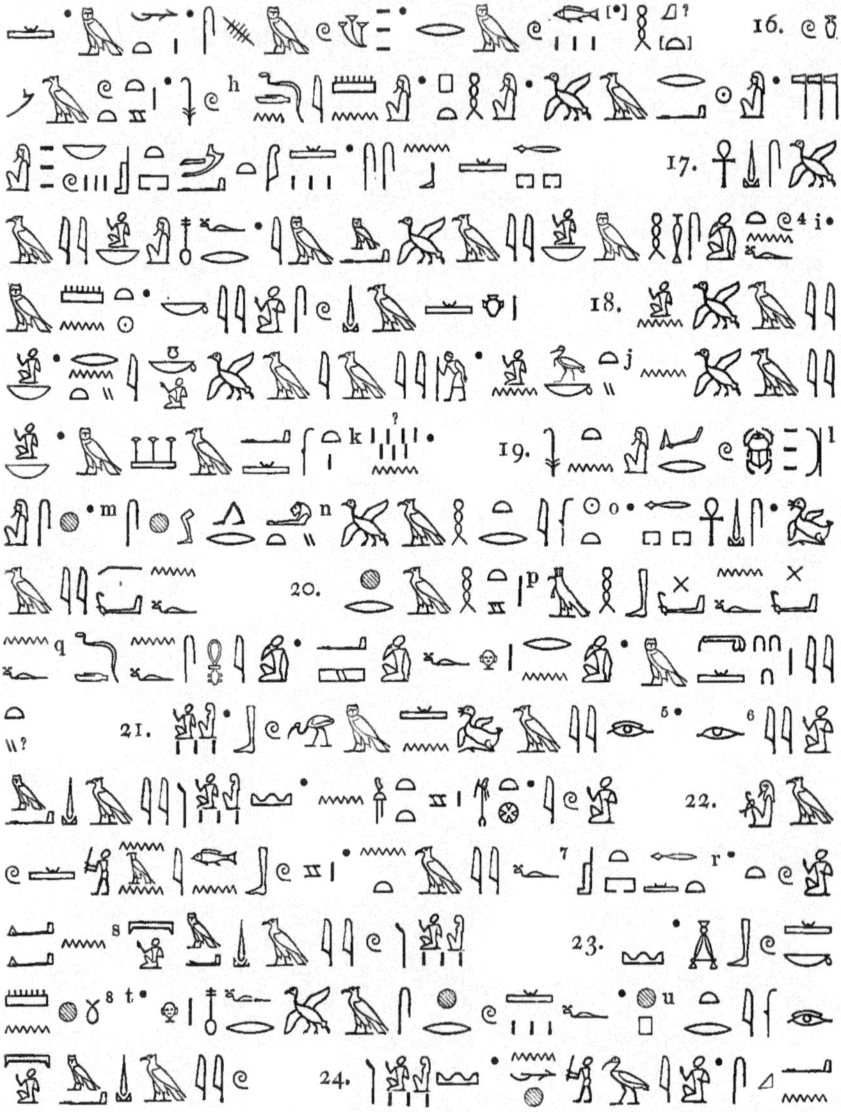

25. [hieroglyphs]

26. [hieroglyphs]

27. [hieroglyphs]

28. [hieroglyphs]

29. [hieroglyphs]

30. [hieroglyphs]

**Notes on the hieratic.**   [1] Above the line is ⌣⌣ which has been erased; upon this has been written a sign like �téné or ⟫. [2] ⟡ | above the line. [3] ⌒ has the appearance of ꖦ. [4] ꭗ is surcharged on ⌣. [5] �'s is a correction. [6] Written over ｜. [7] ｜｜ ꭗ is a correction. [8] ⅄ is a correction. [9] ⌒ written over ꭗ. [10] Like the sign of the old man, but without any stick. [11] ⌒ surcharged upon ꭗ. [12] Corrections. [13] Under ｜｜ are visible the deleted signs ꗥ ｜. [14] ⌒ is almost like hieratic ⌣. [15] Corrections. [16] 𝒦 is a correction. [17] Corrections.

**Critical notes.**   a Read *nb-⟨f⟩*. b Read ⌒⌣ as in 22; so too 24. c Read *nty r*. d Emend ⌣⌣ for *twf*, as above 10. e Some words seem to be omitted. f Read ⟫ⅰⅰⅰ. g Read ｜ ⌒ⅰⅰⅰ. h Surely ⌒ꭦ should be

c**

substituted. [i] Emend *ḥst-(tw)f.* [j] For  read . [k] Emend . [l] *Dsr-ḫprw-Rʿ* is clearly meant. [m] The verse-point is misplaced. [n] Read . [o] For  substitute , an easy corruption. [p] Corrupt? [q] Dittograph? [r] Read 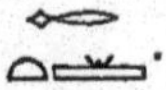. [s] Read *r*? [t] Read 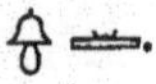. [u] Read  *ptri.* [v] Read . [w] *Ḫft* is a not uncommon confusion for *ḥr-f*, e.g. *Leipzig Ostracon* 16; so, too, at the beginning of the next line. [x] *Ḥn*, imperative? [y] Read . [z] Read *nʾy-i*? [aa] Read *Mntw-rḫ*, like *'Inḥr-rḫ*, *Bologna 1094*, 2, 7. [bb] *N* omitted.

The chief of the Mazoi . . . . . . . . . . . salutes ⟨his⟩ lord, the Overseer of the City and Vizier Khay. In life, prosperity, health! It is a communication to inform my lord! Again a salutation to my lord, to the effect that the great place of Pharaoh which is under the charge of my lord is in proper order; the walls in the district . . . . . . . . . are safe and sound. ⟨As to the⟩ delivery of the yearly dues, they are in proper order, wood, vegetables, fish and beer . . . . . . . I (?) say unto Amon, Ptah, Prē, and the gods of the Place of Truth, 'Preserve Pharaoh, my good lord, in health, and may my lord be in his favour daily.' Again a salutation to my lord, to the effect that I am the aged servant of my lord since the seventh (?) year of King Haremheb. I (?) ran before the horses (?) of Pharaoh. I brought to him . . . . . . . . . . I yoked (his steeds) for him (?). I made report to him, and he inquired of my name before the courtiers; and no fault was found in me. I acted as Mazoi of the west of Thebes, and guarded the walls of his great place. I was made (?) chief of Mazoi, thy excellent recompense because . . . . . . . . . Now behold the chief of the Mazoi Nakht-Thout; ruined (?) is the great place of Pharaoh in which I am . . . . . . . . . . . . . my lord . . . . . . . . . . . . . . . . 'I am small,' said he to me, 'do thou equip (?) this place; thou art . . . . . . . . ,' said he to me. He took away my fields in the country. He took away 2 . . . . . vegetables (?), belonging to my lord as the share of the Vizier, and gave (them to) the chief of the Mazoi Ment-rakh, and gave the remainder to the high-priest of Mont. He took away my grain, which was stored in the country. It is a communication to inform my lord.

The draughtsman Si-Amon.

This model letter is addressed by a chief of Mazoi, i.e. a head-policeman or head-ghaffir, to the well-known Vizier Khay, who was a contemporary of Rameses II. The first part of the letter, down to line 18, consists of the customary greetings and assurances that the writer's duties are being properly performed. The remaining twelve lines are so corrupt as to be barely intelligible. In ll. 18–23 the writer seems to enumerate his past services, doubtless in the hope that the grievances spoken of in ll. 23–30 may receive the more attention. It is difficult to make out what the complaints are about. Another chief Mazoi Nakht-Thout is named, after which the text becomes wholly incomprehensible; in ll. 27–30 reference is apparently made to some property that this official has taken away, and allocated to wrong people.—There is only one difficulty of vocabulary, *šk͑n* in l. 24, which is not improbably corrupt. For the formula *ssnb Pr-͑*; (l. 16), cf. *Anast.* v. 19, 5; see too here, *verso* 24.

### LETTER III (*verso* 1–13).

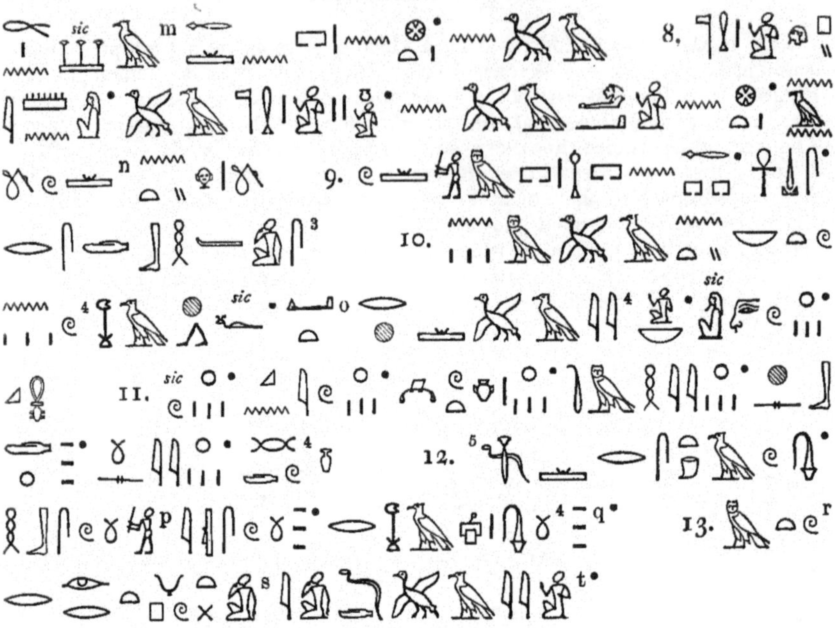

**Notes on the hieratic.** [1] corrected from . [2] corrected from . [3] over , which however is preferable. [4] Here corrections. [5] For the phrases at the beginning of this and the next lines see after the twelfth letter.

**Critical notes.** [a] For *ḥr swḏ; ỉb n.* [b] Read *t;y ḫwy-t ḥr wnmy* ⟨*n ni-swt*⟩, cf. below, 14. [c] is dittographed and the words *ỉst m s-t m;ᶜ-t* probably borrowed from line 1; but cf. below, l. 15. [d] Read *r rdỉ-t rḫ p;y-ỉ nb.* [e] ⟨*Nb*⟩ omitted, as once above and often below. [f] Emend *m n; n ỉs-wt?* [g] I suspect that *ḥr wn ḏrỉw m-dỉ-s-n;-* is merely a corruption of the familiar adjectives *ḏrỉw mnḫ.* [h] ⟨ ⟩ omitted. [j] Read *nfrw* . [k] Emend *h;b r dỉ-t ᶜm Pr-ᶜ;.* [l] *M* superfluous. [m] Read , for which the scribe has wrongly substituted the similar-looking sign . [n] Read . [o] For *r rdỉ-t.* [p] For read . [q] Read

ᛁ 𓅿 𓂝 . <sup></sup>ᴿ Read *mtw-ḥ* or *mtw-n*. ˢ ⟨*Nb*⟩ omitted.

ᵗ ⟨*Nb*⟩ omitted, as above, note ᵉ.

The workman in the Place of Truth, Enherkhow salutes his lord, the Fanbearer to the Right ⟨of the King⟩; the Overseer of the City and Vizier, who does Justice, Khay. In life, prosperity, health! It is a communication to inform my ⟨lord⟩. Again a salutation to my lord, to the effect that we are working ⟨in⟩ the place that my lord said should be excellently adorned. Let my lord ⟨cause⟩ me to perform his good purposes, and let a message be sent to cause Pharaoh to know. And let a dispatch be sent to the Estate-superintendent of Thebes, to the high-priest and second priest of Amon, to the toparch of Thebes, and to the controllers who control in the Treasury of Pharaoh, so as to supply us with all that we require. To inform my lord! *Ḥnt*; *ḳnỉ*; *;w-t-ỉb*; *ỉmḥy*; lapis lazuli; *šsy*; fresh fat for burning; old clothes for lamps; and we will perform ⟨every⟩ commission which my lord has said.

This is a letter supposed to be written by one of the workmen at the Theban Necropolis, doubtless one of those engaged in work at the Royal Tombs, to the well-known Vizier Khay, the addressee of letter No. 2. The upshot of the text when shorn of its ceremonious phraseology is a request for certain pigments and materials required in the decoration of the tombs.—The only unusual words that occur are in the list of desiderata. *Ḥnt* and *ḳnỉ* are well-known names of pigments; *;wt-ỉb* occurs *Ebers* 54, 18; *ỉmḥy*, cf. *Harris I*, 62 b, 14; 70 a, 11; MAR., *Dendera IV*, 36, 50; 39.

## LETTER IV (*verso* 13–25).

about ½ line lost

**Notes on the hieratic.** [1] Corrected from  ? [2] Here a correction.

**Critical notes.** [a] For these titles, here again corruptly written, see *verso*, l. 1. [b] See above *verso* 1–2 and critical note thereon. [c] *F* is superfluous. [d] Emend *pꜣy-ỉ* ⟨*nb*⟩. [e] *Pꜣy-ỉ* does not seem right and is perhaps corrupt.

The scribe Neb-rē salutes his lord, the Fanbearer to the Right of the King, the . . . . . . . . . . . ; the Overseer of the treasury, the Overseer of the priests of the Gods of Upper Egypt; the Overseer of the City and Vizier, who does Justice, Psiūr. In life, prosperity, health! It is a communication to inform my ⟨lord⟩. The town of Pharaoh which is under the control of my lord is in good condition; every wall which is in its neighbourhood is safe. The servants of Pharaoh who are therein are given my (?) revenues, which [my lord] has granted to them. [I say unto Amon, Ptah [Prē] . . . . . . . . . [May] Pharaoh be kept in health . . . . . . . . . . . . . May it (?) be given to thee here eternally . . . . . . . . .

A letter very similar to the first, addressed by a scribe to the Vizier Psiūr, who was Khay's predecessor.  No information is given in the letter beyond the statement that the ' town of Pharaoh ' is prospering.

A few very short lines are inscribed in front of *verso* 12 *et seqq.*, and appear to contain a consecutive text.  These lines which I letter (*a*), (*b*), (*c*), &c., are as follows :— (*a*) [hieroglyphs]    (*b*) [hieroglyphs]

(*c*) [hieroglyphs]    (*d*) [hieroglyphs]    (*e*) [hieroglyphs]    (*f*) [hieroglyphs]

[hieroglyphs]    (*g*) [hieroglyphs]    (*h*) [hieroglyphs]

(*i*) [hieroglyphs]    (*j*) [hieroglyphs]    (*k*) [hieroglyphs]

[hieroglyphs]    (*l*) [hieroglyphs]    (*m*) [hieroglyphs]. ' In the praise of . . . . . . Again salutations to my lord, to the effect that . . . . . . . . of my lord . . . . . . . . . . . . To inform my lord . . . . . . . . . . . . . . . . ' What is intelligible of this is couched in the usual epistolary phraseology.

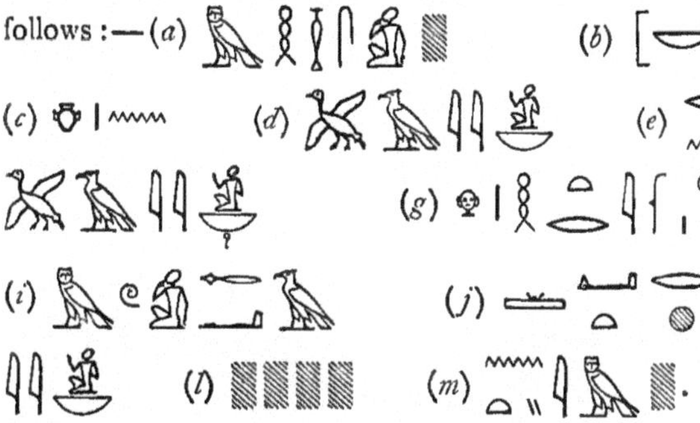

# II

# DEMOTIC TEXTS

## TABLE

# INTRODUCTION

No large collection of demotic ostraca has ever been published and treated systematically in the way in which Wilcken has dealt with the Greek ostraca. This is probably due mainly to two reasons—the difficulty of reading them and consequently the uselessness of publishing transcriptions or translations without reproducing the originals; and any mechanical reproduction on a large scale has until recently been very expensive.

The difficulty of reading them arises from various causes—the perishable nature of the writing, the cursive nature of the script on documents originally of small importance, and the little care taken of such fleeting records. These considerations affect the Greek ostraca equally. Peculiar to the demotic ones are the inherent difficulty of the writing with its immense number of separate signs, many of which have a tendency to run into closely similar forms, and our limited knowledge of the vocabulary of the language, and more especially of the abbreviations used in these often hurriedly written memoranda. The only way to overcome these obstacles is to publish as accurately as possible a large number of ostraca so that by the comparison of numerous specimens of the various types of formulae we may eventually arrive at definite results as to their meaning. It is hoped that the present collection may form a small contribution towards such a corpus.

M. Revillout in this, as in other departments of demotic work, has been a pioneer; he has published by far the largest number of demotic ostraca hitherto. He transcribed several from the

Louvre, British Museum, and Berlin in the *Revue Égyptologique*, vols. iv and vi (1885–8), and the *P.S.B.A.* xiv (1891), but these are mostly demotic dockets to Greek ostraca. In 1895 he published in his *Mélanges sur la Métrologie*, &c., over 120 ostraca of different kinds, many being of great interest; unfortunately his hand-copies are very imperfect; it is difficult sometimes to accept his readings and impossible to control them, for he often omits the number and not infrequently the resting-place of the original.

In 1891 H. Brugsch published thirty-six from the Berlin Museum in hand-copies in his *Thesaurus*, as well as three from Ghizeh in the *A. Z.* xxix.

Wiedemann in 1881 (*Revue Égyptol.* ii) had already given a short account of a collection he made at Karnak, which has since passed into the Berlin Museum, but he gave no examples.

Chardon in his *Dictionnaire Démotique*, 1893–7, published about a dozen examples from the Louvre and one from the British Museum in hand-copies.

In 1902 Magnien published 'Quelques reçus d'impôts agricoles', comprising nine ostraca from the Louvre with hand-copies and translations. In the same year Hess published three from Berlin in the notes to his edition of the Rosetta inscription, and Spiegelberg has published three or four incidentally in various publications (*A. Z.* xlii. 57, xlvi. 112; *Pap. Elephantine*, p. 13; *Pap. Libbey*, pl. III). Up to the present time, however, only one single example—that in *Pap. Libbey* above—has been reproduced by photography.[1] On the plates of the present volume will be found untouched photographs of forty-five specimens, which perhaps will be an encouragement to others,

[1] Since the above was written Prof. Spiegelberg has reproduced four more by photography in *A. Z.* xlix, pl. VI.

so that the best of these documents may be preserved. The chief causes of their destruction in museums or private hands are exposure to light and especially to dust. If each ostracon is wrapped in paper before being stored, it will, if it have no salt in it, remain legible for an indefinite period; but if they are left unwrapped in drawers, the dust fills the fine pores of the clay and the inscription becomes illegible.

The present demotic collection consists in all of nearly 400 specimens, including a large number of fragments and many in very poor condition. They all come from Thebes. About 300 are serviceable and from these I have selected forty-four. The number was necessarily restricted by considerations of expense of reproduction; but the selection gives a very fair idea of the more interesting ones. A considerable proportion contains only lists of names and many are only partly legible and afford small information as to their meaning.

I must be allowed here to offer my thanks to my collaborators in this volume who generously gave up nearly the whole of their share of the plates in order to allow of as many demotic examples as possible being reproduced, and also to Mr. Horace Hart of the Oxford University Press, who by his skill has overcome the difficulties of reproduction with marked success. In order to adapt them to the plates, the ostraca are given on a scale of approximately two-thirds of the size of the originals.

H. T.

## OSTR. D 5 (Pl. I). TAX RECEIPT.[1]

1. a.ʾn P-šr-Mnt s Pa-Mn a p sḫ̆n n n ʿy-w
2. šbte-w ẖr p ḥt ʿpe.t n ḥsp 2.t n Zme sttr 1.t
3. a qt 1.t a sttr 1.t wtḥ (?) ʿn sẖ n ḥsp 2.t n Gys ʿ.w.s.
4. ʾbt-4 pr ss 3 ʾbt-1 šm ss 1 ẖr p ḥt ʿpe.t sttr 1.t a qt 1.t a sttr 1.t wtḥ (?) ʿn
5. . . . . ʾbt-1 šm ss 26 ẖr p ḥt ʿpe.t sttr 1.t a qt 1.t a sttr 1.t wtḥ (?) ʿn . . . .
6. ʾbt-2 šm ss 24 ẖr p ḥt ʿpe.t sttr 1.t a qt 1.t a sttr 1.t wtḥ (?) ʿn
7. . . . . ʾbt-4 šm ss 3 ẖr n tʾ-w qt 1.t t s.t
8. ʾywn qt 1.t a qt ½ a qt 1.t ʿn

'Psenmonthes, son of Paminis, has paid[2] to the bank of the merchants' houses[3] for the silver[4] (of the) poll(-tax) of the year 2 in Jême[5] stater[6] 1 = kite 1 = stater 1 refined (?)[7] (silver) again. Written in year 2 of Gaius,[8] Pharmuthi day 3.

Pachons day 1, for the silver (of the) poll(-tax) stater 1 = kite 1 = stater 1 refined (?) (silver) again.

Item,[9] Pachons day 26, for the silver (of the) poll(-tax) stater 1 = kite 1 = stater 1 refined (?) (silver) again.

Item, Payni day 24, for the silver (of the) poll(-tax) stater 1 = kite 1 = stater 1 refined (?) (silver) again.

Item, Mesore day 3, for the *apomoira*[10] kite 1, the bath(-tax)[11] kite 1 = kite ½ = kite 1 again.'

[1] Taxes were usually paid by instalments and each instalment, as it was paid, was acknowledged by the banker on the same ostracon, which the tax-payer doubtless kept at home and brought with him on each occasion to the bank with his money. The chief taxes mentioned at this time (early Roman empire) are poll-tax, *apomoira*, bath- and dyke-tax.

[2] lit. 'bring': it is the technical word for paying money.

[3] The bank is no doubt the royal bank to which taxes payable in money were

paid. The name it bears here, 'bank of the merchants' houses,' probably refers to the locality in Thebes where it was situated. These 'merchants' houses' are mentioned on six ostraca in this collection besides others known to me. I suspect it is the district known from Greek ostraca as the ἀγοραί, from an unpublished bilingual, but the demotic reading is not certain. For the use of *ʿy-w*, 'houses,' as the name of a district, cf. *n ʿy-w mḥt*, *Rec. tr.* xxxi, pp. 92 and 103, n. xii, and *n ʿy-w n ʾY-m-ḥtp* in Ostr. Louvre 9069 (Revillout, *Mélanges*, p. 147 note). For the reading *šbte*, see Griffith in *P.S.B.A.*, xxxi, pp. 51–2; Spiegelberg adopts the transcription *stȝ* (*Cat. Gén. du Mus. du Caire: die demotischen Papyrus*, p. 1 and elsewhere), which he derives from H. Brugsch, *Wörterb.*, p. 1335.

[4] At first sight the reading here appears to be *p ʿpe.t*, but *ʿpe.t* is a feminine word, and the full phrase is *p ḥt n ʿpe.t*, 'the silver of poll(-tax),' which occurs on D 69 in this collection. Usually the words *p ḥt* are run together by the scribe so as to resemble a *p* with a small additional stroke as here; occasionally it is still further reduced to a sign resembling *p* rather than *ḥt*: but as *p ʿpe.t* is impossible, there is little doubt it must be read *ḥt ʿpe.t*.

[5] A district of Thebes on the west bank of the Nile called in the Greek papyri and ostraca the Μεμνόνεια.

[6] The stater at this time was equivalent to four drachmas, the kite to two. The Egyptian in financial documents, in order to avoid errors, after mentioning a sum, wrote down half the amount and then repeated the original amount. Hence, though he uses a sign meaning =, it is not a real equivalence, and after the first = the words 'its half' must be understood.

[7] These two signs seem to be an abbreviated form of writing the word *wtḥ*, 'refined' (silver). Cf. Griffith, *Cat. Rylands Demotic Papyri*, Glossary, p. 344, and his notes there referred to. The words *ḥt wtḥ*, 'refined silver,' are written out in full on a Berlin Ostracon published by Brugsch, *Thes.*, p. 1059, though from his translation he has misread the words as *e-f wt-w*.

[8] A.D. 38. The Emperor's name is followed by the three signs representing 'life, health, strength', which were always attached to the names of the ancient Pharaohs, and in demotic they follow every imperial title and epithet, but it is not necessary to translate them.

[9] There is no doubt as to the meaning of the Egyptian word: it is clearly the same as the Greek ὁμοίως, but the reading is very uncertain.

[10] This was a tax of one-sixth of the produce of vineyards and orchards (cf. Grenfell, *Revenue Laws*, p. 119; Wilcken, *Gr. Ostr.*, i, p. 157; Otto, *Priester u. Tempel*, i, p. 340; *Pap. Tebtunis*, i, p. 37). In demotic it is always used in the plural (Rosetta inscr., l. 9, where, however, the Greek has τὰς ἀπομοίρας, and on the three other ostraca in this collection, D 37, D 52, D 69). The plural is employed probably because the tax was levied on two classes of land. It is literally 'the portions'.

[11] *s.t ʾywn*, Coptic ϲιοονι, 'bath,' here used for the tax = βαλανικόν, cf. Wilcken, *u. s.* i, p. 165; *Pap. Hibeh*, i, p. 284. The amount of the tax seems to have varied at different times and, perhaps, localities. On Theban demotic ostraca the amount is usually, as here, two drachmas; but numerous unpublished tax receipts from Dendera (belonging to Mr. J. G. Milne) show that the amount there in the reign of Tiberius was 40 drachmas per annum.

## OSTR. D 29 (Pl. I). TAX RECEIPT.

1. a.wt ʾMns s Glymqs (?)
2. ẖr ḥt ʿpe n ḥsp 29 sttr 2.t wtḥ (?) n ḥsp 29 n Gsrs
3. ʾbt-2 šm ss ʿrq n ʾbt-3 šm ss 4 sẖ . . . . s Gphls (?)

'Ammonius, son of Kallimachus (?)[1], has paid[2] on account of the poll (-tax) of the year 29 two staters refined (?) (silver) in the year 29 of Caesar[3], Payni day 30 (and ?) on Epiphi day 4. Written by . . . . son of Kephalos (?).'

[1] The handwriting is difficult, and the names Kallimachus and Kephalos are doubtful. They are certainly Greek, not Egyptian names.

[2] The word *wt* is not infrequently used instead of *ʾn* for 'pay' in the early Roman empire. It seems to have no special significance. Cf. Spiegelberg, *Demotische Papyrus von Elephantine*, p. 13, note xiii.

[3] i. e. Augustus, B.C. 1.

## OSTR. D 16 (Pl. X). TAX RECEIPT.

1. a.ʾn Pa-Mnt p ʿo s Glen a p sẖn n
2. n ʿy-w šbte-w ẖr p ḥt ʿpe.t n ḥsp 25
3. ẖn n rm-w Pa-Mnt s Pa-ʾre sttr 2.t a sttr 1.t a
4. sttr 2.t ʿn sẖ n ḥsp 25 ʾbt-3 šm ss 27
5. . . . n ʾbt-4 šm ss 4 sttr 2.t a sttr 1.t a
6. sttr 2.t ʿn

'Pamonthes the elder, son of Glen,[1] has paid into the bank of the merchants' houses on account of the silver (of the) poll(-tax) of year 25 among the men[2] of Pamonthes, son of Paeris, 2 staters = 1 stater = 2 staters again. Written in year 25, Epiphi day 27.

Item, in Mesore day 4, 2 staters = 1 stater[3] = 2 staters again.'

[1] Κλέων (?).

[2] He was one of the veterans who had *kleroi* allotted to them and was enrolled in a company called after its captain, Pamonthes, son of Paeris.

[3] The last six words of l. 5 are very indistinct, but there is no practical doubt as to the reading.

## OSTR. D 37 (Pl. I). TAX RECEIPT.

1. a.ʾn Py-k s Ḫns-tef-nḫt a p sḫn n n ʿy-w šbte-w
2. ẖr ḥt ʿpe n ḥsp 3.t n Zme sttr 2.t a sttr 1.t a sttr 2.t ʿn
3. sẖ n ḥsp 3.t n Gys ʿ.w.s. Gysrs ʿ.w.s. Sbʿsts ʿ.w.s.
4. Grmnykws ʿ.w.s. ʾbt-3 pr ss ʿrq . . . . ʾbt-1 šm ss 19 ẖr
5. p ḥt ʿpe.t sttr 2.t a sttr 1.t a sttr 2.t ʿn . . . . ʾbt-2 šm ss 23 ẖr
6. n tʾ-w qt 1.t a qt $\frac{1}{2}$ a qt 1.t ʿn t s.t ʾywn qt 1.t a qt $\frac{1}{2}$ a qt 1.t ʿn . . . . ʾbt-4 šm
7. ss 5 ẖr p nbe n ḥsp 3.t sttr 1.t qt $\frac{1}{2}$ (oβ.) 4.t a qt 1.t (oβ.) 5.t a sttr 1.t qt $\frac{1}{2}$ (oβ.) 4.t ʿn

‘Pikos, the son of Khons-tef-nekht,[1] has paid to the bank of the merchants' houses for silver (of the) poll(-tax) of year 3 in Jême, 2 staters = 1 stater = 2 staters again. Written in year 3 of Gaius Caesar Sebastos Germanicus, Phamenoth day 30.[2]

Item, Pachons day 19, for the silver (of the) poll(-tax) 2 staters = 1 stater = 2 staters again.

Item, Payni day 23, for the *apomoira* 1 kite = $\frac{1}{2}$ kite = 1 kite again; the bath(-tax) 1 kite = $\frac{1}{2}$ kite = 1 kite again.

Item, Mesore day 5, for the dyke-tax[3] of year 3, 1 stater $\frac{1}{2}$ kite 4 obols[4] = 1 kite 5 obols = 1 stater $\frac{1}{2}$ kite 4 obols again.’

[1] The same individual as on D 52 infra.

[2] A.D. 39.

[3] The word *nbe* is not a new one, though its reading and meaning have not hitherto been fully recognized. The ostraca here published furnish fresh evidence on these points. It occurs on four demotic ostraca, D 37, D 52, D 69, D 117, and on one bilingual, G 222 (unpublished), and doubtfully on a second, G 427. From these, especially G 222, there is no doubt that the reading is *nbe* 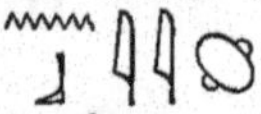. The word occurs on two published papyri in the Louvre (below), but only on one published ostracon, a bilingual at Berlin, no. 1113. The latter was published by Revillout and Wilcken in the *Revue Égyptologique*, vi, p. 11, and the Greek text

again by Wilcken in his *Griechische Ostraka* under no. 1025, and it explains one meaning of *nbe* for us. The Greek text is

Lκβ απειργασται
εις το διακομμα $\overset{o}{\nu}$ λ ερμοφιλος

'Year 22 work done on the breach in the dyke, 30 naubia, Hermophilus.'

διακομμα is clearly a breach in a dyke (χῶμα, περίχωμα), or rather in the bank of a canal which is raised above the surrounding fields (διῶρυξ, *Pap. Tebtunis*, no. 13 and notes). See Mahaffy-Smyly, *Petrie Papyri*, iii, nos. 37 a. ii. 19, b. iii. 9, and 45. (2). 5. The two lines of demotic underneath the Greek read, so far as one can be sure from the hand-copy,

sẖ Ḥr . . . . s Hry a nbe 30
sẖ . . . . s S-wsr nb 30

'Written by Hor . . . . son of Erieus for 30 *nbe*; signed by . . . . son of Senwosre for 30 *nb*.'

Wilcken, *Griech. Ostr.* i. 259–60 discusses the question whether the Egyptian *nbt* (as Revillout read it) can be the same as the Greek word ναύβιον, of which it is here clearly the equivalent, and leaves it unsettled. This is settled for us not only by the material published here, but also by over thirty unpublished demotic ostraca known to me, the large majority of which come from Dendera and belong to Mr. J. G. Milne. The Greek word which is unknown to classical literature and has long been a subject of discussion since its appearance in the papyri and ostraca, is now known to be a cubic measure of soil equal to a cube whose side is a royal double cubit (*Pap. Lille*, i, p. 15). No reasonable etymology has, I believe, been suggested for it; if so, there is the more reason for regarding it as a graecized Egyptian word, if we can find an origin for *nbe*. Now there is an old word  (Brugsch, *Wtb.* 327–8, 749, Suppl., 662) meaning a stake which was employed in staking out the ground in the representations of temple foundation scenes. It is not difficult to see that such a stake should be, or become, of a recognized length and form the origin of a measure for excavating earth generally.

The above bilingual accounts for the number of naubia of earth removed. Thirty naubia seem to have been the amount of forced labour on dykes which the government could demand (Mahaffy-Smyly, *u. s.* p. 344), and probably represents the five days' work which constituted the corvée (Wilcken, *u. s.* p. 338). In two papyri in the Louvre of the 36th year of Amasis (535 B.C.) this corvée is mentioned as *p nbe n ḥte* 'the compulsory *nbe*' (*Corpus Papyrorum*, Louvre, no. 14, pl. xv, ll. 14, 15, and no. 15, pl. xvi, l. 7), a tax on land the payment of which has to be specifically provided for in agreements relating to the transfer of land. Even at that early date it would seem that the corvée could be commuted for a money payment. It was certainly so in Ptolemaic and Roman times, when the tax in money form was known in Greek as χωματικόν (Wilcken, *u. s.* p. 338), and in demotic it is the tax we have here, in D 37, as *nbe*. That these are the same is evident from the amount of the tax, which for the χωματικόν was the peculiar sum of 6 dr. 4 obols annually (Wilcken, *u. s.* p. 334, *Pap. Brit. Mus.* ii, p. 107, iii, p. 55, *Pap. Tebtunis*, ii, p. 188), thus distinguishing this tax from all others. In our ostracon (D 37) the payment, it is true, is only 5 dr. 4 obols, but in D 52 and in D 69 the payments, though paid by instalments, in each case amount together to 6 dr. 4 obols. Conclusive evidence, however, is furnished by Mr. Milne's Dendera ostraca, since out of twenty-nine *nbe*-ostraca (unpublished) twenty-four are for precisely 6 dr. 4 obols and three of the remainder are for exactly half the amount.

[4] This reading of the demotic word is uncertain. Dr. Griffith in his *Cat. Rylands Demotic Papyri*, iii, p. 400, suggests *qt* (?) with doubt; but as this may lead to confusion with the silver kite, I have preferred to use the Greek ὀβολός in a bracket, seeing that there is no doubt as to the meaning.

## Ostr. D 52 (Pl. I). Tax Receipt.

1. a.ʾn Py-k s Ḫns-tef-nḫt a p sẖn

2. n n ʿy-w šbte-w ẖr p ḥt ʿpe.t n ḥsp 2.t n Zme sttr 1.t

3. a qt 1.t a (?) sttr 1.t wtḥ (?) ʿn sẖ n ḥsp 2.t n Gys ʿ.w.s. ʾbt-2 pr ss 26

4. .... n ʾbt-3 pr ss 3 ẖr p ḥt ʿpe.t sttr 1.t a qt 1.t a sttr 1.t wtḥ (?) ʿn

5. .... n ss 25 ẖr p ḥt. ʿpe.t sttr 1.t a qt 1.t a sttr 1.t wtḥ (?) ʿn .... n

6. ʾbt-4 pr ss 19 ẖr p ḥt ʿpe.t sttr 1.t a qt 1.t a sttr 1.t wtḥ (?) ʿn

7. .... ʾbt-1 šm ss 26 ẖr n tʾ-w qt 1.t a qt ½ a qt 1.t ʿn .... t s.t ʾywn qt 1.t

8. a qt ½ a qt 1.t ʿn .... ʾbt-4 šm ss 3 ẖr p nbe qt 1½ (oβ.) 4½ a qt ½ (oβ.) 5.t

9. a qt 1½ (oβ.) 4½ ʿn .... ss 24 ẖr p nbe qt 1.t (oβ.) 8.t ½ a qt ½ (oβ.) 4.t ¼

10. a qt 1.t (oβ.) 8.t ½ ʿn

'Pikos, son of Khons-tef-nekht, has paid to the bank of the merchants' houses for the silver (of the) poll(-tax) of year 2 in Jême, 1 stater = 1 kite = 1 stater refined (?) (silver) again. Written in year 2 of Gaius,[1] Mechir day 26.

Item, Phamenoth day 3, for the silver (of the) poll(-tax) 1 stater = 1 kite = 1 stater refined (?) (silver) again.

Item, on day 25, for the silver (of the) poll(-tax) 1 stater = 1 kite = 1 stater refined (?) (silver) again.

Item, Pharmuthi day 19, for the silver of the poll(-tax) 1 stater = 1 kite = 1 stater refined (?) (silver) again.

Item, Pachons day 26, for the *apomoira* 1 kite = ½ kite = 1 kite again.

Item, the bath(-tax) 1 kite = ½ kite = 1 kite again.

Item, Mesore day 3, for the dyke-tax 1½ kite 4½ obols = ½ kite 5 obols [2] = 1½ kite 4½ obols again.

Item, day 24, for the dyke-tax 1 kite 5½ obols = ½ kite 2½ obols [3] = 1 kite 5½ obols again.'

[1] A.D. 38.

[2] Strictly 5¼ obols, but the scribes often neglect small fractions in these equivalences.

[3] Strictly 2¾ obols.

## Ostr. D 4 (Pl. VIII). Receipt for Arrears of Taxes.

1. Ws-ḥ s Hry
2. Ns-Mn s Pa-by
3. n nt z n Pa-Zme
4. s Pa-Wn wn . . . . Pr-ʿo
5. 1 a ½ a 1 ʿn e.ʾn-k s a
6. p pr-ḥt Pr-ʿo n N
7. n ḥsp 35 ʾbt-3 pr ss 18 ẖn
8. n sp-w
9. sẖ ḥsp 35 ʾbt-3 pr ss 18

'Weser-he, son of Erieus (and) Zminis, son of Pa-by, say to Pasemis, son of Phagonis: there is[1] . . . .[2] of the King (artaba?) 1 = ½ = 1 again, which thou hast paid to the treasury[3] of the King in the City (Thebes) in year 35, Phamenoth day 18, among the arrears. Written year 35,[4] Phamenoth day 18.'

[1] i.e. 'we have', 'we acknowledge'. The receipt is given by two *sitologoi* probably to the tax-payer.

[2] At first glance this group looks like a date, but this it cannot be here, and

I can only suggest—but with great diffidence—that it may be a writing of *pr*, corn, with a 'prosthetic *alif*' to represent the initial vowel of **ⲉⲃⲣⲁ** (**ⲉⲃⲣⲉ**, **ⲉⲃⲣⲓ**), pl. **ⲉⲃⲣⲏⲧⲉ**.

[3] 'Treasury' is not, perhaps, the most appropriate word, but it is the customary translation of *pr-ḥt* = ταμιεῖον (for this equation see Spiegelberg, *Demot. Pap. Berlin*, p. 4 note). According to Wilcken (*Griech. Ostr.* i, reff. in index, s.v. ταμιεῖον) the latter is a general word for the royal (and imperial) 'treasury', which included both the banks (τράπεζαι), for receipts and payments in money, and the magazines (θησαυροί, storehouses, granaries) for the like in kind, whether live stock, or grain, oil, &c. In Ptolemaic times the usual word for ταμιεῖον was simply τὸ βασιλικόν. In demotic *sḫn n pr-ʿo* = τράπεζα βασιλική and *r n pr-ʿo* = θησαυρὸς βασ. Here we have the less common and more generalized term *pr-ḥt n pr-ʿo* = ταμιεῖον βασ., which in this case is more probably = θησαυρός than τράπεζα. Had it been a money payment into the bank, the nature of the sum, whether teben, stater, or kite, would probably have been stated.

[4] From the handwriting I should be inclined to date the ostracon as late Ptolemaic. If so, the 35th year would be either of Philometor or Euergetes II, 147/6 or 136/5 B.C.

## OSTR. D 61 (Pl. VIII). RECEIPT.

1. Ws-ḥ s Hry Ns-Mn s Pa-by
2. n nt z n P-šr-ʿo-pḥt s Ns-Mn wn
3. . . . . Pr-ʿo 1 a ½ a 1 ʿn e.ʾn-k s
4. a p pr-ḥt n Pr-ʿo n N n ḥsp 35
5. ʾbt-3 pr ss 18 ẖn p wbt (?)
6. sẖ ḥsp 35 ʾbt-3 pr ss 18

'Weser-he, son of Erieus, (and) Zminis, son of Pa-by, say to Psenapathes, son of Zminis: there is . . . . of the King (artaba ?) 1 = ½ = 1 again, which thou hast paid to the treasury of the King in the City (Thebes), in year 35, Phamenoth day 18, among the . . . .[1]. Written year 35, Phamenoth day 18.'

[1] This ostracon is of exactly the same date and in the same handwriting as D 4, see notes there. The givers of the receipt are the same, but the individual to whom the document is given is different and also the subject of the receipt. What *wbt* (or *wbʿ* ?) is, I cannot guess.

## Ostr. D 28 (Pl. II). Tax (?) Receipt.

1. a.ʾn Pa-Mnt s P-msḥ a p r
2. Pr-ʿo ʿ.w.s. n t (?) nsytykwn n ḥsp 2.t
3. ẖr Zme yt (?) $\frac{1}{3}$ $\frac{1}{12}$ a yt (?) $\frac{1}{6}$ $\frac{1}{24}$ a yt (?) $\frac{1}{3}$ $\frac{1}{12}$ ʿn
4. n p ẖy n ʾyp.t sẖ n ḥsp 3.t n
5. Twmʾtyns ʿ.w.s. nt ẖwe
6. [ʾbt-. .] ʾẖ ss 21

'Pamonthes, son of Pempsais, has paid to the royal thesaurus for the ......[1] of year 2 for Jême barley (?) (artaba) $\frac{1}{3}$ $\frac{1}{12}$ = barley (?) $\frac{1}{6}$ $\frac{1}{24}$ = barley (?) $\frac{1}{3}$ $\frac{1}{24}$ again by the measure of the oiphi.[2] Written in year 3 of Domitian, who is august[3] [month- . . of] verdure,[4] day 21.'

[1] This should be the name of a tax or other reason for payment. The reading of the demotic word (which is obviously a Greek word transliterated) is certain except for the second letter *s*. Demotic *ns* is the customary transliteration of ζ and the word which naturally suggests itself is ζυτικόν. There is some obscurity attaching to this tax which rarely occurs under this name (see note in *Pap. Tebt.* ii, p. 335), the usual word being ζυτηρά, but both taxes were paid in money, whereas here the payment is made in corn of some kind; for though there is some doubt about the symbol for 'barley', the reference to the measure of the oiphi and the payment into the θησαυρὸς βασιλικός are conclusive as to its being grain in some form.

[2] The οἶφι was equal to four χοίνικες, cf. Wilcken, *Gr. Ostr.* i, 750–1. It occurs not infrequently in demotic documents; in Coptic, Crum, *Coptic Ostr.* no. 499.

[3] lit. 'who protects'. The word *ẖw*, originally 'protect', seems in Ptolemaic times to have come to mean simply 'sacred' when applied to divine beings. In the bilingual inscriptions it is used as the equivalent of ἱερός (Brugsch, *Wtb.* 1061). The formula *nt ẖw* is found on the cartouche of Domitian and many other Roman emperors, and presumably represents σεβαστός (Augustus). On Greek ostraca Domitian is usually qualified as ὁ κύριος or καῖσαρ ὁ κύριος.

[4] i.e. a month between Thoth and Choiak inclusive.

## Ostr. D 19 (Pl. II). Receipt for Rent.

1. a.ʾn P-me s Ḥr-Mnt ẖn p sḥn
2. a.ʾr-f n t qnb.t (?) n p tme n p wḥ (?) ʾs
3. n p wḥ (?) ʾMn P-ʾhe n ḥsp 22 m (?) sẖ wy mbḥ

4. ʾMn-Rʿ-nsw[1]-ntr-w rtb sw 50 a sw 25 a sw 50 ʿn
5. n p qws n ḥmt n ḥ.t-ntr N e-w swt
6. st šp ʾp sẖ Ns . . . . . Z-ḥr
7. sẖ ḥsp 22 ʾbt-1 pr ss 24 . . . . .
8. s P-ẖl-Ḫns ẖr-f (?)

'Pmois, son of Harmonthes, has paid under (?) the (contract of) lease which he made with the council (?) of the village of "The old Estate (?)"[2] on the estate (?) of Amon[3] (called) Pois,[4] in year 22,[5] by deed of cession[6] before Amonrasonther,[7] 50 artabas of wheat = 25 (artabas of) wheat = 50 (artabas of) wheat again by the bronze χοῦς-measure[8] of the temple of Thebes, they being delivered.[9] They are received by reckoning (?).[10]

Written by Ns . . . ., (son of) Teos. Written in year 22, Tybi day 24, by . . . . . son of Pkhelkhons, on his account (?).'

[1] Sethe, *A. Z.* xlix. 15. His arguments for this reading seem to me convincing.

[2] The reading and meaning of *wḥ* are doubtful. The word occurs frequently in place-names. Spiegelberg reads it *ḥr* 'face', 'aspect', and gives references (*Rec. trav.* xxxi, pp. 98 and 104, n. xxix) to its use with the words 'North' and 'South'. But this meaning does not satisfy other contexts, and the sign may equally well be read *wḥ*, possibly with a meaning akin to ⲟⲩⲱϩ 'dwell, dwelling-place', though as it is here applied to a landed property containing a village, it must have a wider significance than a mere house or group of houses. This village is named also in D 24 and D 100.

[3] This property of the great Temple of Amon at Thebes is mentioned on other documents, viz. Pap. dem. Berlin 3116, col. 6, l. 21, and Ostr. Louvre 9086 (Revillout, *Mélanges*, p. 80), and another unnumbered (ibid. p. 191, *p wḥ* (?) *ʾhy*), and Pap. dem. Brussels 5 (Spiegelberg, *Demot. Pap. Mus. Roy. du Cinquantenaire*, pp. 20 and 24, note 21, *p ʾhy* only).

[4] Pois is the Greek form of the demotic *p ʾhy* given by the Pap. Casati 14/5 (Bibl. nat. no. 5, only in the genitive πωεως). It means 'the stables', no doubt large erections for the great herds of cattle belonging to the Temple. Cf. Spiegelberg, *Pap. Reinach*, p. 196. In Peyron, *Pap. gr. Taurin*, ii, p. 45, we have ποενπωις, perhaps *p wḥ* (*ḥr* ?) *n p ʾhy*. Cf. *Philologus*, lxiii, p. 530.

[5] Judging by the writing I think the date is probably late Ptolemaic, but as several kings reigned twenty-two years and over, it is not possible to be more precise.

[6] See Griffith, *Cat. Rylands Demot. Pap.* iii, p. 255.

[7] i. e. confirmed by oath in the great Temple of Amon at Karnak.

[8] Cf. Griffith, *u. s.* p. 397 ; also Spiegelberg, *Pap. Reinach*, 3 9, 4/14 (he reads *ḥnws* ?), Ostr. Louvre 9083, 9066 (Revillout, *Mélanges*, pp. 92, 110). M. Revillout was the first to read the word as *kos* (= *qws*). As to the 'bronze' measure, see *Pap. Hibeh*, i, p. 229.

[9] 'They', i.e. 'the wheat'; *swt* probably implies actual delivery at the cost of the tenant, cf. Spiegelberg, *u.s.* p. 183.

[10] The exact significance of this frequently recurring sentence is not clear. The full phrase is *st šp n 'p* and seems to mean that the amount has been received after being counted or measured.

## OSTR. D 45 (Pl. V). RECEIPT FOR RENT.

1. ʾn Hrklts
2. s ʾRystypws
3. ẖr p šm pe-f (?) km n t mrwt
4. ʾpy nt sẖ wy mbḥ ʾMn-Rʿ-nsw-ntr-w
5. p ntr ʿo ḥnʿ pe-f ʾrp a wʿ km
6. ʾrp 2 ẖr pe-f km
7. n p ʾbr (?) rt ʾrp ½
8. a ʾrp 2½ st šp n (?) ʾp
9. sẖ . . . . s Ḫf-Ḫns ḥsp 15 a ḥsp 12
10. ʾbt-1 ʾẖ (?) ss 25 sẖ Ḥr . . . -Ḫns
11. sh Wn-nfr s Ḥr sẖ Z-ḥr Ḫf-Ḫns

'Herakleitos,[1] son of Aristippus, has paid for the rent [2] of his garden in the corn-land [3] of Ophi,[4] which was conveyed [5] before Amonrasonther the great god, together with his wine(-tax?) for a garden 2 (keramia of) wine [6] for his garden (and) for the . . . . (of) the produce half a (keramion of) wine, making 2½ (keramia of) wine. They are received by reckoning (?).

Written by . . . . son of Khapokhonsis, year 15 = year 12,[7] Thoth (?) day 25.

Written by Horus, (son of) . . . -khons.

Written by Onnophris, son of Horus.

Written by Teos, son of Khapokhonsis.

[1] Or Heraklides.

[2] Cf. Spiegelberg, *Pap. Reinach*, pp. 181–2, 240. If further proof were required that *šm* = *ἐκφόριον*, it is given by a bilingual in this collection, G. 131, where the two words correspond.

[3] Cf. Griffith, *Cat. Rylands Pap.* iii, p. 266, n. 15.

[4] i.e. the modern Karnak.

[5] Usually *sẖ wy* means a deed conveying all the property in the land possessed by the owner. Here it seems to be a lease.

[6] For this use of *'rp* as a measure of wine, cf. Rosetta, l. 18.

[7] This double date applies to the regnal years of Cleopatra III and Alexander I = 102 B.C.

## OSTR. D 216 (Pl. V). RECEIPT FOR RENT.

1. Tḥwt-stm s
2. By-ʿnẖ
3. p nt Z n Ḥr-py-kʾ s
4. Pa-n-nẖt.w (?) erme P-ʾhy s
5. P-ẖm-bk wn sttr.t 2.t
6. a sttr.t 1.t a sttr.t 2.t ʿn
7. šp n ʾp ẖr p šm n
8. T-sgt (?) sẖ n ḥsp 6.t
9. tp-šm ss 14 (*2nd hand*) sẖ Tḥwt-stm
10. s By-ʿnẖ

'Thotsutmis, son of Bienchis, saith to Harpikos, son of Panekhates (?), and Pois (?), son of P-khem-bekis: there are[1] 2 staters = 1 stater = 2 staters again received by reckoning (?) for the rent of Tseget (?). Written in year 6, Pachons day 14. Signed Thotsutmis, son of Bienchis.'

[1] i.e. 'I have' = ἔχω of the Greek tax-collectors' receipts (Wilcken, *Griech. Ostr.* i, p. 61 sq.).

## OSTR. D 49 (Pl. XI). NOTICE OF PAYMENT OF RENT.

1. Ššnq s Pa-ʾMn p nt z n P-hb
2. s P-šr-Mnt te-y mḥ p ḥwe Ḥr-nẖt
3. n t t.t $\frac{1}{4}$ n p yḥ tkm a.ʾr-k t (?) wp.t ḥr zz
4. p mʾ n t msḥ n ḥsp 10 ẖr T-šr.t-ʾMn-ḥtp (?)
5. ta Ns-Mn e-y st ty . . . . a hn
6. ḥsp 9 sẖ Ššnq s Pa-ʾMn n ḥsp 9 ʾbt-3 šm ss 19

'Sheshonk, son of Pamounis, saith to Phibis, son of Psenmonthes, I am paying the surplus of Ho-nekht[1] for the quarter share of the land (under) oil-crop, of which thou doest the work,[2] on the canal[3] of the Crocodile for year 10 on behalf of Senamenothis (?), the daughter of Zminis. I will discharge (?)[4] this . . . . until year 9. Signed Sheshonk, son of Pamounis, in year 9,[5] Epiphi day 19.'

[1] The name of a farm—more clearly written in D 107 (pl. XI). Perhaps it should be read *wḥ-nḫl*, cf. D 19, note 2 above. The farm was probably worked in common by Sheshonk and Phibis under a farming agreement such as we have in Griffith, *Cat. Rylands Pap.* nos. xxvi, xxxiv (and see reffs. there, pp. 155–6).

[2] i. e. in the full phrase *t wp.t wyᶜ* (ειεποτοει) 'tillage'. It means here the work on the crop, not 'work on the canal', the *ḥr zz* refers to the locality of the farm.

[3] The word *m'*, the old word for a canal (Griffith, *u. s.* p. 170, n. 3, and p. 299, n. 7), is only known to me in published demotic documents in the compound *me-wr* = μοῖρις (Griffith, *u. s.* and p. 423; Spiegelberg, *A. Z.* xliii. 84) and once alone (Spiegelberg, *Demot. Pap. Mus. Roy. du Cinquantenaire*, no. 4, l. 3). It seems to have survived chiefly in place-names. In this collection, besides the present instance, we have in D 35 *p m' t zlᶜ* 'the canal of the Scorpion', D 147 *p m' u Ḥr-p-K* (?) 'the canal of Horus-the-bull'. From the context it seems usually, however, to denote a tract of land named after the canal bounding it (?). 'The crocodile' has the feminine article and must refer to a crocodile-goddess, cf. D 22, note 4.

[4] lit. 'avert'. The meaning of this phrase is probably 'I will be responsible for the payment of rent till the end of year 9, if you do the work on the land'.

[5] Phibis, son of Psenmonthes, occurs on a number of these ostraca, including D 6 below, and as he is doubtless the same person in both, it is likely that this is the ninth year of Augustus.

## Ostr. D 107 (Pl. XI). Receipt for Rent.

1. [a.]ʾn P-hb s P-šr-Mnt
2. ẖn p ḥwe Ḥr-nḫt
3. p yḥ tkm a ʾr-f ḥ-zz
4. t msḥ ẖr ḥsp 10.t tkm
5. 12 ẖr t tʾ.t $\frac{1}{6}$ p yḥ rn-f
6. e-f šp ʾp sẖ Nḫt-Mnt
7. s Ḫf-Ḫns n ḥsp 10.t ʾbt-1 šm ss 25

'Phibis, son of Psenmonthes, has paid from among the surplus of Ho-nekht[1] the land (under) oil crop which he worked[2] on the Crocodile[3] on account of year 10, oil (artabas) 12 for the $\frac{1}{6}$th share of the land named. It is received by reckoning (?). Signed Nekhthmonthes, son of Khapokhonsis, in year 10, Pachons 25.'

[1] Cf. D 49, note 1.

[2] *'r-f* here is evidently equivalent to *'r t wp.t* in D 49.

[3] = the place known as the 'Canal of the Crocodile' in D 49. This ostracon is much abbreviated and would be unintelligible without D 49. Note the writing *ḥ-zz* for *ḥr-zz*.

## Ostr. D 55 (Pl. IX). Receipt for a Tax (?).

1. E-f-ʿnḫ s Wm-p-mw (?)
2. p nt z n Py-k s E-f-ʿ[nḫ]
3. wn sttr 2.t p ms šp n ['p ?]
4. ḫn pe-k t'y (?) n ḥsp 16 . . .

'Apynkhis, son of Wem-pmou (?),[1] saith to Pikos, son of Apynkhis: there are 2 staters (and) the interest received by reckoning (?) for thy tax (?)[2] of year 16 . . . .'

[1] The name is incomplete owing to the left-hand corner of the ostracon having been broken away; but it can hardly be anything else. The tip of the determinative of *mw* 'death' remains. The name, which is new to me, means 'Death has consumed' and is parallel to *Sy-p-mw* (σιεπμους) 'Death is sated' (cf. Griffith, *Cat. Rylands Pap.* iii, p. 131, n. 7). The name *P-šr-p-mw* 'the child of death' occurs on an ostracon (D 81) in this collection.

[2] This seems to be the same word as in Brugsch, *A. Z.* xxix. 67–8, and Spiegelberg, *Rec. trav.* xxxi. 102; cf. Id., *Pap. Reinach*, pp. 181–2. It is written very like *šm* 'rent', but the determinative is different. Here I think it is the silver determinative.

## Ostr. D 56 (Pl. IX). Receipt for Money.

1. Pa-Mnt s Pa-p-zyt sme a
2. Pa-Zme s Py-k wn krkr 5
3. erme p . . . . šp n 'p ḫr P-'šwr
4. s P-šr-'Np
5. sḫ n ḥsp 29 'bt-1 pr ss 14

'Pamonthes, son of Papzoit,[1] sends greeting to Pasemis, son of Pikos. There are 5 talents and the . . . .[2] received by reckoning (?) for Pesuris, son of Psenenupis. Written in year 29, Tybi day 14.'

[1] lit. 'he of the olive tree', a name I have not met elsewhere.

[2] This word begins with *w*; the gender prevents it being *wz.t* 'interest'. It may be the same as the obscure word in l. 5 of D 61 (*wbt*?).

## OSTR. D 22 (Pl. II). ACKNOWLEDGEMENT OF WHEAT-LOAN (?).

1. ḥsp 18 ꜥbt-1 šm ss 12
2. Pa-Mnt s P-šr-ꜣMn-ꜣpy p nt z
3. n P-šr-ꜣMn s My-ḥs wn nte-k
4. rtb n sw 22½ a ꜥ-y nte-y
5. t šp-w a p qws n Mn-k-Rꜥ (?)
6. s (?) Pa-Mnt p srtyqws erme
7. ne-w hwe-w ẖr (?) wn n yḥ a-te-k n-y
8. ẖn p gsmꜣ n t
9. msḥ.t n ḥsp 18
10. n ḥtr ꜣt mn

'Year 18, Pachons day 12, Pamonthes, son of Psenamenophis, saith to Psenamounis, son of Miusis, there are (belonging) to thee[1] 22½ artabas of wheat in my charge and I will cause them to be received at the χοῦς-measure of Menkere (?),[2] son (?) of Pamonthes, the strategus, together with their interest (?)[3] according to (?) (the) list of fields which thou gavest me in the "canal-land (?) of the Crocodile"[4] in the year 18 compulsorily without delay.'

[1] i.e. 'I owe thee', cf. Spiegelberg, *Pap. Reinach*, p. 199.

[2] For corn-measures known by the names of individuals cf. *Cat. Greek. Pap. Brit. Mus.* ii, p. 257. The reading of the name Menkere (only the final syllable is doubtful) I owe to Dr. F. Ll. Griffith. Nothing else is known of this strategus unless, as Dr. Griffith suggests, he be the same as Menkere, the father of Hamsauf (?), whose tomb-papyrus ('Book of the Dead') we have in the Rhind papyrus (ed. H. Brugsch, 1865). Menkere is there called governor (hieratic *wr*, demotic *ꜥo* 'great one') of Hermonthis, but his father's name is not given, only that of his mother. His son was born in the thirteenth year of Ptolemy Neos Dionysos,

69–8 B.C.; and if the eighteenth year of the ostracon be taken to refer to the same king (64–3 B.C.), I should not be inclined to contradict it on palaeographical grounds, though it could perhaps be earlier.

[3] The meaning of *hw* is uncertain. The word itself is very general, 'excess, addition.' It might mean cost of carriage, or in connexion with the measurement (cf. Spiegelberg, *Pap. Reinach*, 1/13, p. 176), but is more likely interest on the loan (Spiegelberg, *Pap. Strassb.* no. 44/5, *Pap. Berlin*, no. 3103/7, *Rec. trav.* xxxi, p. 92, and Griffith, *Cat. Rylands Pap.* no. xxi, l. 11).

[4] The word *gsm*ʾ is obscure. It has the determinative of water, and being written out alphabetically it suggests a foreign word. It possibly might stand for χάσμα, though the transliteration of χ by *g* is unusual. But it may also be a demotic writing for a hieroglyphic 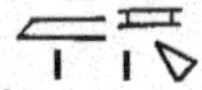 'side of a canal' (for *m*ʾ = , see D 49, note 3 above), and be equivalent to περίχωμα 'land bounded by a dyke or canal', *Pap. Tebt.* i, p. 80. The 'canal-land (?) of the Crocodile (fem.)' is a place-name, the crocodile being no doubt a local goddess; with *t-msḥ.t*, cf. Lake Timsah. See also D 175, note 1, p. 54 infra.

## Ostr. D. 24 (Pl. II). Acknowledgement of Receipt of Wheat.

1. Twt s Še-ny p mr pr-st.t (?)
2. n pr ʾMn n s 2-n sme a n rt-w n
3. t šme.t wn rtb n sw 35 a sw 17½ a sw 35 ʿn
4. e-te s n-y Ns-Mn s P-a.te-ʾMn-nsw-tw Z-ḥr s Mnḥs
5. n sḥn-w n p wḥ (?) ʾs n ḥsp 30 ẖn pe ʾp
6. n s 2-n st šp n ʾp
7. Sẖ ḥsp 30 ʾbt-2 šm ss 2

'Totoes, son of Shenai,[1] the chief baker[2] of the Temple of Amon, of the second[3] phyle, greets the bailiffs of the stock-farm (?).[4] There are[5] 35 artabas of wheat = 17½ (artabas of) wheat = 35 (artabas of) wheat again, which Zminis, son of Petamestous, and Teos, son of Menhes,[6] the collectors[7] of "The Old Estate (?)",[8] gave to me for year 30 in my account of the second phyle. They are received by reckoning (?).

Written in year 30, Payni day 2.'

[1] The literal meaning of the name as written is 'These have departed', but what the mythological reference is, I do not know. Perhaps the Greek transcription is σεναιης (*Cat. Greek Pap. Brit. Mus.* iii, p. 164—a woman's name there).

[2] The same title is found in *Pap. Dem. Berlin*, 3116, col. 2, l. 18, with the

Greek equivalent ἀρτοκ[όπος] in *Pap. Casati*, vi, l. 1, and in Petrie, *Denderah*, pl. XXVI. A 28, 29, lit. 'overseer of the fire-chamber', i.e. kitchen or bakery. The reading of this last may perhaps be *ʿ-st.t* (?), cf. Spiegelberg, *Cat. Cairo Dem. Pap.* no. 30801.

[3] The numeral is written with the old form of the ordinal numbers, cf. Griffith, *Cat. Rylands Pap.* p. 417. In what sense Totoes belonged to the second phyle is not clear, probably not as Chief Baker (cf. Otto, *Priester u. Tempel im Hellenistischen Aegypten*, i. 283), but he may have been priest as well, though it does not seem probable in so large an institution as the Temple of Amon at Thebes.

[4] This word occurs again on two other ostraca in this collection (D 78, D 157) and Ostr. Louvre 9083 (Revillout, *Mélanges*, p. 92). Perhaps it is only a variant of the word *šmyme.t* which is found on an ostracon at Cairo (*A. Z.* xxix. 70), and which Brugsch translates *Gehöft* 'farm-buildings', deriving it doubtless from  which is found on the Pianchi stela with the meaning 'stables' or 'stud-farm', cf. Brugsch, *Wtb.* 1390, *Suppl.* 1186.

[5] i.e. 'I have in my charge', 'I account for'. The rent-collectors of the village which was on the estate of the Temple (p. 32 supra) would ordinarily hand over the rents, which were paid in kind, to the Temple-bailiffs; but in this instance they handed these 35 artabas direct to the Chief Baker for his use, and hence he addresses this ostracon to the bailiffs.

[6] These two officials are named also on D 100 and the former of them on D 103 also. On D 100 the name Menhes is clearly written in its more familiar form Menkhes.

[7] Cf. Spiegelberg (*A. Z.* xlii. 57), who takes the *sḫn* to have been 'finance officials', perhaps taxation officials, corresponding to the λογευταί who were the ordinary tax-collectors of Ptolemaic times (Grenfell and Hunt, *Fayum Towns*, p. 323). Here they are clearly collectors of rents or other dues belonging to the Temple.

[8] Cf. p. 32 supra, D 19 and notes 2, 3 ibid.

## OSTR. D 51 (Pl. II). ACKNOWLEDGEMENT OF RECEIPT OF WHEAT.

1. Ššnq s Ḥr . . . . . . . . . .
2. s Ššnq n nt z n P-šr-Mnt (?)
3. s P-šr-ʾMn-ʾpy wn rtb sw 1½ n p qws
4. n 29 e-te-k s n-n ẖr P-a.te-ʾMn (?) p mr šn Mnt
5. p ḥm-ntr 2-n ẖn n sw a.te-f n-n n p ẖʿ Mnt
6. ḥsp 9 st šp n ʾp sẖ n ḥsp 9 ʾbt-1 šm ss 26

'Sheshonk son of Hor (?), [and X.] son of Sheshonk, say unto Psenmonthes son of Psenamenophis: there are[1] 1½ artabas of wheat by the

29-χοῦς measure [2] which thou hast given to us on behalf of Petamounis (?), the chief priest [3] of Montu (and) second prophet, among the wheat which he gave us for the festival of Montu [4] of the 9th year. They are received by reckoning (?).

Written in year 9, Pachons day 21.'

[1] i. e. 'we have'.

[2] The artaba varied in size locally and hence was frequently defined. What was the meaning of this particular measure, which occurs frequently, is obscure. It is discussed in Griffith, *Cat. Rylands Pap.* iii, p. 397, and references given there.

[3] The *mr-šn* is represented in the Canopus and Rosetta decrees by ἀρχιερεύς, and etymologically by the word λεσῶνις. He was administrator as well as chief priest of the temple and was elected annually (*Arch. f. Papyrusforschung*, ii, p. 122; cf. Griffith, *u. s.* p. 65, note 3).

[4] There is, as far as I know, no record of the date of the annual feast of Montu at Thebes. From this it would appear that it was possibly in Pachons.

## OSTR. D 100 (Pl. II). ACKNOWLEDGEMENT OF RECEIPT OF WHEAT.

1. Še-ny s Ḫns-p-ẖrt p gwt n pr Mnt nb
2. .... s tp p nt z n Ns-Mn s P-a.te-ʾMn-nsw-tw
3. Z-ḥr s Mnḫ n sḥn-w n p wḥ (?) ʾs wn rtb
4. n sw 10 a sw 5 a sw 10 ʿn e.te-tn n-y ẖr
5. p fy pr Mnt nb .... s tp
6. st šp ʾp
7. sẖ n ḥsp 30 ʾbt-1 šm ss 21

'Shenai, son of Khespokhrates, the *gwt* [1] of the temple of Montu, lord of .... [2] (of) the first phyle saith to Zminis, son of Petamestous, (and) Teos, son of Menkhes,[3] the collectors of "The Old Estate": there are 10 artabas of wheat = 5 (artabas of) wheat = 10 (artabas of) wheat again, which you have given me on account of the bread-rations [4] (of) the temple of Montu, lord of .... (for) the first phyle. They are received by reckoning (?). Written year 30, Pachons day 21.'

[1] Cf. Spiegelberg in *A. Z.* xxxvii. 36. The meaning is uncertain; from similar hieroglyphic titles Spiegelberg thought it might mean a workman, but in demotic

at any rate the title is always associated with a temple or a god. In his later *Cat. Demotic Papyri at Cairo* (no. 31080) Spiegelberg translates it '*kut*-Priester', and as its holder is described as belonging to a phyle (D 103 below), he was probably a priest.

[2] Montu is usually 'lord of Wese (Karnak)' or 'of Hermonthis', or rarely 'of Totun' (*Cat. Dem. Papyri Cairo, u. s.*), but I cannot read any of these in the present signs.

[3] See D 24 and notes 6 and 7, p. 39, supra. For the 'Old Estate', cf. D 19, note 2 (p. 32).

[4] Cf. D 31, note 6, infra, p. 52.

## OSTR. D 103 (Pl. II). ACKNOWLEDGEMENT OF RECEIPT OF WHEAT.

1. Še-ny s Ḫns-p-ẖrt p gwt n pr
2. Mnt s . . . . p nt z n Ns-Mn s P-a.te-ʾMn-nsw-tw
3. [p] sḥn n (?) t (?) my.t rs n ḥsp 30 wn rtb n sw $5\frac{1}{2}\ \frac{1}{12}$
4. [a sw] $2\frac{1}{2}\ \frac{1}{4}\ \frac{1}{24}$ a rtb n sw $5\frac{1}{2}\ \frac{1}{12}$ ʿn e.te-k [n-y]
5. [ẖr p] fy n pr Mnt nb . . .
6. sẖ ḥsp 30 ʾbt-4 pr (?) . . .

'Shenai, son of Khespokhrates,[1] the *gwt* of the temple of Montu, (of the) . . . . phyle[2] saith to Zminis, son of Petamestous,[3] the collector of the Southern Island[4] for year 30: there are $5\frac{1}{2}\ \frac{1}{12}$ artabas of wheat [= wheat (artabas)] $2\frac{1}{2}\ \frac{1}{4}\ \frac{1}{24} = 5\frac{1}{2}\ \frac{1}{12}$ artabas of wheat again, which thou hast given [to me on account of the] bread-rations (?)[5] of the temple of Montu, lord of . . . .

Written in year 30, Pharmuthi (?) . . . .'

[1] Cf. D 100, supra, p. 40.

[2] In D 100 Shenai is said to belong to the first phyle. Here the reading looks like 'fifth phyle', but the number is faint, and I do not venture to insert it. It would be unprecedented to find a man belonging to two phylae in succession (cf. Otto, *Priester u. Tempel*, i. 31) except in the circumstances arising out of the formation of the fifth phyle (Canopus decree), and the date does not allow of that explanation here; but see *P.S.B.A.* xxxi. 219, where a priest appears to belong to two phylae at once. A few months only separate this ostracon and D 100.

[3] Cf. D 24.

[4] Not referred to elsewhere, I believe.

[5] Cf. D 31, note 6, p. 52 infra.

## Ostr. D 135 (Pl. V). Order to Deliver Wheat.

1. a.nw a p gy n t rtb n sw 2
2. Py-k s My a ẖ p tbḥe nte-y
3. ṯ.t-f (?) n-t.t-k δοθηναι πικωτι
   τας δυο αρταβ(ας)

'See[1] to the giving[2] of two artabas of wheat (to) Pikos, son of Moui, according to the petition which I have received (?) from thee. (*Greek*)[3] To be given to Pikos, the two artabas.'

[1] The old form of imperative retained in the Coptic ⲁⲛⲁⲩ.
[2] *ϭⲓⲛϯ actio dandi: so far only the Bohairic form ϫⲓⲛϯ seems to have occurred (Peyron).
[3] Mr. Milne has kindly read the Greek. There is room for the two missing letters at the end, and possibly a trace of them exists.

## Ostr. D 12 (Pl. III). Land Measurement.

1. ḥsp 11.t ꜣbt-4 ꜣḫ ss 20 n ẖy-w n P-twl
2. n P-šr-ꜣNp s Py-k erme (?) pe-f ꜣre nt ẖn
3. p yḥ ʿŠ-ꜣẖy mḥ-1 n rs
4. $\frac{1}{2}\ \frac{\bullet}{1\frac{1}{4}}\ \frac{1}{2}\ \frac{1}{16}$ a tmt (?) $\frac{1}{2}\ \frac{1}{8}\ \frac{1}{32}$
5. te-f (?) . . .
6. $\frac{1}{2}\ \frac{1}{8}\ \frac{1\frac{1}{4}\ \frac{1}{8}}{1\frac{1}{4}\ \frac{1}{16}}\ \frac{1}{2}\ \frac{1}{4}$ a tmt (?) $\frac{1}{2}\ \frac{1}{4}\ \frac{1}{8}\ \frac{1}{16}$
7. ybt (?) . . .
8. $\frac{1}{2}\ \frac{1}{4}\ \frac{1}{8}\ \frac{1}{1\frac{1}{4}}\ \frac{1}{2}\ \frac{1}{4}\ \frac{1}{32}$ a tmt (?) $\frac{1}{2}\ \frac{1}{4}\ \frac{1}{8}\ \frac{1}{16}$
9. te-f (?) . . .
10. $\frac{1}{4}\ \frac{1}{16}\ \frac{\frac{1}{2}\ \frac{1}{8}\ \frac{1}{16}}{\bullet}\ \frac{1}{2}\ \frac{1}{8}\ \frac{1}{16}$ a tmt (?) $\frac{1}{4}\ \frac{1}{16}$

'Year 11, Khoiak day 20, the measurements of Ptollis for (?) Psenenupis, son of Pikos, and (?) his companion, which are in the first field of Asychis on the South.[1]

$\frac{1}{2}\ \dfrac{1\frac{1}{4}}{1\frac{1}{4}}\ \frac{9}{16}$ = total (?)[2] $\frac{21}{32}$ (arura)[3]

its adjacent (?)[4] (piece)

$\frac{5}{8}\ \dfrac{1\frac{3}{8}}{1\frac{5}{16}}\ \frac{3}{4}$ = total (?) $\frac{15}{16}$ (arura)

East (?) . . .

$\frac{7}{8}\ \dfrac{1}{1\frac{1}{4}}\ \frac{25}{32}$ = total (?) $\frac{15}{16}$ (arura)

its adjacent (?) (piece)

$\frac{15}{16}\ \dfrac{\frac{11}{16}}{\frac{11}{16}}\ \frac{11}{16}$ = total (?) $\frac{5}{16}$ (arura).'[5]

[1] This system of recording land measurements has been explained by Kenyon in his *Cat. Greek Pap. Brit. Mus.* ii, p. 129. The dimensions of the sides of each plot are written round a line representing the plot. The unit of measurement is the *ḫ.t* = 100 cubits linear *, or should be, strictly speaking, as the scribe employs the fractions of the arura here and in all the instances I have met with, the arura having a set of symbols for its fractions distinct from those for ordinary fractions, which should properly be used for those of the *ḫ.t*. Since the arura was $100 \times 100$ cubits, or a square *ḫ.t*, it comes to the same thing for practical purposes, though it is logically indefensible, if he says $\frac{1}{2}$ (ar.) $\times \frac{1}{2}$ (ar.) $= \frac{1}{4}$ arura, when he means $\frac{1}{2}$ (*ḫ.t*) $\times \frac{1}{2}$ (*ḫ.t*) $= \frac{1}{4}$ arura. It is only a substitution of the symbols he is working with. The area is obtained by multiplying together the means of the two opposite numbers. When the two opposite sides of a plot have the same length, the figure is written out once and a dot placed on the other side of the line.

Other examples of land measurement may be found in *Cat. Greek Pap. u. s.* and *Pap. Tebt.* no. 87 (Greek), in Brugsch, *Thesaurus*, iii. 567 (hieroglyphic), Hall, *Greek and Coptic Ostraca*, p. 128 (Coptic), and in demotic, in this collection are several examples.

[2] A symbol having a strong likeness to the fraction $\frac{1}{8}$ (ar.) followed by a dot comes in each case between the preposition *a* ('amounting to') and the result. It must stand for 'total' or 'superficies'.

[3] None of the fractions are carried beyond the nearest $\frac{1}{32}$. Strictly the first result should be $\frac{85}{128}$, i.e. $\frac{1}{128}$ more than is set down. The second result is overstated by $\frac{7}{512}$, the third by $\frac{3}{512}$, and the fourth is understated by $\frac{1}{32}$. On other ostraca the measurements are carried down to $\frac{1}{64}$ arura.

[4] This is speculative: I cannot read it.

* This *ḫ.t*, the linear measurement, must not be confused with the *mḥ ḫ̌t* or square cubit, a unit of surface. This *ḫ̌t* is a different word altogether.

[5] Against each of the first three measurements some notes are recorded in the margin; but as I do not feel at all sure of their reading, I give them under reserve here. To the first: *sp* .... *mḥ* 50(?) *n ḫt* 'remainder .... 50 square cubits', and below it *a st* $\frac{1}{2}$ $\frac{1}{8}$ .... '= $\frac{5}{8}$ arura', which I take to mean that 50 square cubits have for some reason or other been omitted from the measurement and also $\frac{5}{8}$ ar. of land unfit to be included owing to it being desert, salt-marsh, &c., indicated by the word I cannot read. To the second: *sp a mḥ* 80 (?) 'remainder 80 (?) cubits' and .... *st* $\frac{1}{4}$ $\frac{1}{16}$ '.... arura $\frac{5}{16}$'. To the third: *sp* .... *mḥ* 80 (?) 'remainder .... 80 (?) cubits'.

## OSTR. D 23 (Pl. IV). ALLOTMENT (?) OF LAND.

1. a.rḫ-w a P-šr-Mnt s P-hb st 3 a st 1$\frac{1}{2}$ a st 3 ʿn
2. sẖ ʿO-pḥt s Ḥr-s-ʾS ḥsp 30 ʾbt-4 šm ss 2
3. sẖ Ḫns-Tḥwt s P-šr-Mn a st 3 a ẖ p nt sẖ ḥry
4. sẖ P-a.te-p-šy s Ḥr-Tḥwt
5. a st 3 a ẖ p nt sẖ ḥry
6. sẖ S-wsr s ʿNḫ-Ḥʿp
7. st 3 a st 1$\frac{1}{2}$ a st 3 ʿn

'There have been adjudged (?)[1] to Psenmonthes, son of Phibis, 3 aruras = 1$\frac{1}{2}$ aruras = 3 aruras again. Written by Apathes, son of Harsiesis, year 30,[2] Mesore day 2.

(2nd hand) Written by Khesthotes, son of Psenminis, for 3 aruras as is above written.

(3rd hand) Written by Petepsais, son of Harthotes, for 3 aruras as is above written.

(4th hand) Written by Senwosre,[3] son of Ankh-Hapi, 3 aruras = 1$\frac{1}{2}$ aruras = 3 aruras again.'

[1] *rḫ*, primarily 'to know', 'recognize', seems to have a technical meaning here. It is followed by *a* (ⲉ) and apparently means 'to recognize as belonging to', 'measure out to', 'adjudge', just the meaning of the Coptic verb ⲣⲱϣⲉ which is found followed by ⲉ in the same sense, e. g. Z. 419, ϥⲥⲟⲟⲩⲛ ⲅⲁⲣ ϫⲉⲛⲕⲱϩⲧ ⲛⲧⲅⲉϩⲉⲛⲁ ⲛⲁⲣⲱϣⲉ ⲉⲛⲉⲧⲉⲙⲡⲟⲩⲟⲩⲱϣ ⲉⲥⲱⲧⲙ 'for he knows that the fire of Gehenna will be meted out to those who have refused to hearken'. The derivation of ⲣⲱϣⲉ is unknown and may come from this special use of *rḫ*. (The

other verb ⲡⲱϣⲉ 'to see to', 'consider', is associated with *rḫ* by Brugsch, *Wb.* p. 868, and by Griffith, *Cat. Rylands Pap.* iii. 367, but this word, whether it have the same origin or not, has become differentiated in meaning.) Dr. Griffith has kindly referred me to what is perhaps a similar use of the word *rḫ* in earlier times, *Beni-Hasan*, i, p. 59, where Chnemhotep relates how the king 'came . . . . and caused one city to know its boundary with another city, establishing their landmarks as heaven, reckoning their waters (*rḫ mw-sn*) according to that which was in the writings', &c., i.e. allotting their rights in the water for irrigation purposes. Probably the sense is approximately the same here, and these ostraca may refer to rectifications of boundaries of land disturbed by the inundation. The amount of land is sometimes so small as to exclude the idea that they can be allotments of *kleroi* or of farms to royal *georgoi*.

This ostracon is one of a considerable group. Revillout has published four examples from the Louvre, nos. 8007, 9070, 9083, and 9152 (*Mélanges*, pp. 108, 97, 92, 99), but I cannot agree with many of his readings. There are sixteen examples in this collection, and five others, unpublished, are known to me. They usually state that so much land has been adjudged (?) to X. This formula is expanded in Louvre 9083, 9152 to 'there has been adjudged (?) to the (land-) measurements' (*a n ḫy*) of X, &c., and in D 41 here we have 'there has been adjudged (?) for the compensation of the measurements (*n p 's n ḫy-w*) of the year 23 of Caesar to X'. In Louvre 9070 we read 'There have been adjudged (?) to X for the tillage (*wp.t wyʿ*) of the temple of Montu, lord of Thebes' so many aruras. These documents are usually signed by three officials, but their status is not revealed. The land is always agricultural land but its locality is nowhere more closely defined than 'in Jême'. Some few of the ostraca give further details, which only make the subject more obscure; they will be discussed in the notes as they occur.

[2] I am inclined to think that the whole group dates from about the same period. The regnal years fall into two groups, one ranging from 2 to 9, the other from 22 to 37, with a single one of year 17 between them. Only one, D 41 (not published here because it is partly obliterated), bears a definite date, year 23 of Augustus. But another, D 82 below, bears the name of a man, Pikos the younger, son of Permamis, who is almost necessarily identified with a group of Greek ostraca which Mr. Milne attributes to the years 94 to 75 B.C. (Part III, no. 12 note). On palaeographical grounds I should be content to accept Mr. Milne's date also for my group, except perhaps for D 44, which looks to me Roman; but I confess to having little confidence in my ability to put anything like an accurate date to these demotic hands on ostraca, and as I cannot distinguish D 41 with its certain Augustan date from the rest of the group, I must leave the problem open.

[3] This official signs four other ostraca in this group ranging between years 29 and 36. His name is the same as that of the 12th dynasty kings which used to be transliterated as Usertesen, and of which Sethe gave the correct reading and interpretation (*Untersuchungen*, ii; *A. Z.* xli, p. 45), equating it with the Sesostris of the Greeks. For the demotic form, see Spiegelberg, *Rec. trav.* xxviii, p. 195. I have refrained from using the Greek form of the name as it does not occur as a proper name in Ptolemaic or Roman times.

## OSTR. D 1 (Pl. IV). ALLOTMENT (?) OF LAND.

1. a.rḫ-w ʾPwlnys s Thʾm
2. rtb sw 10 (?) $\frac{1}{4}$ Zme q st 3 a st 1$\frac{1}{2}$ a st 3 ʿn
3. sẖ S-ws(r) s ʿNḫ-Ḥʿp n ḥsp 35 ʾbt-2 pr
4. sẖ Ḥr-s-ʾS s Ḫns-te-f-nḫt a q st 3
5. a st 1$\frac{1}{2}$ a st 3 ʿn n ḥsp 35
6. sẖ P-šr-Ḥr s P-šr-Ḫns a q st 3 a st 1$\frac{1}{2}$ a st 3 ʿn
7. sẖ P-šr-ʾMn-ʾpy s Ḥr-Tḥwt st 3
8. a st 1$\frac{1}{2}$ st 3 ʿn a ẖ p nt ḥry

'There have been adjudged (?) (to) Apollonius, the son of Teham[1] ......[2] (in) Jême high-land 3 aruras = 1$\frac{1}{2}$ aruras = 3 aruras again. Written by Senwosre, son of Ankh-Hapi, year 35 Mechir.

(2nd hand) Written by Harsiesis, son of Khons-tef-nekht, for high-land 3 aruras = 1$\frac{1}{2}$ ar. = 3 ar. again in the year 35.

(3rd hand) Written by Psenuris, son of Psenkhonsis, for high-land 3 aruras = 1$\frac{1}{2}$ ar. = 3 ar. again.

(4th hand) Written by Psenamenophis, son of Harthotes, 3 aruras = 1$\frac{1}{2}$ ar. (=) 3 ar. again according to the above.'

[1] The final letter of this name may perhaps be *n* instead of *m*; if so, it could represent Θέων.

[2] The words *rtb sw* 10 (?) $\frac{1}{4}$, '10$\frac{1}{4}$ (?) artabas of wheat', look as though they had been inserted later, probably after the ostracon was signed. It may represent a rent reserved on the land allotted, but if so, it is a very high one. Cf. D 44, note 2, p. 49 infra.

[3] Cf. Spiegelberg, *Pap. Elephantine*, p. 15, note ii.

## OSTR. D 25 (Pl. IV). ALLOTMENT (?) OF LAND.

1. a rḫ-w a P-ẖr s Ns-ne-w-ḫmn-ʾw Zme
2. q st 1$\frac{1}{2}\frac{1}{8}\frac{1}{16}$ a st $\frac{1}{2}\frac{1}{4}\frac{1}{16}\frac{1}{32}$ a st 1$\frac{1}{2}\frac{1}{8}\frac{1}{16}$ sẖ S-ws(r) s ʿNḫ-Ḥʿp
3. [ḥsp] 29 2-pr ss 4
4. [sẖ . . . -]Tḥwt ḥnʿ Pa-zme a st 1$\frac{1}{2}\frac{1}{8}\frac{1}{16}$ a st $\frac{1}{2}\frac{1}{4}\frac{1}{16}\frac{1}{32}$ a st 1$\frac{1}{2}\frac{1}{8}\frac{1}{16}$ ʿn

5. [sẖ . . . . . . .] st $1\frac{1}{2}\frac{1}{8}\frac{1}{16}$ a st $\frac{1}{2}\frac{1}{4}\frac{1}{16}\frac{1}{32}$ a st $1\frac{1}{2}\frac{1}{8}\frac{1}{16}$ ʿn a ẖ p nt sẖ ḥry

6. [sẖ . . . -]Tḥwt a st $1\frac{1}{2}\frac{1}{8}\frac{1}{16}$ a st $\frac{1}{2}\frac{1}{4}\frac{1}{16}\frac{1}{32}$ a st $1\frac{1}{2}\frac{1}{8}\frac{1}{16}$ ʿn

'There have been adjudged (?) to Pkhoiris, son of Snakhomneus,[1] (in) Jême high-land $1\frac{11}{16}$ aruras = $\frac{27}{32}$ ar.[2] = $1\frac{11}{16}$ ar. Written by Senwosre, son of Ankh-Hapi, [year] 29, Mechir 4.

(2nd hand) [Written by . . . . -]Thoout and Pasemis for $1\frac{11}{16}$ aruras = $\frac{27}{32}$ ar. = $1\frac{11}{16}$ ar. again.

(3rd hand) [Written by . . . . . .] $1\frac{11}{16}$ ar. = $\frac{27}{32}$ ar. = $1\frac{11}{16}$ ar. again as is written above.

(4th hand) [Written by . . . . -]Thoout for $1\frac{11}{16}$ ar. = $\frac{27}{32}$ ar. = $1\frac{11}{16}$ ar. again.'

[1] This name, which is not uncommon in the Theban district, means 'devoted to Nakhomneus', the latter being a surname of Amon. But what the surname means as an epithet of Amon it is difficult to say. Its literal meaning is 'They of *Ḫmnw* are coming', i.e. the gods or spirits of Shmun, the eight elemental gods, children of Ra, who were associated with Thoth in his worship at Hermopolis (Brugsch, *Dict. Geogr.*, p. 750). The form of the name is comparable with Thoteus, 'Thoth is coming', and several others.

[2] The two signs for the fractions $\frac{1}{16}$ and $\frac{1}{32}$ of an arura are sometimes ligatured when they follow one another, and this has caused them to be read as a single sign. Griffith (*P.S.B.A.* xiv, p. 410 table, and ibid. xxiii, p. 295, and *Cat. Rylands Pap.* iii, p. 414) reads the group as $\frac{2}{16}$ in order to make an equation when the fraction $\frac{1}{2}$ is divided into its component parts. In a similar context it occurs in *Pap. Strassburg* no. 7, line 3. But I believe the Egyptian was satisfied to equate the $\frac{1}{2}$ to as many smaller fractions as he knew, viz. $\frac{1}{4}\frac{1}{8}\frac{1}{16}\frac{1}{32}$. When he wanted to express $\frac{1}{64}$, he adopted another system, see D 6, note 2. , probably the first letter of , and not | (as Griffith, *Cat. Rylands Pap.* p. 414) = $\frac{1}{16}$ arura; and , abbreviated often to | (hierogl. ) = $\frac{1}{32}$.

## OSTR. D 6 (Pl. IV). ALLOTMENT (?) OF LAND.

1. a.rḫ-w a P-hb s P-šr-Mnt n Zme q
2. tkm st $\frac{1}{32}$ a st $1\frac{1}{2}$ a st $\frac{1}{32}$ ʿn sẖ Hry n ḥsp 7.t
3. sẖ Hry ḥnʿ Pa-Mnt a q st $\frac{1}{32}$ a st $1\frac{1}{2}$ a st $\frac{1}{32}$ ʿn ḥsp 7.t
4. sẖ P-šr-Mnt ḥnʿ P-šr-Mnt a tkm st $\frac{1}{32}$ n ḥsp 7.t
5. sẖ Ḥr-p-Rʿ a ẖ p nt sẖ ḥry n ḥsp 7.t

'There have been adjudged (?) to Phibis, son of Psenmonthes, in Jême high-land (under) oil-crop [1] arura $\frac{1}{32}$ = (land-cubit) $1\frac{1}{2}$ [2] = arura $\frac{1}{32}$ again. Written by Erieus in year 7.

Written by Erieus and Pamonthes for high-land arura $\frac{1}{32}$ = (land-cubit) $1\frac{1}{2}$ = arura $\frac{1}{32}$ again, in year 7.

Written by Psenmonthes and Psenmonthes for oil-crop arura $\frac{1}{32}$ in year 7.

Written by Harpres in conformity to that which is written above, in year 7.'

[1] *tkm*, the final letter is written with a stroke so small as to be little more than a mere dot—and this occurs elsewhere as well as here—so as to raise a question whether the reading should not be *tk* = *tgy* of Rosetta, l. 9, where *yḥ-w tgy* = παράδεισοι, 'orchards'. But since, so far as I know, *tgy* does not occur alone without *yḥ* and as in one of this group (D 26) the word is undoubtedly *tgm*, I have preferred to take it so here. The *tgm*-plant produced an oil which was extensively used by the Egyptians. Loret (*Flore Pharaonique*, ed. 2, p. 49) identifies it with *Ricinus communis*, mainly on the authority of Revillout; but the identification is not free from doubt.

[2] Apparently there was no symbol for $\frac{1}{64}$ arura. We know the hieroglyphic words for the fractions of the arura down to and including $\frac{1}{32}$, but none is known for $\frac{1}{64}$ (cf. Griffith, *P.S.B.A.* xiv, table, p. 410). So it is expressed in *mḥ ytn* 'land-cubits' (the *mḥ ytn* being one-hundredth of an arura) as $1\frac{1}{2}$ 'land-cubits'; strictly speaking $\frac{1}{64}$ arura = 1·5625 land-cubits.

## Ostr. D 44 (Pl. IV). Allotment (?) of Land.

1. a.rḫ-w a Z-ḥr s Py-k
2. n Zme st (?) q st $7\frac{1}{2}\frac{1}{4}\frac{1}{8}$
3. a st $3\frac{1}{2}\frac{1}{4}\frac{1}{8}$ a st $7\frac{1}{2}\frac{1}{4}$ ʿn sẖ Pa-Mnt n ḥsp 17
4. sw $33\frac{1}{2}$ bt (?) $2\frac{1}{8}$ a sw 1
5. tkm $1\frac{1}{2}\frac{1}{4}$

'There have been adjudged (?) to Teos, son of Pikos, in Jême aruras (?) (of) high-land $7\frac{7}{8}$ aruras = $3\frac{7}{8}$ ar. = $7\frac{3}{4}$ [1] ar. again. Written by Pamonthes in year 17. Wheat $33\frac{1}{2}$ (artabas) [2], spelt (?) [3] $2\frac{1}{8}$ (artabas) to wheat 1 (artaba). Croton-oil $1\frac{3}{4}$ (artabas) [4].'

[1] These figures do not correspond, though the reading is quite certain. Either the first must be corrected to $7\frac{3}{4}$ by omitting the final fraction; or if $7\frac{7}{8}$ be accepted, then $3\frac{7}{8}$ should be $3\frac{15}{16}$, and $7\frac{3}{4}$ becomes $7\frac{7}{8}$.

[2] If this be the entire rent, it is doubtless a round figure. If the land was $7\frac{3}{4}$ ar. in extent, it means $4\frac{1}{3}$ art. wheat per arura, which would work out exactly at $33\frac{7}{12}$ artabas rent. If the land was $7\frac{7}{8}$ aruras, it means $4\frac{1}{4}$ artabas per arura, working out exactly at $33\frac{15}{32}$. In either case the result is not far removed from the average rent of crown-land at Tebtunis somewhat earlier than this (*Pap. Tebt.* i, p. 564).

[3] The reading is very uncertain. Cf. Griffith, *Cat. Rylands Pap.*, p. 412, for the same group, who reads it *bt* (?) or *šs* (?). The ratio would be about that for ὄλυρα, cf. *Pap. Tebt.*, p. 560, value of wheat to olyra = 5 : 2, or as the ratio is put on the ostracon, spelt $2\frac{1}{2}$ art. = wheat 1 art.*

[4] Presumably this is the ratio of croton-oil to wheat.

## Ostr. D 2 (Pl. IV). Allotment (?) of Land.

1. ḥsp 4.t a.rẖ-w a P-šr-Mn s P-šr-ʾS ne-f yḥ
2. Ptlwmys s ʾMnys ẖn
3. st $9\frac{1}{2}\frac{1}{8}$ sw $4\frac{1}{2}$ st $\frac{1}{2}$ . . . . 2.t st $2\frac{1}{2}$ k.t (?) ẖn st 25
4. sw $3\frac{1}{6}$ . . . . 1.t $2\frac{1}{2}$ a st 5 a st $2\frac{1}{2}$ a st 5 ʿn sẖ P-šr-Mn
5. s ʿO-pḥt
6. sẖ ʾY-m-ḥtp s Hry st 5 a st $2\frac{1}{2}$ a st 5 ʿn n ḥsp 4.t
7. sẖ Gphln s Ḥr-p-bk st 5 a st $2\frac{1}{2}$ a st 5 ʿn n ḥsp 4.t
8. *πτολεμαιος σε(σημαιωμαι) (ετους) δʹ*

'There have been adjudged (?) to Psenminis, son of Psenesis, (as ?) his lands[1] from (?) Ptolemy,[2] son of Ammonius, among $9\frac{5}{8}$ aruras (at ?) $4\frac{1}{2}$ (artabas of) wheat,[3] $\frac{1}{2}$ arura (at ?) 2 . . . . . .,[4] $2\frac{1}{2}$ aruras;[5] another, among 25 aruras (at ?) $3\frac{1}{6}$ (artabas of) wheat, 1 . . . . ., $2\frac{1}{2}$ (aruras), making 5 aruras = $2\frac{1}{2}$ aruras = 5 aruras again. Written by Psenminis, son of Apathes.

(2nd hand) Written by Imuthes, son of Erieus, 5 aruras = $2\frac{1}{2}$ aruras = 5 aruras again, in year 4.

(3rd hand) Written by Kephalon, son of Harpbekis, 5 aruras = $2\frac{1}{2}$ aruras = 5 aruras again, in year 4.

(*Greek*) I, Ptolemy, have signed, year 4.'

* In *P.S.B.A.* 31/50 Dr. Griffith rejects the reading *bδti* (ὄλυρα) but agrees that it represents some grain or other. Spiegelberg (*Rec. trav.* 28/187; *Cairo Cat. Demot. Pap.* p. 2) treats it as a measure = *κεράμιον*.

[1] Elsewhere *n ne-fyḥ* (D 68) 'for his lands' or 'as his lands'.

[2] In two other instances (ostraca in private possession unpublished) a name is inserted here—in one case preceded by *n*—but what its relation is to the preceding name is by no means clear. Perhaps the land assigned to Psenminis had belonged to Ptolemy. In any case, the latter is presumably the man who signs in Greek at the foot. In neither of the instances quoted does the corresponding individual sign the ostracon.

[3] Probably the annual rental per arura of the ground out of which an allotment is being made.

[4] This group, which I cannot read, occurs also in D 68 and D 82 in the same connexion as here. It is a feminine substantive and is always followed by a number which ranges between 1 and 3 and admits of fractions (ordinary fractions, not those of the arura). I suspect that it is the name of some crop other than the wheat which always precedes it. Sometimes it is written so as to be indistinguishable from the word *s.t* 'seat' (without its determinative), but usually it is a little more 'curly' in its upper part. It is not impossible that it reads *rnp* 'year'

[5] This is the amount actually allotted; but in all the examples I know of this group of ostraca, there is never any relation between the number so allotted and the larger number 'among' or 'from' which it is taken, nor any relation to the other numbers involved. Here we have two plots of $2\frac{1}{2}$ aruras allotted, making a total of five.

## Ostr. D 82 (Pl. IX). Allotment (?) of Land.

1. ḥsp 23 a.rḫ-w a Py-k p ḫm s P-rm-mm (?) ẖn st 3
2. n sw $6\frac{1}{4}$ .... 1.t (?) $\frac{1}{4}$ st 1 ẖn st 10 n sw 6 .... 1.t (?) $\frac{1}{3}$ (?) $\frac{1}{8}$ st 1
3. ẖn st 15 n sw 3 .... 3.t st $1\frac{1}{2}$ a st $3\frac{1}{2}$ a st $1\frac{1}{2}$ $\frac{1}{4}$ a st $3\frac{1}{2}$ ʿn
4. sẖ ʾSklʾ Gphln
5. sẖ Hrmys s Phyln st $3\frac{1}{2}$ a st $1\frac{1}{2}$ $\frac{1}{4}$
6. a st $3\frac{1}{2}$ ʿn n ḥsp 23

'Year 23, there have been adjudged (?) to Pikos the younger, the son of Permamis,[1] among 3 aruras of $6\frac{1}{4}$ (artabas of) wheat ..... $1\frac{1}{4}$, 1 arura; among 10 aruras of 6 (artabas of) wheat ..... $1\frac{1}{24}$ (?), 1 arura; among[2] 15 aruras of 3 (artabas of) wheat ..... 3, $1\frac{1}{2}$ arura, making $3\frac{1}{2}$ aruras = $1\frac{3}{4}$ aruras = $3\frac{1}{2}$ aruras again. Written by Asklas, son of Kephalon.

(2nd hand) Written by Hermias, son of Philon, $3\frac{1}{2}$ aruras = $1\frac{3}{4}$ aruras = $3\frac{1}{2}$ aruras again in year 23.'

[1] This is a not infrequent name on Theban ostraca in its Greek form περμᾶμις, fem. τερμᾶμις: but hitherto it has only occurred twice in demotic publications, on an ostracon in the Louvre, no. 8112 (ap. Chardon, *Dict. Démotique*, p. 113), and on the *verso* of the Pap. Brit. Mus. 1201 (*Rec. trav.* xxxi, pl. v, l. 16). I do not think there can be serious doubt as to the reading. The hieroglyphic transcription is , perhaps 'the man of the *dûm*-palm'. For περμ- = *p rm* cf. Spiegelberg, *A. Z.* xliii, pp. 89, 158. The same name πικῶς νεώτερος περμάμιος occurs on six Greek ostraca (see Part III, no. 12 note), and this Pikos being the only one distinguished by the epithet 'the younger', it is natural to conclude that the same person is named on the Greek and demotic ostraca.

[2] The stroke which looks like *nt* before *ẖn* is continuous with the top stroke of *sẖ* in l. 4, and I believe it is merely a flourish belonging to it, especially as it was written over, and therefore after, the horizontal stroke of *ẖn*. In line 3 the number 15 is certain.

## Ostr. D 31 (Pl. III). Transfer of Temple Services.

1. [P-šr ?]-Mnt s P-a.te-Ḫns-p-ẖrt p nt z n yt-ntr Yr.t-Ḥr-ar-w s sp-sn

n ʾbt-4 pr ss 28 a ʾbt-1 šm ss 27

2. [sḥn-y] n-k pe ʾbt n ḥ.t-ntr n s tp nte-k ʾr ne-f šms-w
3. [ne-]f ʿrš-w ne-f ḥʿ-w e.bnp-k t ʿš-w m-s-y n mt
4. n p t e.nte-k s p fy p ḥnq hn nḥ
5. 3 sw $\frac{1}{6}$ ẖn t wpre.t e-w wm nt nb
6. nk nb nt a ẖp n p ʾbt rn-f e-w wm
7. p ky n p tre ʾbt-4 pr ss 15
8. sẖ n ḥsp 12 (?) n Kʿmyts ʿ.w.s.
9. pr-ʿo nt ḫwe

'Psen(?)-monthes, son of Petekhespokhrates, saith to the divine father[1] Inaros,[2] son of Inaros, [I have leased][3] to thee my temple-month[4] in the first phyle *of Pharmuthi day 28 to Pachons day 27* that you may do its services,[5] its celebrations (and) its feasts without your making any claim for them against me in any respect whatsoever, since to you belong the solid offerings (?)[6], the beer,[7] three *hin* of oil (and) one-sixth (artaba of) wheat in the . . . . when they[8] eat, (and) everything whatsoever that shall accrue during the month aforesaid when they eat the . . . . of the . . . .[9] of Pharmuthi day 15.

Written in year 12 (?) of Commodus, the King who is august.'[10]

[1] A general title of honour given to any priest who held no special rank. Cf. Canop. 3, where  = οἱ ἄλλοι ἱερεῖς = dem. *n ky-w wʿb-w.*

[2] Spiegelberg, *Rec. tr.* xxviii. 197.

[3] Restored from D 175 below, and from a very similar demotic ostracon at Brussels (E 353) of the fourteenth year of Tiberius. The verb *sḥn* is used of a temporary assignment (lease or pledge) of land in *Pap. Strassb.* no. 9, l. 7; *Pap. Reinach,* no. 5, l. 30; and Ostraca Louvre, nos. 9081, 9052 (Revillout, *Mélanges,* pp. 175–6); or of chattels, *Pap. Reinach,* no. 4, l. 9 (cows). The same temporary quality of transfer applies in these instances of priestly offices.

[4] This with similar expressions in other ostraca here proves that the term of service of each phyle was one month, which was not so clearly stated before (Otto, *Priester u. Tempel,* i. 24–5). The words between asterisks are written above the line in the original.

[5] For the meanings and Greek equivalents of these words see Griffith, *Cat. Rylands Pap.* iii, p. 319.

[6] *fy* is that which is brought, any offering. It seems likely, however, that the temple offerings were largely a matter of contract, or at any rate not wholly voluntary; and when they were in the shape of food they became the perquisites of the priests. Perhaps the *fy* were largely bread (cf. Brugsch, *Wtb.* p. 536).

[7] In view of the frequent occurrence of *ḥnq* in later demotic = ϩⲛⲕⲉ : ϩⲉⲙⲕⲓ(ⲛ) 'beer', and its spelling, both here and elsewhere, with *q,* I have not ventured to depart from that translation, though I have a suspicion that it rather represents the old word *ḥnk* 'liquid-offering' here, which in the temples meant wine and milk rather than beer.

[8] i.e. the priests.

[9] Cf. D 122, l. 8. The reading is certainly *tre,* but I cannot give any interpretation. It is not possible to read *pre* 'dream'.

[10] Cf. D 28, note 3, p. 31, supra. [In connexion with this group of ostraca, see one just published by Prof. Spiegelberg, *A. Z.* xlix. 37, and his valuable notes.]

## OSTR. D 122 (Pl. III). TRANSFER OF TEMPLE SERVICES.

1. [P-šr-Mnt (?) s P-a.te-] Ḫns-p-ẖrt p nt z n yt-ntr . . . .
2. [. . . . . s . . . . sḥn-y]n-k pe ᵓbt n ḥ.t-ntr n s 3-n šty
3. ]ᵓbt-1 ᵓḥ ss 14 nte-k ᵓr ne-f šms-w
4. ]-w e.bnp-k t ʿš-w m-s-y n mt n p t
5. [e.nte-k s p] fy p ḥnqe p kft (?) glm

6. ] pe (?) ʾbt nṭe-y ṯ.t-w ḥ.t-y
7. ] ḫp nte-y t n-k ty (?)
8. . . . . . . .]pe-k (?) ʾbt n s 4-n ḥnʿ p qy (?) n p tre
9. ḥnʿ . . . . . . nt a ḫp n-k e-w p fy
10. . . . . .]nte-k t n-y p sp . .
11. pe ʾbt ʾbt-4 šm . . . .
12. sẖ
13. nt ḫwe

'[Psenmonthes (?), son of Pete]khespokhrates, saith to the divine father [X, son of Y, I have leased] to thee my month of the temple in the third phyle (and its) dues[1] [of Mesore day 15 to] Thoth day 14 that thou mayest do its services, [its celebrations, its feast]s (?) without your making any claim for them against me in any respect whatsoever [since to you belong the] solid offerings (?), the beer, the . . . .[2] wreaths [which shall accrue during] my month and I will take them myself . . . . . . . . . happen and I will give thee . . . . . [in exchange for (?)] thy month in the fourth phyle[3] together with the . . . . . ,[4] and the . . . . . . . which shall accrue to thee, they being (?) the solid offerings (?) [and the beer (?)] and thou shalt give me the remainder . . . . . . my month of Mesore . . . . . . Written . . . . . . . . . . Augustus.'

[1] *šty*, see Griffith, *Cat. Rylands Pap.* iii. 319.
[2] The reading seems to be *kft* or possibly *kfn*, in either case an unknown word. If it could be read *kf*, it might be ⲕⲁϥ : ϫⲁϥ 'branches', especially of palm-trees, but as against this the determinative looks like a vessel.
[3] This must mean an exchange of duties between the two priests for their respective months.
[4] Cf. D 31, l. 7.

## OSTR. D 175 (Pl. III). TRANSFER OF TEMPLE SERVICES.

1. yt-ntr Ḥr . . . s ʾMn (?)-ḥtp p nt Z n (?)
2. Ns-pe-w-t s Bs sḥn-k n-y pe-k
3. ʾbt n Qsm n ʾbt-4 pr
4. ss 9 a ʾbt-1 šm ss 9 n Bs s (?) Ns-pe-w-t pe-k šr

5. n te-y ʾr ne-f šms ne-f ʿrš w e.bnp-y
6. t ʿš-k m-s-y n mt p t (?) nte-K
7. t n-y (?) p (?) ·sw (?) . . hn nḥ (?) 2 (?) $\frac{1}{12}$ (?)
8. . . . . . ʾbt-4 (?) pr ss 9

'The divine father Hor . . . ., son of Amenothes (?), saith to Spotous, son of Besis, thou hast leased to me thy month of Qesm[1] of Pharmuthi day 9 till Pachons day 9 belonging (?) to[2] Besis, son of (?) Spotous thy son; and I will do its services (and) its celebrations without causing thee to make any claim upon me for anything on earth, and thou shalt give[3] me (?) the . . (artabas) of wheat (and) $2\frac{1}{12}$ (?) *hin* of oil (?) . . . . Pharmuthi (?) day 9.'

[1] Written , probably the name of the temple of some goddess. This can hardly be the same as the *gsmʾ* of D 22.
[2] It is not clear how the 'month' could belong both to Spotous and to his son.
[3] From here to the end the text is a palimpsest and very difficult to decipher.

## Ostr. D 221 (Pl. X). Transfer of Temple Services.

1. yt-ntr . . . . . . . .
2. p nt z n yt ntr Ḥf-Ḫns s . . . sḥn[-y]
3. n-k pe ʾbt n ḥ.t-ntr n s 3-n
4. n ʾbt-4 šm mte-k ʾr ne-f šms-w ne-f ʿr
5. šw e-bn (?)-k t ʿš m-s-y n mt p t
6. mte-k ṯ p fy p ḥnq
7. hn n nḥ 2 ef sw (?)
8. n t mte.t yt-ntr p ʾbt . . . . sẖ
9. n ḥsp 11.t n n pr-ʿo-w nt ḫwe
10. ʾbt-4 šm ss 1

'The divine father . . . ., son of . . . ., saith to the divine father Khapokhonsis, I have leased to thee my temple-month of the third phyle for Mesore so that thou mayest do its services (and) its celebrations; thou shalt not cause any claim to be made against me in regard of anything on earth, and thou shalt take the solid offerings (?) (and) the beer, two *hin* of oil, meat (and) corn (?) as the due (?) [1] of a divine father (for) the temple-month aforesaid (?). Written in year 11 of the august kings,[2] Mesore day 1.'

[1] This may be only an unusual way of writing *mt* = ⲙⲛ̄ⲧ-, 'the beer, &c., of the office of a divine father.'

[2] The only joint emperors to whom such a date can apply are Septimius Severus and Caracalla. The eleventh year of their joint reign would be A. D. 208–9.

## Ostr. D 235 (Pl. X). Transfer of Temple Services.

1. [A s B p nt z n C s D]
2. [sḥn-k] n-y (?) ne-k ʾbt-w n tẖb (?) n (?) ḥ-t-ntr n
3. [n ?] rpy-w [n] ḥ.t[-w-ntr]. . . . Zme (?) ʾPy pr-Mnt nb To-tn (?)
4. [n ḥsp . .] Wspšyns Sbsts (?) ʾbt-1 pr ss 4 šʿ p mnq n rnp (?) . .
5. . . . 3.t n Wspšyns ʾbt-1 pr ʿn nte-y ʾr ne-w šms-w ne-w ʿrš-w
6. e.bnp-y t ʿš-w m-s-k n mt nb (?) p t e.ʾnk s nt nb nk nb nt e-w a ḫp n n ʾbt-w
7. . . . . . . nt sẖ ḥry ḫp nte . . . -k n . . ʾbt-w nt (?) ḥry (?)
8. . . . . . . . . . t ʿš-y m-s-k n mt n p t e.bn-y rḫ
9. . . . . . . . . . . . nte-k ʾr syḫ
10. . . . . n n škr erme-k ẖr n ʾbt-w
11. . . . . . škr ẖr-w sẖ n
12. . . . . . . . . . . . . . .

'[A, son of B, saith to C, son of D, thou hast leased] to me (?) thy months [1] of temple-duties [2] of the shrines and temples in (?) Jême (?),[3] Ophi, (and) the temple of Montu in To-tun (?) for the [second ?] year of Vespasian Augustus (?), Tybi day 4, until the completion of the year (?), [being year] 3 of Vespasian, month of Thoth again ; [4] and I will perform their services (and) their celebrations, without my making claim for them against thee in any respect whatsoever, since to me [5] belongs everything which shall accrue in the months . . . . . . . above mentioned. If [anything shall come to thee in?] the months above mentioned [or any one should?] cause me to make a claim on thee for anything whatsoever, I shall not be able [to claim it of thee?], and thou shalt keep possession [thereof and I shall not have any question] with thee as to the rent (?) [6] of the months [aforesaid] . . . . . the rent (?) on account of them. Written . . . . .'

[1] The only instance I know of a lease for more than a month's service.

[2] The reading is uncertain; but if it be *tḥb*, it is doubtless the same word that we have in the Canopus decree *n gy n tḥb* (Tanis, l. 31 = El hisn, l. 9) = αἱ ἁγνεῖαι, i.e. the payment of the priests for their religious services (Otto, *Priester u. Tempel*, ii. 32). For another instance of the same word see Spiegelberg, *Cairo Cat. Demotic Papyri*, no. 30611, l. 10. In the Canopus decree it means the payment for services, here it is the services themselves, called after one of the principal duties, viz. that of 'sprinkling' the statues of the gods (Moret, *Rituel du culte divin*, p. 171 sq.).

[3] Jême was the Memnoneia on the west bank, Ophi was Karnak on the east bank, and To-tun was the site of a temple of Montu somewhere close to Thebes (cf. Spiegelberg, *Cairo Cat. u. s.* p. 258, n. 4).

[4] i.e. for the eight months from Dec. 30, A.D. 69, to Aug. 29, A.D. 70.

[5] The scribe began writing *mte-k* and altered it *'nk*.

[6] This word is found in the decrees of Canopus and Rosetta as = πρόσοδοι 'the revenues of the state', especially those derived from sources other than the taxes—chiefly rents; and this is the meaning also of ϣⲕⲁⲣ in Coptic (Crum, *Copt. MSS. Fayyum*, p. 79; Id., *Coptic Ostraca*, Ad. 15, p. 23; Krall, *C.P.R. Kopt. Texte*, pp. 72, 107).

## OSTR. D 197 (Pl. V). LIST OF PHYLAE.

1. n s . . . . . wʿb 12
2. n s tp wʿb 12
3. n s 2-n wʿb 12
4. n s 3-n wʿb 11
5. n s 4-n wʿb 12
6. n s 5-n wʿb 10

'To each (?) phyle, 12 priests.[1]
To the first phyle, 12 priests.
To the 2nd phyle, 12 priests.
To the 3rd phyle, 11 priests.
To the 4th phyle, 12 priests.
To the 5th phyle, 10 priests.'

[1] I cannot read the critical word in this line. I suppose it is a statement of the normal number in each phyle and we should expect *n s nb ṯn wʿb* 12. The fifth phyle was instituted by the decree of Canopus, 238 B.C.; but the writing here seems to me to be Roman. The inscription is apparently complete.

## OSTR. D 88 (Pl. VI). OATH.

*Recto* 1. h̲ p ʿnḫ nte P-hb s Ḥr . . .
2. a ʾr-f pr Ḫns nb ʿḥ ḥsp 10 (?) ʾbt-1 šm (?) ss 19
3. n Ḫns-Tḥwt s P-a.te-ʾy-m-ḥtp (?) z ʿnḫ
4. Ḫns nb ʿḥ nt ḥtp ty erme ntr nb
5. nt ḥtp erme-f p hw šp te-k
6. t.t $\frac{1}{4}$ a.ʾr-y a (?) ʿpr (?) bp-s . . . .
7. ḥn-y (?) e.ʾr-k t pr.t sḫ.t
*Verso* 8. nte-w wy ar-f
9. e-f ʾr p ʿnḫ nte Ḫns-Tḥwt
10. t t pr.t sḫ.t e-f st
11. a tm ʾr-f nte P-hb t
12. sw rtb $2\frac{1}{4}$
13. te-w (?) p ʿnḫ a rt
14. Pa-Mnt

'Copy of the oath which Phibis, son of Hor . . ., shall[1] make (in) the temple of Khons, lord of time,[2] in year 10 (?), Pachons (?) day 19, to Khesthotes, son of Petimuthes (?), saying, "As liveth Khons, lord of time, who dwelleth here, and every god who dwelleth with him,[3] (since) the day I received[4] your quarter share for storage (?)[5] it has not . . .
If you give seed corn, let no claim be made upon him. If he make the oath, let Khesthotes give the seed corn; if he fail to make it, let Phibis give $2\frac{1}{4}$ artabas of wheat."
(2nd hand) The oath was given to Pamonthes.'[6]

[1] The future tense seems undoubted, though we should rather expect the oath to be made verbally first and then recorded as having been taken. The demotic is exactly the Sah. ⲡⲁⲛⲁϣ ⲉⲧⲉⲣⲉⲫⲓⲃⲓⲥ ⲉⲁⲁϥ. Cf. Spiegelberg, *Demot. Pap. Strassburg*, p. 34, 'Eid welchen A. leisten wird,' quoting Wilcken, *Gr. Ostr.*

no. 1150, ὅρκος ὃν δεῖ ὀμόσαι Ἡρακλείδην; and another Greek example has recently been published in *A. Z.* xlviii, p. 168.

[2] As the moon-god Khons was 'lord of time'. Lanzone, *Mit.* pl. 343, 2. His temple at Thebes seems to have been known as the Χεσεβαιῆον (*A. Z.* xlviii, p. 173), and Wilcken raises the question whether this can involve the above title *Ḫns nb ʿḥ* (or *nb ha,* as Revillout transliterated it). Though I know no parallel for the elision of the *n* of *nb,* I think Wilcken's suggestion must be correct. The Coptic form of *ʿḥ* is ⲁϩⲉ : ⲁϩⲓ, which would be quite right for -*αιη*-. The n. pr. *πετεχενσεβαις* is also known (Wilcken, *Gr. Ostr.* ii, p. 480).

[3] = *σύνναοι θεοί.*

[4] lit. 'the day of receiving thy ¼ share which I did'.

[5] *ʿpr,* a word unknown to me in demotic elsewhere; it is perhaps the hieroglyphic 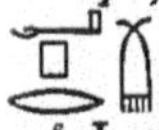, but the meaning here is very doubtful.

[6] I suppose Pamonthes was the temple official before whom the oath was taken. *a rt* = ⲉⲣⲁⲧⲡ̄-.

## Ostr. D 32 (Pl. VI). Oath.

1. ḫ p ʿnḫ nte ʾr Pa-zme s P-šr-ʾNp
2. [n X. s] Py-k mbḥ Mnt ḥsp 2.t (?)
3. ʾbt-4 (?) ʾḫ ss 23 (?) z ʿnḫ Mnt nt ḥtp ty
4. [erme] ntr nb nt ḥtp ty erme-f ty sttr.t 8.t
5. [a.]ʾn-w n-t.t-y my ʾp n-t.t-k e-f ʾr p ʿnḫ (?)
6. nte-f wy n-f e-f mḥ t sttr.t 8.t nt ḥry
7. e-f st a tm ʾr-f nte-f ʾy e.ʾr-ḥr p rt
8. [nte-f] t ʿḥ (?) p ʿnḫ

'Copy of the oath which Pasemis, son of Psenenupis, shall make [to X, son of] Pikos, before Montu in the year 2 (?), Khoiak (?) day 23 (?),[1] saying, "As liveth Montu who dwelleth here [and] every god who dwelleth here with him, these 8 staters [which] were paid to me, let them be reckoned to thee." If he (i. e. Pasemis) makes the oath, let him make no claim on him (i. e. X), he paying the 8 staters aforesaid. If he fails to keep it, let him go before the Steward,[2] [and let him] confirm (?) the oath.'

[1] The month is either Athyr or Khoiak and the day is one of the twenties.

[2] The steward of the priests of the temple of Montu, the usual representative of the priests in business matters. In Wilcken, *Gr. Ostr.* no. 1150, an oath of

134 B.C. before Khonsu of Thebes, we have the phrase εἰ δὲ μὴ ἔρχεσθαι ἐπὶ τὸν ἐπιστάτην, i.e. no doubt the ἐπιστάτης τοῦ ἱεροῦ. This officer is named in the Canopus decree (Kom-el-hisn, Greek, l. 62), and is equivalent to the demotic (l. 20) *p rm nt šn*, who is found making oaths (not receiving them as here) on behalf of the priests in Spiegelberg, *Pap. Elephantine*, no. 5.

## Ostr. D 104 (Pl. VI). Oath.

1. ẖ p ʿnḫ nte Py-k s Ḫns-Tḥwt a ʾr-f
2. n ḥfth n Zme a ʾr-f n ḥfth n Zme
3. n ḥsp 20.t ʾbt-3 šm ss 11 n Ne-w-ḥwe ta 4-Mn
4. ʿnḫ ʾMn na-ḫmn-ʾw nt ḥtp ty erme ntr nb
5. nt ḥtp ty n t̠ n p še a.ʾr Twt s sp-sn pe-t
6. hy a bl ty bnp-y prq tkm
7. ẖn pe-t tkm bnp-y nw a ge e-f prq
8. bnp ʾḫ.t nte-y wm-f sẖ n ḥsp 21.t . . . . .

'Copy of the oath[1] which Pikos, son of Khesthotes, shall make in the dromos of Jême[2] shall make in the dromos of Jême (*sic*) in the year 20,[3] Epiphi day 11 to Neuhoue (νεχουα?), the daughter of Phthouminis[4]: "As liveth Amon Nakhomneus,[5] who dwelleth here together with every god who dwelleth here, since the departure which Totoes, the son of Totoes,[6] thy husband, made from here, I have not rooted up (any) castor-oil plant among thy castor-oil (crop); I have not seen any one else rooting (it) up; no cow belonging to me has eaten it." Written in the year 21 . . . . . . .'

[1] There is another copy of this same oath in this collection, D 180, but made by another individual. It is in the same handwriting. In l. 1 after *ʿnḫ* we have *nt e.ʾr My-ḥs s P-a.te* . . . ., then a fracture till *n ḥfth n Zme n ḥsp* . . . ; thereafter the text begins in l. 3 at *ʾbt-3 šm*; the name *4-Mn* is broken away. In l. 4 the words *nte-t z* (which must be a blunder for *nte-f z*) are inserted before *ʿnḫ*. In l. 5 *erme-f* is inserted after *ty*, while *s sp-sn* is omitted, and thenceforward the text is the same except that after 20.*t* the rest of the date *ʾbt-4 šm ss* 11 is added; this may be lost by fracture in D 104. The translation of D 180 is as follows: '[Copy of the] oath which Miusis, son of Pete . . . ., [shall make in the] dromos of Jême in year [21?], Epiphi day 11, to Neuhoue, daughter of [Phthouminis], and he (?) shall say: As liveth Amon Nakhomneus who dwelleth here and every god who dwelleth here with him, since the departure which Totoes, thy husband, made

from here, I have not rooted up (any) castor-oil plant among thy castor-oil (crop); I have not seen any one else rooting (it) up; no cow belonging to me has eaten it. Written in the year 21, Epiphi day 11 (altered from day 2).'

[2] Presumably the dromos of a temple of Amon—since the oath is taken before him—in Jême, i. e. on the west bank of the river at Thebes; possibly the great temple of Deir-el-bahri, which was dedicated to him, though his title of Nakhomneus occurs nowhere on the inscriptions there.

[3] '20' must be a mistake for '21', as that is the date clearly written on D 180, as well as at the foot of the present ostracon.

[4] This name means 'the four Mins', Min being one of the gods having a manifold form; there are also references to four or more Montus and a corresponding name φθουμωνθης.

[5] Cf. note 1 to D 25, p. 47, supra.

[6] lit. 'Totoes, son of ditto', a frequent method of abbreviation.

## Ostr. D 179 (Pl. XI). Oath.

1. ẖ p ʿnḫ nte a.ꜣr Ḥr-wz
2. s P-šr-Mnt a ꜣr-f ḥr (?) Zme n ḥsp 30
3. ꜣbt-3 šm ss 6 (?) [n] P-šr-Mnt s Ws-
4. Mʿ.t-Rʿ z ʿnḫ ꜣMn ne-w-ḫmn-ꜣw nt
5. ḥtp ty erme ntr nb nt ḥtp ty erme-f
6. bnp-y t (?) ʿz a.ꜣr-k z p ꜣsy
7. nt e-y ꜣr-f ḥr (?) ny sw-w nt (?).ne-ḥr (?)
8. p srtyqws e-y t-s e-f
9. ꜣr p ʿnḫ nte-f wy ar-f e-f st
10. a tm ꜣr-f nte-f t sw $\frac{1}{3}$ $\frac{1}{12}$ $\frac{1}{24}$
11. sẖ (?)

'Copy of the oath which Haruothes, son of Psenmonthes, shall make[1] in (?) Jême in year 30, Epiphi day 6 (?), [to] Psenmonthes, son of Osimarres,[2] saying, "As liveth Amon Nakhomneus who dwelleth here and every god who dwelleth here with him: I have not lied to thee (?),[3] for the damage which I have done to this wheat,[4] which is before (?) the strategus, I will pay (for) it." If he (i. e. Haruothes) makes the oath, let him (Psenmonthes) make no claim on him; if he fail to keep it, let him give $\frac{1}{2}\frac{1}{4}$ (artaba) wheat. Signed (?).'[5]

[1] *a.'r* is written, but as it is followed by *a 'r-f*, it can only be the same as *'r* ϵpϵ.
[2] Cf. *A. Z.* xlii, p. 46 and pl. IV.
[3] Cf. *Pap. Insinger*, xxvii. 12.
[4] lit. 'these wheats' in the plural. Cf. D 111 *pass.* and Coptic Texts no. 30, note 4, Pt. IV, p. 200, infra.
[5] No name was ever written after *sẖ*, if it be *sẖ*.

## Ostr. D 9 (Pl. VII). Letter.

1. ʾY-m-ḥtp s Ns-Ptḥ n Mn-ʾS (?) te šr.t
2. e.ʾr-t gm ʾnqer e.ne-ʿn-f my te-w
3. mzʼ 2.t n-y nte.t t ʾn-w-s n-y a.ʾr-t gm
4. kwk ʿn my te-w . . 2.t (?) ne-a.ʾr-t gm n p ʿy
5. n t šr.t n Ḥr s Ns-Ḫns-p-Rʿ (?) m-s (?) ḫp b-ʾr-y rḫ
6. zhe a.wn ty ḥr-y ṯ-w ne-ʾr ḫp n-y a Rʿ-qty
7. n wʿ ḫbl nte-y . .
8. te-y gm ʾnqer ty n qb (?)
9. my mze $\frac{1}{4}$

'Imuthes, son of Nesptah, to my daughter Menese (?). If thou findest (any) excellent *anker*,[1] let two *maṭia* be given to me, and do thou have it sent to me. If thou findest *dûm*-palm dates also, let two (*matia*) of those which (?) thou findest be given to the daughter of Hor, son of Nesikhons-prê (?) . . . . . . I cannot touch anything (?) here.[2] I have taken those which I have to Rhacotis (Alexandria) in a parcel (?) [3] of mine (?).

I find (some) *anker* here . . . . . Send a quarter of a *mation*.'

[1] This is probably a foreign word, being spelt out. It has the determinative of a plant, and as the *μάτιον* was a dry measure for small things such as seeds, spices, salt, &c., it probably means some species of seed or nut. *e.ne-ʿn-f* = Copt. **ⲉⲛⲁⲛⲟⲩϥ**.
[2] The translation of this sentence is very doubtful.
[3] A word unknown to me elsewhere.

## OSTR. D 14 (Pl. VII). LETTER.

1. T-šr.t-Bḫy ta T-šr.t (?)-n-Ḫns sme a . . . .
2. s P-4-Mnt ty mbḥ ʾMn p ntr ʿo nte-f a t [nw-y]
3. a ḥr-k ḫn ʿš-sḥn (ne-)nfr nb ḥ.t n mt nb p [t]
4. mn ze.t nm-y a hn a p-hw (?) te-y . . .
5. te-y tbḥ nm-k nte-k t ʾn-w (?) . . . .
6. a rs atbe ḫp te-y mqḥ (?) . . .
7. P-šr-Ḫns s Z-ḥr (?) nte-k t . . .
8. ty n p ʿyš šn (?) a mʿ (?) . . .
9. sḫ n ḥsp 12.t n Twmty[n] . . .

'Senbukhis,[1] the daughter of Senkhonsis (?), greets . . . . the son of Phthoumonthes [2] here before Amon the great god, who shall [3] cause [me to see] thy face in all prosperity (?) [4] before everything [on earth]. There is nothing to reproach me with [5] up to to-day (?). I . . . . I pray thee to let them send . . . . southwards on account of what has happened (?). I am in trouble (?) [6] [with regard to ?] Psenkhonsis, son of Teos (?). Do thou give . . . . . , here to the *ʿyš*-priest (?) [7]; inquire in [every ?] place (?) . . . . . Written in the 12th year of Domitian [8] . . . .'

[1] For the god Bukhis, the name of the sacred bull of Hermonthis, and its form in demotic, see Spiegelberg, *Rec. trav.* xxiv. 30.

[2] See D 104, note 4.

[3] The future here no doubt implies an optative.

[4] Or perhaps 'success'. The words *ʿš-sḥn nfr*—or *sḥn-nfr*, they seem to be used interchangeably—occur often as an element in the valedictory phrases of letters (cf. Spiegelberg, *Cat. Demot. Pap. Cairo*, p. 201, note) and especially in petitions to the gods.

[5] lit. 'there is no fraud in me'—a common formula. Cf. *A. Z.* xlii, pp. 57–8.

[6] Copt. ⲙⲕⲁϩ (?).

[7] The word *ʿyš* has occurred so far only as a title or description of some members of a priestly college. Spiegelberg (*u. s.* nos. 30618, 30619) translates '*ʿiš*—Priester'. The context does not allow of any certainty as to whether it is the same word here.

[8] A. D. 92–3. The month and day have disappeared with the portion of the ostracon broken away.

## OSTR. D 111 (Pl. VII). LETTER.

(*Recto*) 1. Ns-Mn sy Z-ḥr p nt z pe-f sme a (?) ʾY-m-ḥtp
2. s P-a.te-ʾMn-Rʿ-nsw-t . . . . . mbḥ ʾMn p-hw ss 5
3. te-y ʾn-w n-k sw $\frac{1}{3}$ erme wʿ.t ble zʿ t st (?)
4. Ta-wbst.t t rm.t Ns-p-wt sy Ns-Mn bnp Wn-nfr
5. ʾy n-y n sf (?) erme (?) wʿ . . . z ʾw-f
6. a N ʿn wʿ . . . p-e.ʾr fy n sw-w a ʾPy
7. e-y yʿb m-šs e.ʾr Wn-nfr ʾy
8. n-y ṯ p . . . a.ʾr-y n ʾPy e-y t
9. n-f ke sw $\frac{1}{3}$ a mḥ sw $\frac{2}{3}$ hb n-y n rst-
10. -e n . . . e-f ḫp e.ʾn-w-s
11. n-k mte-k t ʾw Wn-nfr
12. n rste m-s p ke
13. sw $\frac{1}{3}$ a mḥ p rtb sw 1
14. ḫp bnp
(*Verso*) 15. T-šr.t-Mn ta P-a.te-ʾMn-Rʿ-nsw-t
16. wḫ p sw $\frac{1}{4}$ a.hb-k a.tbe.t-f
17. my ʾn-f p bre 2 a.ʾn-w n-k ḫr
18. n sw.w n p-hw e-f ʾw a N n rste
19. t mt.t ʿo.t hb n-y n rste n p wḥ
20. n n sw.w n p-hw z n-y ʾn-w-s n-k
21. n nte ʾr-k wḫ-s hb n-y nʾm-s (?)
22. sḫ ḥsp 28 3-ʾḫ ss 5

'Zminis, son of Teos, utters his greeting to Imuthes, son of Petamestous[1] . . . . ., before Amon to-day, the 5th (of the month). I am sending them to you, $\frac{1}{3}$ (artaba) wheat and a basket[2] of chaff (?).[3] Give them (?) to Taubastis, the wife of Nes-pwôt, son of Zminis. Onnophris did not come to me yesterday . . . . . . . . ., because (?) he went back to the City (Thebes) . . . . a . . . , who took the wheat to Ophi. I am very ill. When Onnophris comes to me from the . . . . . . in Ophi, I will give (?)

him another $\frac{1}{3}$ (art.) wheat to make up $\frac{2}{3}$ (art.) wheat. Write to me to-morrow . . . . if it is brought to thee, and send Onnophris to-morrow for the other $\frac{1}{3}$ (art.) wheat to complete the one artaba of wheat. If Senminis, the daughter of Petamestous, has not asked for the $\frac{1}{4}$ (art.) wheat which thou hast written about, let him bring the two baskets, which were brought to thee with the wheat to-day, when he goes to the City to-morrow. The chief thing is (to) write to me to-morrow, in addition (?) to the wheat to-day, (to say) that it has been brought to thee, that which thou didst ask for. Write it to me. Written year 28, Athyr day 5.'

[1] The Greek equivalent is not quite accurate. It represents *P-a.te-'Mn-nsw-t*, whereas here, and in l. 15 also, Amon-Ra takes the place of the usual Amon.

[2] This word is distinctly written with a feminine article here and with *l*, and yet it can hardly be different from the word *bre* with a masculine article in l. 17. Copt. ⲃⲓⲣ is feminine.

[3] *ẓ*ᶜ qy. ϫⲏ : ϫⲏⲓ.

## OSTR. D 220 (Pl. VIII). MEMORANDUM.

1. z-yt (?) n-f n rn n
2. ᶜo ḥwt ḥnᶜ p sym
3. a.ʾn-y etbe ḥt e.ʾr
4. Hgr

'I have spoken (?)[1] to him in the matter of the male ass and the fodder which I bought from (?)[2] Akoris.'[3]

[1] I cannot explain the final *t*, if it be one; it closely resembles in form the *ḥn*ᶜ of the following line, but that is impossible here. The phrase *z-yt n-f* is used as our word 'called' ('Simon called Peter'), see Griffith, *Cat. Rylands Pap.* iii, p. 407, and probably also *P.S.B.A.* xxiii, May, 1901, pl. II, *f.* 1, which Dr. Griffith explains as a participle. Here it can hardly be other than the first person singular of the *stm-f* form.

[2] Cf. Griffith, *u.s.* no. xv, A/2, B/3. Following *e.'r* is a sign resembling *ḥt* which I do not understand.

[3] I think certain, but the first two letters are written over an earlier error perhaps *Sgr*.

Ostr. D 168 (Pl. IX). Accounts.

1. P-my ʾbt-2 pr ss 25 1
2. p hw ms srtyqws 1
3. ʾbt-4 pr ss 18 2 ss 20 1
4. ʾbt-1 šm ss 2 a p . . . . 1 a 6
5. Pa-ʾMn ʾbt-3 pr ss 10 1
6. p srtyqws 1
7. ʾbt-3 pr ss 10 1
8. . . . . šm ss 3 2
9. a 5 11

'Pmois, Mechir day 25 1[1]
the birthday (of the) strategus 1
Pharmuthi day 18 2 day 20 1
Pachons day 2 for the . . . . 1 = 6
Pamounis, Phamenoth day 10 1
The strategus 1
Phamenoth day 10 1
. . . . day 3 2
= 5 11.'[2]

[1] It does not appear what the units are.
[2] This final summation for lack of space at the bottom is written in the margin between ll. 5 and 6.

# INDEXES

(The numbers refer to the pages.)

## 1. Gods.



## 2. Kings and Emperors.



## 3. Geography.



## 4. Personal Names.

5. Demotic Words.

(A selected list.)

### 6. Foreign Words.

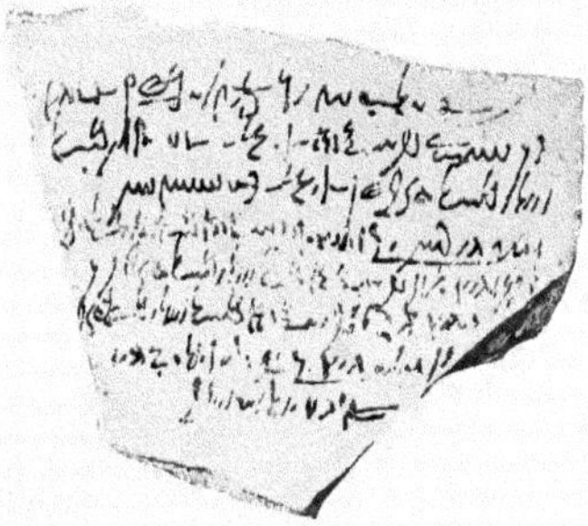

D 5

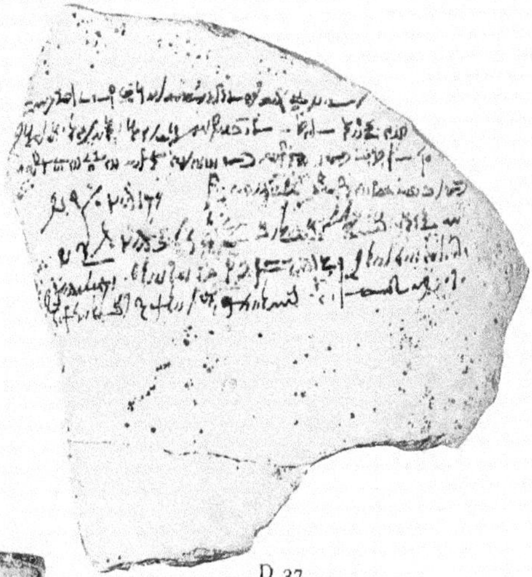

D 37

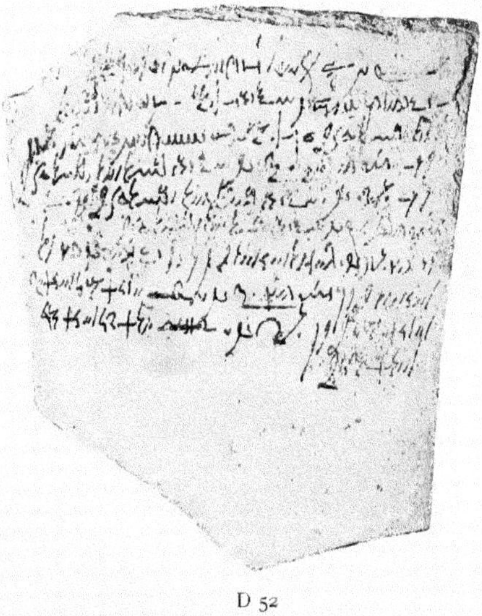

D 52

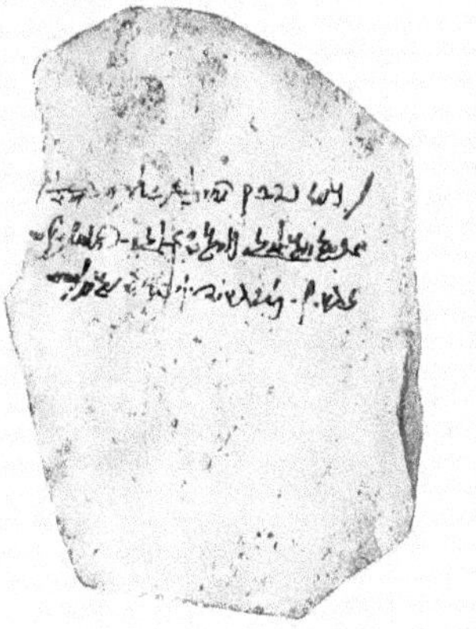

D 29

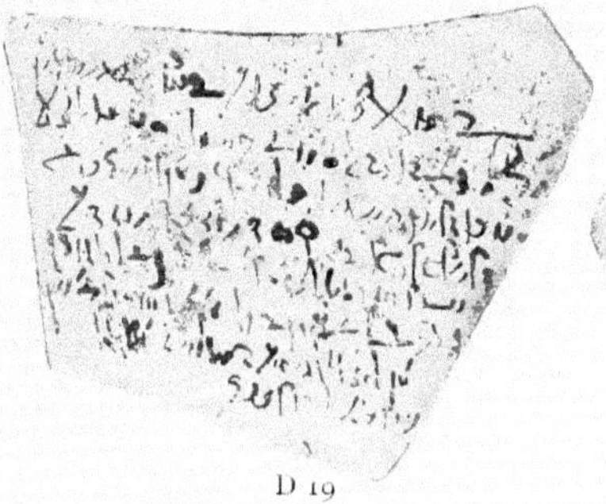

D 19

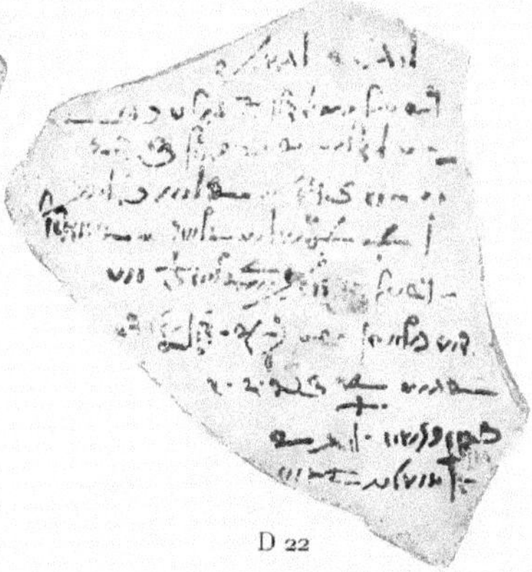

D 22

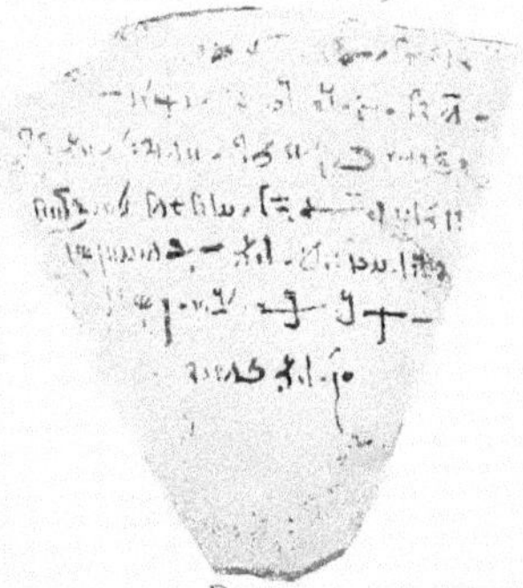

D 24

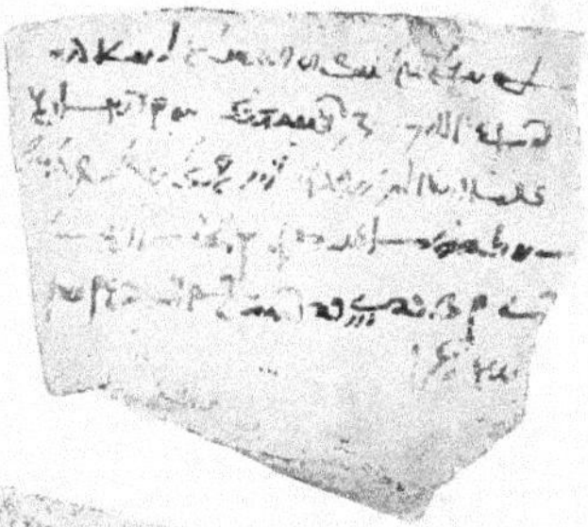

D 28

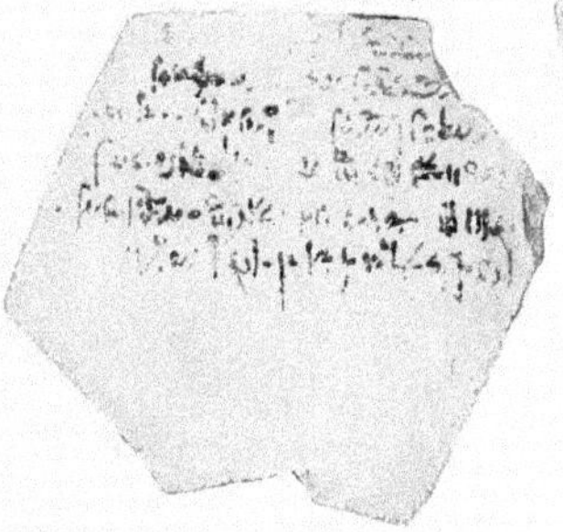

D 51

D 100

D 103

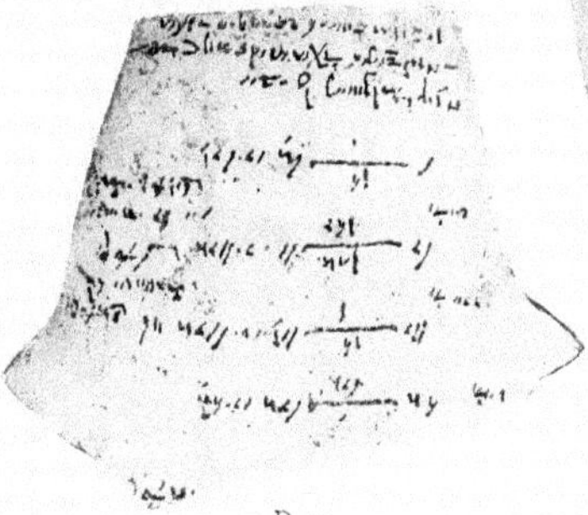

D 12

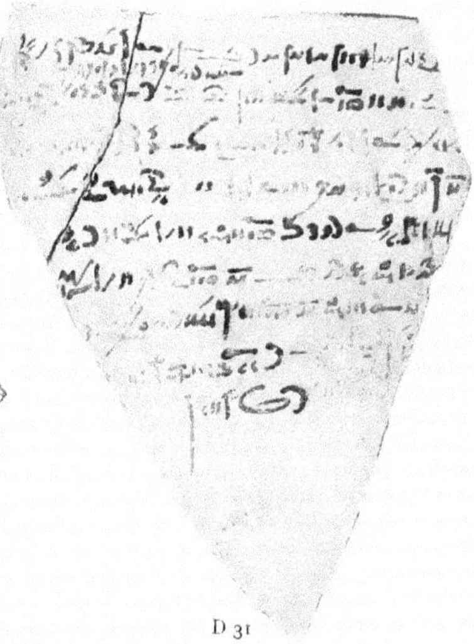

D 31

D 175

D 122

D 2

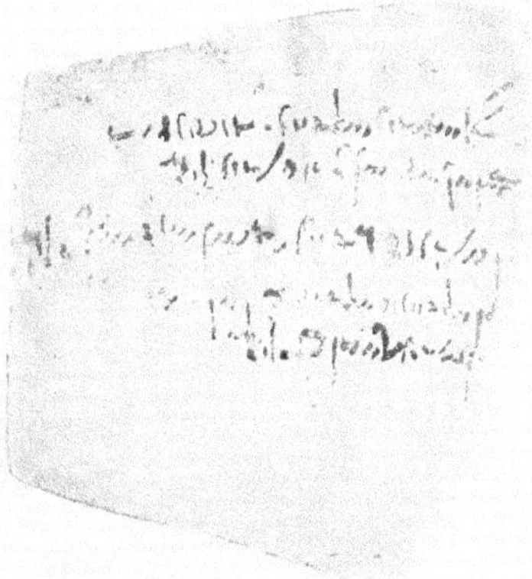

D 6

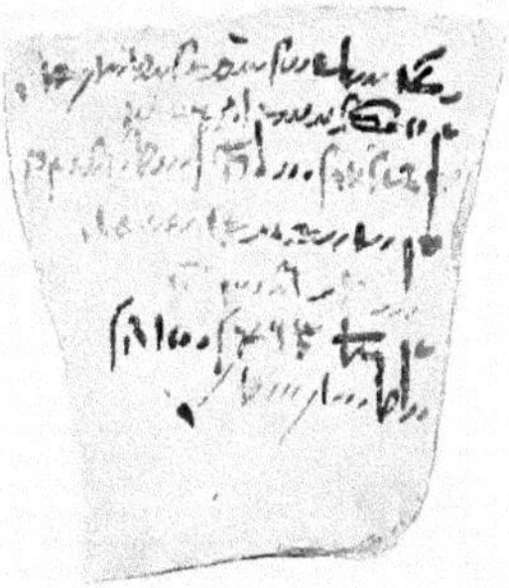

D 23

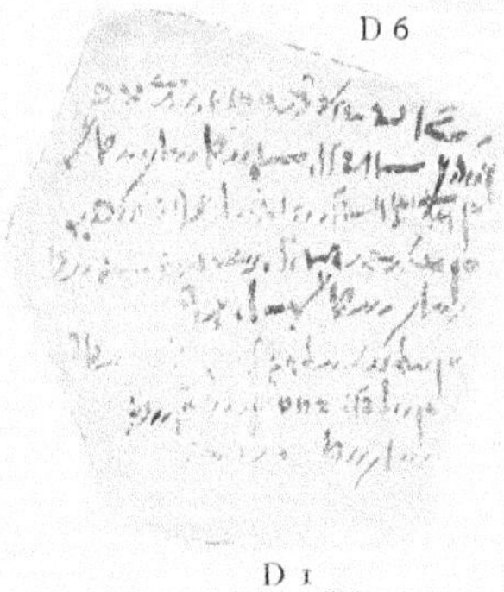

D 1

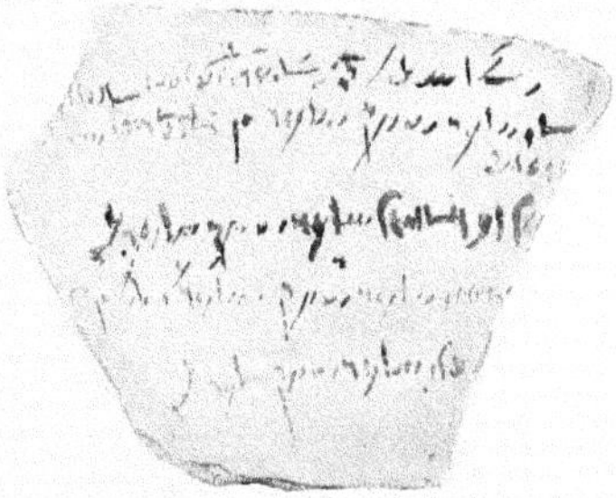

D 25

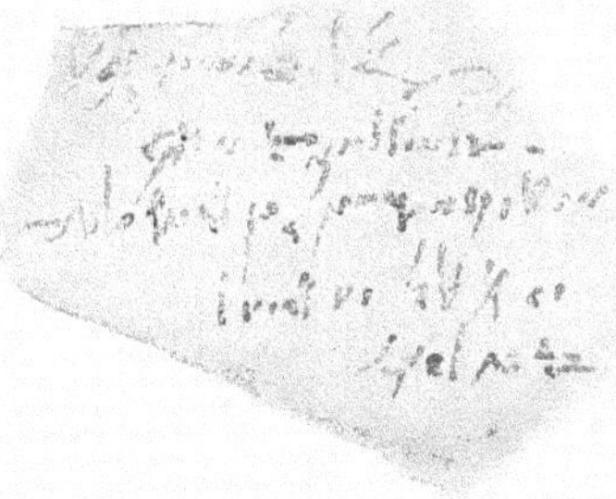

D 44

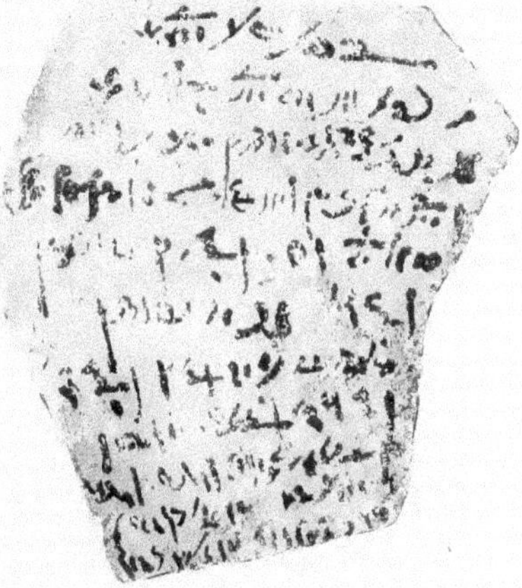

D 45

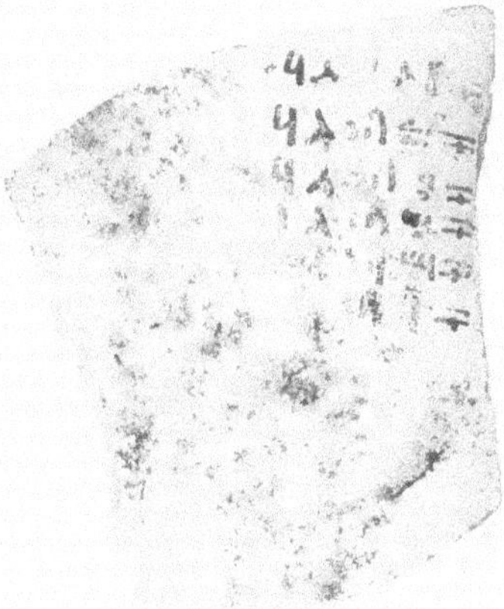

D 197

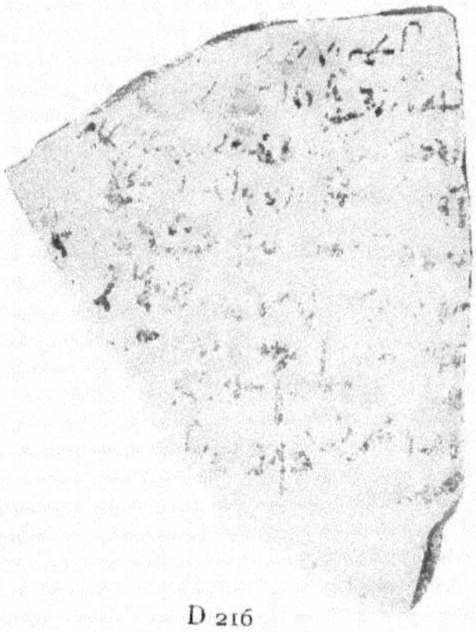

D 216

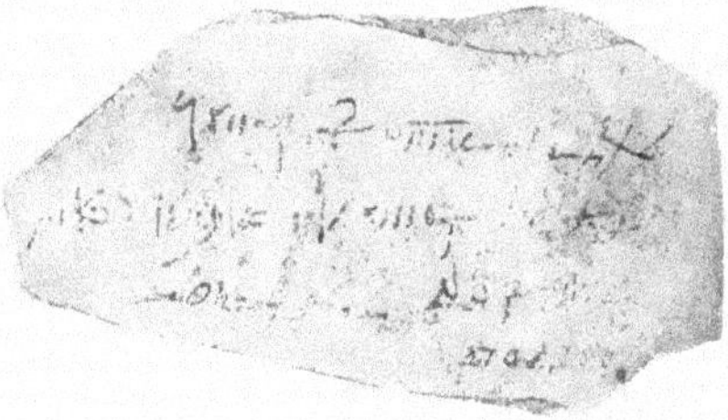

D 135

D 88 *recto*

D 88 *verso*

D 32

D 104

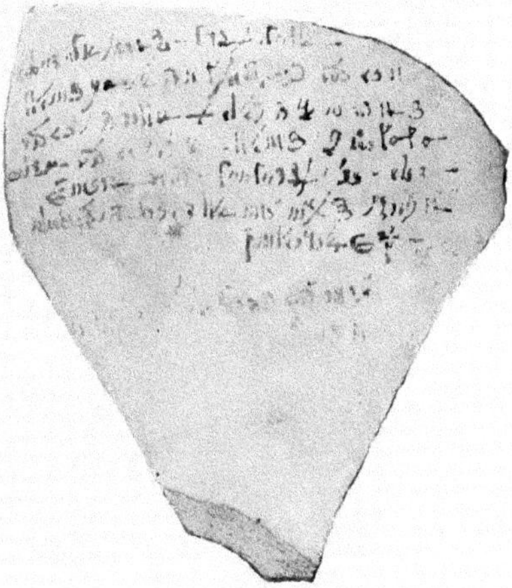

D 9

D 14

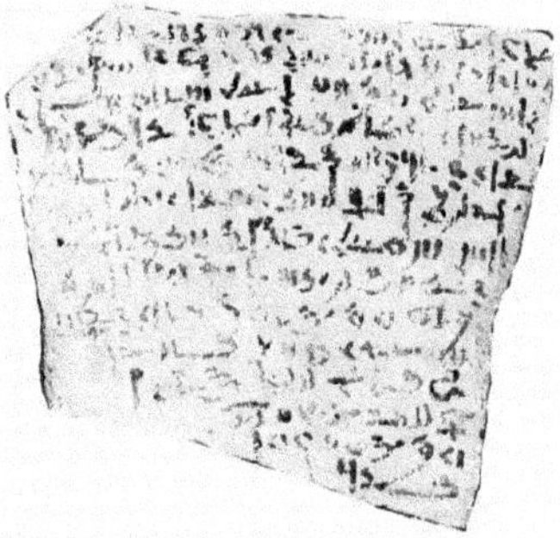

D 111 *recto*

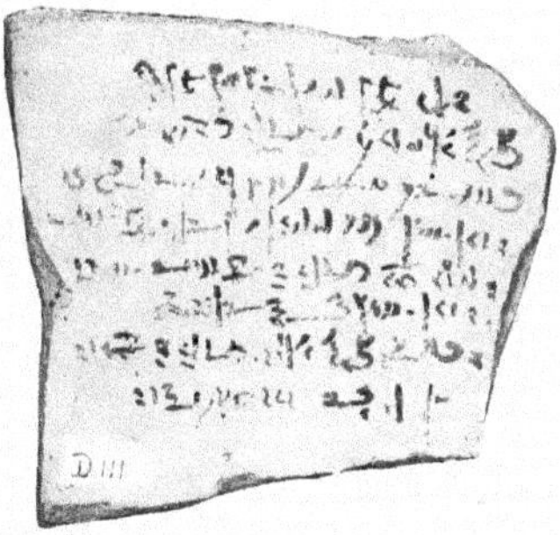


D 111 *verso*

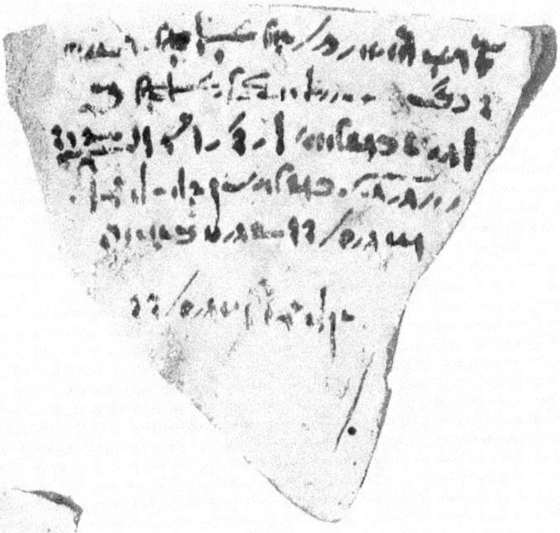

D 61

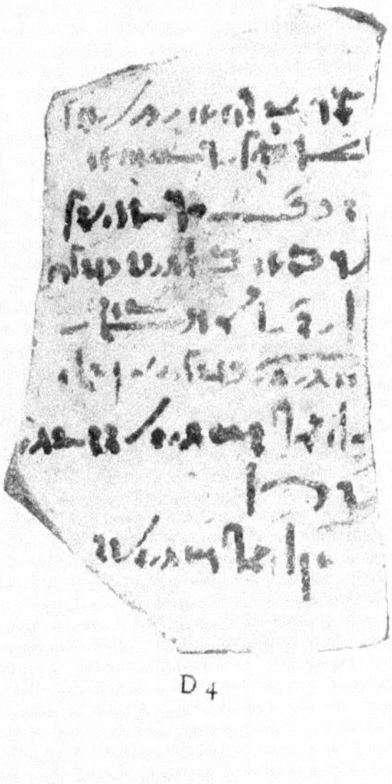

D 4

D 220

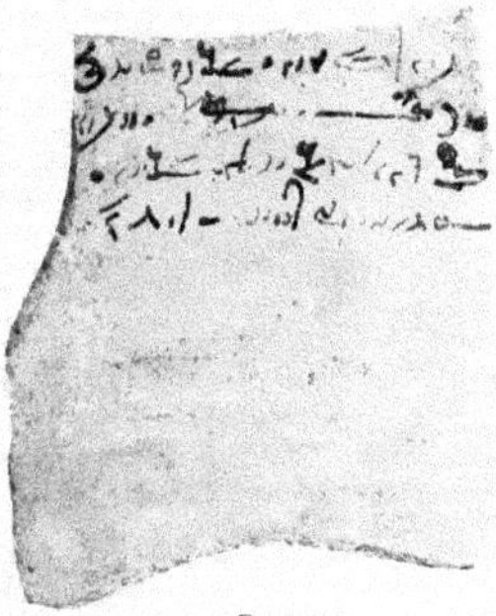

D 55

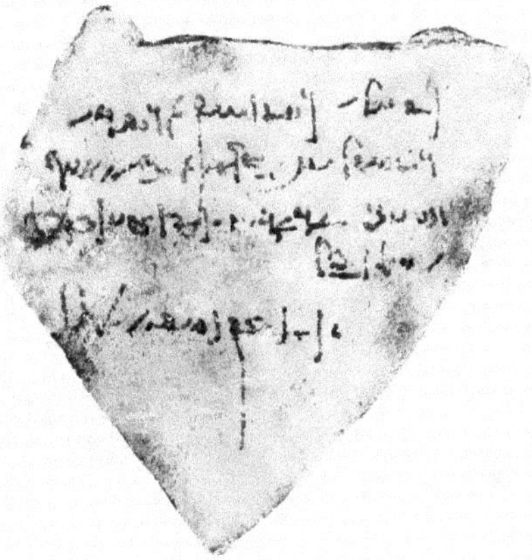

D 56

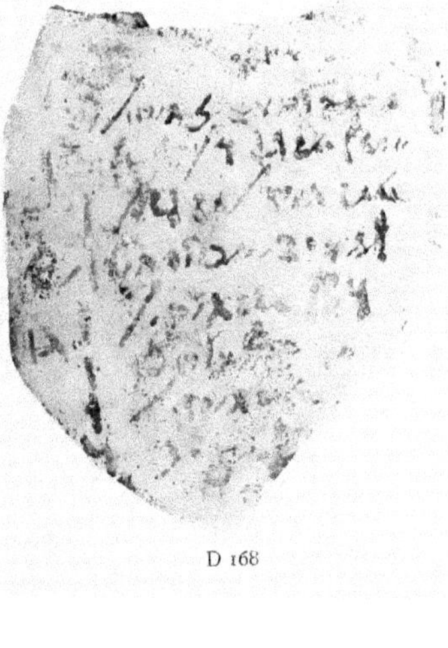

D 168

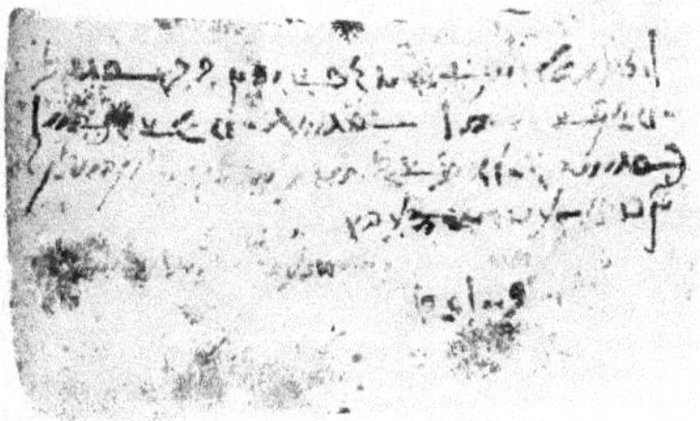

D 82

D 235 (*left half*)

D 235 (*right half*)

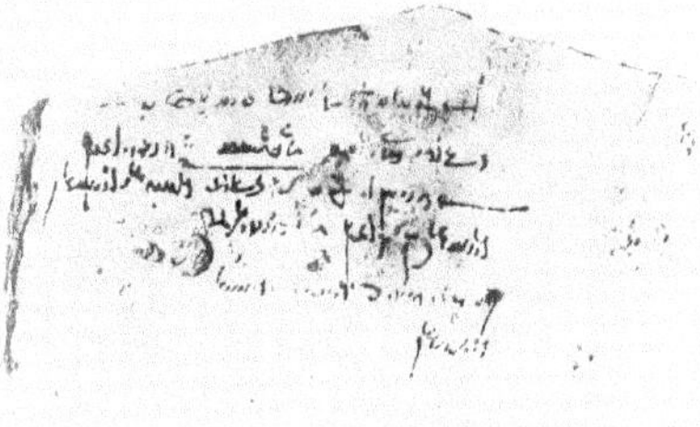

D 16

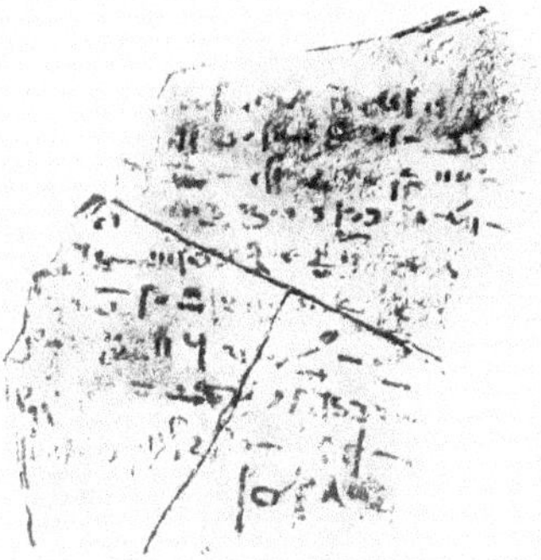

D 221

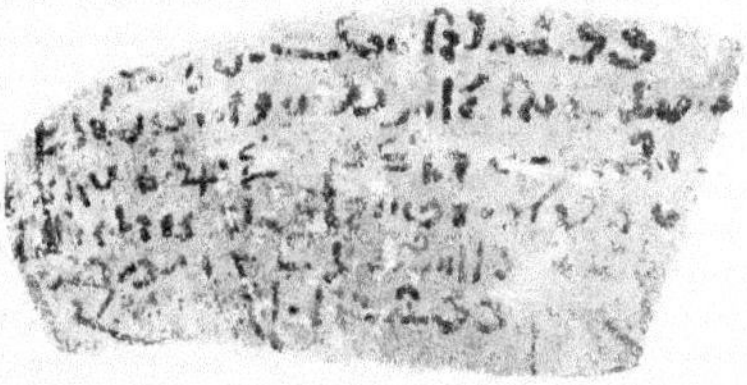

D 49

D 107

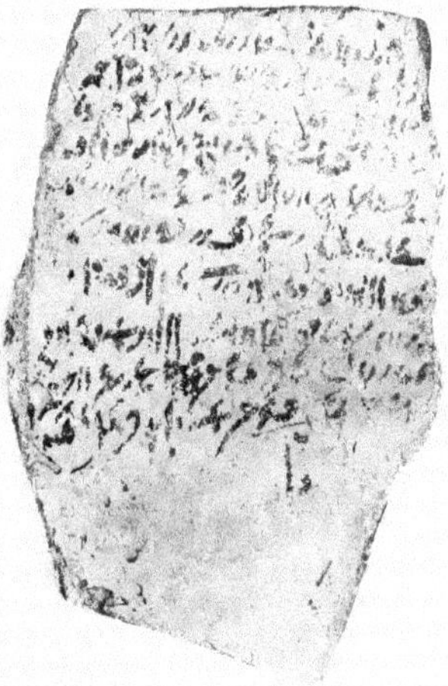

D 179

C 26

# III

# GREEK TEXTS

## A. PTOLEMAIC

I. Receipts for Taxes paid in Money. Nos. 1–9.

II. Receipts for Taxes paid in Kind. Nos. 10–27.

III. Miscellaneous Receipts. Nos. 28–31.

## B. ROMAN

I. Receipts for Taxes paid in Money. Nos. 32–101.

II. Receipts for Taxes paid in Kind. Nos. 102–125.

III. Receipts for Personal Service. Nos. 126–130.

IV. Miscellaneous. Nos. 131–146.

# INTRODUCTION

THE total number of Greek ostraca included in this collection is about 1500. A large proportion of these, however, are fragmentary or partly illegible, and only about 500 appeared to be worth copying. Even of these many are of little interest, especially those belonging to the common class of receipts for corn: and I have therefore selected for publication only such as seemed to give some fact to be added to the evidence accumulating with regard to the economy of Graeco-Roman Egypt.

Any large collection of Greek ostraca must now be treated in the main as supplementary to Wilcken's great publication: and its chiet value is likely to be found in the additional light which it may give upon the taxation of Egypt. For this purpose I have grouped the texts according to the taxes to which they refer, and prefixed to each subsection references to Wilcken or other writers on the subject.

In preparing this work I have received most valuable help from Dr. A. S. Hunt, who has compared the transcripts of most of the Ptolemaic, and several of the Roman, ostraca with the originals, and made corrections and suggestions so numerous that they can better be acknowledged here than in sporadic notes. He has also read through the proofs, and thus assisted further in the improvement of the texts. I am indebted to Sir Herbert Thompson for the transcripts and translations of the demotic parts of the bilinguals.

J. G. M.

# A. PTOLEMAIC

## I. Receipts for Taxes paid in Money.

### (*a*) Ἀσπο(        ).

The receipt in this ostracon refers to a payment, the amount of which is lost, in copper at par on *ασπο*, a contraction which only suggests *ἀσπόρου*: in this case it would appear that a tax on unsown land might be paid in money, contrary to the general principle observed that land-taxes were payable in kind, except for those on ground occupied by fruit-trees. But, as has been shown by Grenfell and Hunt (*Tebtunis Papyri*, i, p. 39), there are instances of money-payments for other land-taxes: and it is not unreasonable to suppose that a tax on land which produced nothing, and so could not furnish material for a payment in kind, was settled in cash.

**1.** (G. 101). ·065 × ·082 (broken below). 156 or 145 B.C.

*Ἔτους κε Μεσορὴ κ*
*τέ(τακται) ἐπὶ τὴν ἐν Ἑρμώ(νθει) τρά(πεζαν)*
*ἐφ' ἧς Ἀπολλώ(νιος) ασπο(       ) κε L*
*Ψεναπάθης [*
*χα(λκοῦ) ἰσονό(μου) [          .*

'Year 25, Mesore 20. Psenapathes has paid into the bank at Hermonthis kept by Apollonios for unsown land (?) for the twenty-fifth year [*x* drachmae] of copper at par.'

1. Ἔτους κε: from the handwriting there can be little doubt that the date is the twenty-fifth year of Philometor or Euergetes II.

3. Ἀπολλώνιος: possibly identical with the Apollonios of G. O. 342, who was in charge of a bank at Hermonthis in the thirtieth year.

### (*b*) Βαλανικόν.

The receipts for bath-tax published by Wilcken are all of the Roman period, and he assumed (*Ostr.* i, p. 170) that the tax was introduced in

Egypt by Augustus. This view has already been shown to be incorrect (Grenfell and Hunt, *Hibeh Papyri*, i, p. 284), and the present ostracon proves the existence of the tax at Thebes in Ptolemaic times. I have another Ptolemaic ostracon from Denderah, which records the payment of 160 copper drachmae for bath-tax.

For notes on the tax in Roman times see p. 99.

**2.** (G. 120). ·090 × ·064. 154 or 143 B.C.

Ἔτους κζ Ἐπεὶφ ῑᾱ
τέ(τακται) ἐπὶ τὴν ἐν Ἑρμ(ώνθει) τρά(πεζαν)
ἐφ' ἧς Ἑρμόφιλος βαλανείο(υ)
κζL Μεμ(νονείων) Ψεμμών-
θης τρισχιλίας
ἑξακοσίας εἴκοσι
/ γ'χκ.
Ἑρμόφιλος
δ'ρπ.

'Year 27, Epeiph 11. Psemmonthes has paid into the bank at Hermonthis kept by Hermophilos for the bath-tax of the twenty-seventh year in the Memnonia three thousand six hundred and twenty (copper drachmae) = 3620 (dr.). (Signed), Hermophilos, 4180 (dr.).'

(*c*) Ἐλαϊκά.

The ostraca relating to payments for oil are almost always in the form of receipts given by the royal banks, into which the sums collected by the government officials from the κάπηλοι were passed (cf. *Rev. Laws*, xlviii. 3). The first three published here refer to oil used for the gymnasium at Thebes: it may be noted that no. 5 is dated five days later than no. 4, and so is in agreement with the direction in the Revenue Laws that oil should be measured out every five days to the dealers, and paid for if possible on the same day. It is not unreasonable to assume that each of these three ostraca refers to the amount of oil required for five days' consumption in the gymnasium: and, as the sums paid are comparatively small, averaging 500 copper drachmae, or approximately one silver drachma, it would not appear that the gymnasium was a very important institution. A similar receipt (G. O. 318) for the price of oil apparently for the use of the baths at Thebes about the same date is for 3000 copper drachmae—i. e. six times the amount spent for the gymnasium. No. 6, which shows a much larger payment, is probably for sums received from the dealers who retailed oil to the general public: the managers of the gymnasium perhaps did not obtain their oil from these dealers, but got it direct from the government officials.

**3.** (G. 102). ·095 × ·109. Possibly 107 B.C.

Lι Φαρμοῦθι κγ τέτακται
ἐπὶ τὴν ἐν Διὸς πόλει τῆι με(γάλῃ)
τρά(πεζαν) ἐφ' ἧς Ἀπολλώνιος ἐλαίου
τοῦ εἰς τὸ γυμνάσιον ιL Σιμάριστος
χα(λκοῦ) ἰσονό(μου) ⊢ τετρακοσίας / υ.
(2 h.) τρα(πεζίτης) Ἀμμώνιος.

'Year 10, Pharmouthi 23. Simaristos has paid into the bank at Diospolis Magna kept by Apollonios for olive oil used in the gymnasium for the tenth year four hundred drachmae of copper at par = 400 (dr.). (Signed), Ammonios, banker.'

1. Lι: from the handwriting the reign of Soter II would seem a probable date for this and the two following ostraca.

**4.** (G. 103). ·086 × ·092. Possibly 107 B.C.

Lι Μεσορὴ κγ τέτακται
ἐπὶ τὴν ἐν Διὸς πόλει
τῆι με(γάλῃ) τρά(πεζαν) ἐφ' ἧς Ἀπολλώνιος
ἀπὸ τιμῆς ἐλαίου τοῦ
εἰς τὸ γυμνάσιον Ἀπολ-
λώνιος Λεωνίδου χα(λκοῦ)
ἰσονό(μου) ⊢ πεντακοσίας
/ φ. Ἡρακλείδης.
(2 h.) Ἡρα(κλείδης).

'Year 10, Mesore 23. Apollonios son of Leonidas has paid into the bank at Diospolis Magna kept by Apollonios as the price of olive oil used in the gymnasium five hundred drachmae of copper at par = 500 (dr.). (Signed), Herakleides. (Countersigned), Herakleides.'

**5.** (G. 128). ·063 × ·097. Possibly 107 B.C.

∟ι Μεσορὴ κη̄ τέ(τακται) ἐπὶ τὴν
ἐν Διὸς πόλ(ει) τῆι με(γάλῃ) τρά(πεζαν) ἐφ' ἧς
Ἀμμώνιος ἐλαϊκῆς ι∟
τοῦ εἰς τὸ γυμνάσιον Ἀπολλώνιος
Λεωνίδου χα(λκοῦ) ἰσονό(μου) ἑξακοσίας
/ ⊢ χ. Ἀμμώνιος.
(2 h.) Νικομạ́χου.

7. l. Νικόμαχος.

'Year 10, Mesore 28. Apollonios son of Leonidas has paid into the bank at Diospolis Magna kept by Ammonios for the dues on olive oil used in the gymnasium for the tenth year six hundred (drachmae) of copper at par = 600 dr. (Signed), Ammonios. (Countersigned), Nikomachos.'

3. Ἀμμώνιος: the relationship between the various bank officials who sign these ostraca is not clear. Presumably the one who is named as 'over' the bank is the head: and, if there was only one bank concerned in the three payments recorded on nos. 3, 4, and 5, it would appear that Ammonios, who signed no. 3 as a subordinate of Apollonios on 23 Pharmouthi, succeeded him in charge of the bank between 23 and 28 Mesore.

**6.** (G. 119). ·064 × ·093 (broken on left). Second to first century B.C.

Φ]αρμοῦθι ιε̄ τέ(τακται) ἐπὶ τὴν ἐν Διὸς πό(λει) τῆι με(γάλῃ)
τράπεζαν . . ] . ἀπὸ τι(μῆς) ἐλαίου καὶ κίκι(ος) Ἑρμογένης
] . ἑξ ⊼ πέντε τρισχιλίας / ⊼ε γ'.
Ἀπο[λ]λώνιο(ς) τρ(απεζίτης).

'[Year *x*], Pharmouthi 15. Hermogenes has paid into the bank at Diospolis Magna [ ] as the price of olive and castor oil [ ] five talents three thousand (drachmae) = 5 T. 3000 (dr.). (Signed), Apollonios, banker.'

3. ἑξ: this presumably relates to the amount of oil.

The next ostracon is rather obscure: as it refers to a payment in respect of sales of sesame, it would appear to belong to the series of receipts dealing with the revenue from oils; but there is an entry, in a position in the formula which would suggest that it was intended to give the general classification of the tax, of the title *νιτρική*. It is difficult to see the connexion between the sale of sesame and that of natron, beyond the fact that the latter very likely, as the former certainly, was a royal monopoly (cf. next section).

**7.** (G. 116). ·065 × ·080. Latter part of third century B.C.

*Lκδ Παῦνι κδ*
*νιτρικῆς Κολ̣. . . . ινοπό(λεως)*
*Θοτεὺς Τασο(ῦτος ?) εἰς τιμὴν*
*σησάμου ⊢ ἓξ / ϛ.*   × ×
*Ἡλιόδωρος.*

'Year 24, Pauni 24. For the tax on natron in Kol[ ]inopolis Thoteus son of Tasous (has paid) as the price of sesame oil six drachmae = 6 (dr.). (Signed), Heliodoros.'

1. Lκδ: the most probable date is in the reign of Euergetes I; the writing would suit this better than the twenty-fourth year of Philadelphus.

2. Κολ̣ . . . . ινοπ: this contraction presumably represents a place-name ending in -πόλεως.

### (*d*) *Νιτρική*.

The *νιτρική*, which is mentioned both on papyri and on ostraca (cf. Wilcken, *Ostr.* i, p. 264), is found on the latter with the addition *πλύνου*. The two examples published by Wilcken, like the one given here, are from Thebes; and it would seem possible that the word *πλύνος* has a local signification, in which case it may be compared with *νιτρική Κολ . . . . ινοπόλεως* in no. 7 above. This interpretation is suggested by Grenfell and Hunt (*Hibeh Papyri*, i, p. 305) in connexion with the occurrence of the word *πλύνος* in P. Hib. 114 and 116, in the latter of which *νίτρον* is also mentioned. The sale of natron was probably a government monopoly, and the ostraca may therefore represent payments into the royal banks of the sums received from the contractors who retailed it. In all three of the ostraca relating to this tax the payments are in copper at a discount (G. O. 329, 60 drachmae *πρὸς ἀργύριον*: G. O. 1497, 600 drachmae accounted as 500: this ostracon, 2400 drachmae accounted as 2085).

**8.** (G. 132). ·090 × ·101. 155 or 144 B.C.

2-šm 15 ʾntrsthns
(tbn) 104 (qt) 2½ tbn 120

*Lκϛ Παῦνι ιε̅ τέ(τακται) ἐπὶ τὴν ἐν Διὸς πό(λει)*
*τῆι με(γάλῃ) τρά(πεζαν) ἐφ' ἧς Πα̣ά̣τ̣ης νιτρικῆς*
*πλύνου κϛL . . ε̣ω̣ν̣ Σ̣ταλ(    ) δισ-*
*χιλίας ὀγδοήκοντα πέντε.*
*/ β'πε. Πα(άτης ?) τρα(πεζίτης)*
*β'υ.*

'Pauni 15. Androsthenes, 104 teben 2½ kite: 120 teben.

Year 26, Pauni 15. [ ]eon son of Stal( ) has paid into the bank at Diospolis Magna kept by Paates (?) for the tax on natron of the washing-place (?) for the twenty-sixth year two thousand and eighty-five (drachmae) = 2085 (dr.). (Signed), Paates (?), banker, 2400 (dr.).'

4. Πα̣ά̣τ̣ης: Dr. Hunt suggests Πάτρης as a possible alternative reading.
5. . . ε̣ω̣ν̣ Σ̣ταλ( ) or . . εωνς Ταλ( ): the name is not to be equated with the Androsthenes of the demotic text: he was probably a clerk.

### (*e*) *Πορθμίδων.*

A tax on ferrymen—*πορευτῶν*—is already known from several ostraca published by Wilcken (*Ostr.* i, p. 280). Probably the same tax is the subject of the following receipt, although in this case it is nominally assessed on the ferry-boats instead of the men. Like Wilcken's ostraca, this shows a payment into the royal bank of sums collected in copper at a discount.

**9.** (G. 115). ·087 × ·108. 134 B.C.

*Lλϛ Μεσορὴ θ̅ τέ(τακται) ἐπὶ τὴν ἐν Διὸς π(όλει)*
*τῆι μεγ(άλῃ) τρά(πεζαν) πορθμίδων ἕκτου καὶ λL*
*'Ισίδωρος ⳨ δύο πεντακισχιλίας*
*ἑκατὸν μ/ ⳨ βε'ρμ. Διογέ(νης) τρα(πεζίτης)*
*⳨ γα'ψκ.*

'Year 36, Mesore 9. Isidoros has paid into the bank at Diospolis Magna for ferry-boats for the thirty-sixth year two talents five thousand one hundred and forty (drachmae) = 2 T. 5140 (dr.). (Signed), Diogenes, banker, 3 T. 1620 (dr.).'

## II. Receipts for Taxes paid in Kind.

### (*a*) Ἀρταβιεία.

The relationship of the various and numerous land-taxes mentioned in papyri and ostraca is still obscure. But there can be little doubt that the ἀρταβιεία was a tax of one artaba per aroura on corn-land; and variants of this may be found in the ἡμιτεταρταρταβιεία of P. Tebt. 346—i.e. a tax of three-quarters of an artaba per aroura—and the ἡμιαρταβιεία of P. Reinach 9 bis. The latter impost occurs in these ostraca, once coupled with the ἀρταβιεία (no. 11), where ἀρταβιεία καὶ ἡμιαρταβιεία may mean a tax of one and a half artabae per aroura, and twice with the ἐπιγραφή (nos. 13 and 15).

**10.** (G. 121). ·065 × ·089. 53 B.C. (?).

Ἔτους κη Παῦνι ιζ με(μέτρηκε)
ἀρταβιείας τοῦ αὐτοῦ L Σελοῦλις
Αὐελέους πυροῦ δέκα / ℘ ι.
Θέων σιτολό(γος).

(on *verso*) ḥr ʼs ḥsp 25 ḥq (?) sw (?) 1 a ½ (?) 1 (?)

'Year 28, Pauni 17. Seloulis son of Aueles has paid for the 1 artaba-tax of the same year ten (artabae) of corn = 10 art. corn. (Signed), Theon, sitologus.'

'For payment of year 25 1 artaba of corn = ½ = 1.'

1. Ἔτους κη: the handwriting is distinctly of later Ptolemaic times, and, as Soter II was not recognized in Egypt during his twenty-eighth year, the date must be of Philometor (153 B.C.), Euergetes II (142 B.C.), or Neos Dionysos (53 B.C.). The attribution to the later reign is supported by no. 11, which contains a payment by the same man in the third year. As a rule, the ostraca in this collection referring to any one individual are fairly close together in date; and it would be more likely that nos. 10 and 11 belong to the twenty-eighth year of Neos Dionysos and

the third of Cleopatra VII and Ptolemy XIV, with an interval of four years, rather than to the corresponding regnal years of Euergetes II and Soter II respectively, with an interval of twenty-eight.

5. The demotic docket on the *verso* relates to a different transaction from that recorded on the *recto*.

**11.** (G. 122). ·066 × ·077. 49 B.C. (?).

Ἔτους γ Παχὼ(ν) ῑϛ̄ με(μέτρηκεν)
εἰς τὴν ἀρ(ταβιείαν) καὶ (ἡμιαρταβιείαν) τοῦ αὐ(τοῦ) L
Σελοῦλις Αὐελέους πυροῦ
εἴκοσι πέντε
/ ⳨ κε.

'Year 3, Pachon 16. Seloulis son of Aueles has paid for the 1½ artaba-tax of the same year twenty-five (artabae) of corn = 25 art. corn.'

1. Ἔτους γ: see note on 10. 1.
2. ἡμιαρταβιείαν: written ∠—.

(*b*) Ἐπιγραφή.

Grenfell and Hunt (*Tebtunis Papyri*, i, p. 39) have shown considerable reason for doubting Wilcken's explanation (*Ostr.* i, p. 194) of ἐπιγραφή as the special term for the land-tax on corn-land; but its exact nature remains obscure. The name is confined to Ptolemaic times, except for a reference on an early Roman papyrus from Hawara (*Archiv* v, p. 397); but the very brief character of the receipts on which the tax is mentioned throw no light on the method of its assessment. In two cases it is coupled with the ἡμιαρταβιεία.

**12.** (G. 126). ·079 × ·064. 94 B.C. (?).

Ἔτους κ Ἐπεὶφ κ̄θ̄
με(μέτρηκεν) εἰς τὴν ἐπιγρ(αφὴν) τοῦ αὐ(τοῦ) L
Πικῶς νεώ(τερος) Περμάμιος
πυροῦ ἀρτάβας τεσσαρά-
κοντα τρεῖς ἥμισυ
τρίτον δωδέκατον
/ ⳨ — μγ∠γ´ιβ´.
Μ̣έμ(νων ?) καὶ Ἑρμί(ας) σιτολ(όγοι).

'Year 20, Epeiph 29. Pikos the younger, son of Permamis, has paid for the epigraphe of the same year forty-three and eleven-twelfths artabae of corn = 43 11/12 art. corn. (Signed), Memnon (?) and Hermias, sitologi.'

1. Ἔτους κ: there are in this collection six Greek ostraca referring to Pikos son of Permamis—nos. 12, 13, 14, 30, and 15, and G. 141 (not published), dated in years 20, 21, 23, 30, 5, and 6 respectively, and one demotic (D. 82) of year 23. In the first three and the demotic he is described as Pikos the younger, but the epithet is dropped in nos. 30 and 15, which may suggest that they are later in date. The only successions of regnal years which would fit this series, without a serious gap, in the later Ptolemaic period are from 94 B.C. to 75 B.C., which covers the twentieth to twenty-sixth years of Alexander I, the twenty-ninth to thirty-seventh of Soter II after his restoration, and (after the brief reign of Alexander II) the opening years of Neos Dionysos—or, as an alternative, 61 B.C. to 46 B.C., which covers the twentieth to thirtieth years of Neos Dionysos and the first to sixth of Cleopatra VII: but against the latter it may be urged that in the fifth and sixth years of Cleopatra VII she was associated with Ptolemy XV, and there should be a double date; the former series is accordingly preferable.

**13.** (G. 104). ·102 × ·128. 93 B.C. (?).

*Ἔτους κα Παῦνι κ̄ με(μέτρηκεν) εἰς τὴν*
*ἐπιγρ(αφὴν) καὶ (ἡμιαρταβιεῖαν) Πικῶς νεώ(τερος) Πορμά-*
*μιος πυροῦ ⁻₀ δέκα δύο τέταρτον*
*/ ⁻₀ ιβδʹ.*
*Κρόνιος σιτολ(όγος).*

2. l. Περμάμιος.

'Year 21, Pauni 20. Pikos the younger, son of Permamis, has paid for the epigraphe and ½ artaba-tax twelve and a quarter artabae of corn = 12¼ art. corn. (Signed), Kronios, sitologus.'

1. Ἔτους κα: see note on 12. 1.
2. ἡμιαρταβιεῖαν: written ∠ ⁻₀.

**14.** (G. 127). ·089 × ·088. 91 B.C. (?).

*Ἔτους κγ Ἐπεὶφ θ̄ με(μέτρηκεν) εἰς τὴ(ν)*
*ἐπιγρ(αφὴν) τοῦ αὐ(τοῦ) L Πικῶ(s) νεώ(τερος) Περμά(μιος)*
*πυροῦ ⁻₀ δέκα ἑπτὰ ἥμισυ τρίτον.*
*ιϛ̄ κ̄ ὁ αὐ(τὸς) δέκα ἑπτὰ τρίτον. Μεσο(ρὴ) λ*
*δύο ἥμισυ τρίτο(ν) / λη.*
*Ἑρμ(ίας) σιτολ(όγος).*

'Year 23, Epeiph 9. Pikos the younger, son of Permamis, has paid for the epigraphe of the same year seventeen and five-sixths artabae of corn. (Epeiph) 16, 20 (?), the same man, seventeen and one-third (artabae). Mesore 30, two and five-sixths artabae = 38 art. corn. (Signed), Hermias, sitologus.'

1. Ἔτους κγ: see note on 12. 1.

**15.** (G. 113). ·079 × ·098. 76 B.C. (?).

*Ἔτους ε Ἐπεὶφ ιβ̅ με(μέτρηκεν) εἰς τὴν*
*ἐπιγρ(αφὴν) καὶ ἡμιαρ(ταβίειαν) τοῦ αὐ(τοῦ) L Πικῶ(s)*
*Περμάμιος πυροῦ $\frac{\quad}{o}$ [μίαν τρί]τον*
*/ ⁊ $\frac{\quad}{o}$ αγ´.*
*Πετε(    ) σιτολ(όγος).*

'Year 5, Epeiph 12. Pikos son of Permamis has paid for the epigraphe and ½ artaba-tax of the same year one and one-third artabae of corn = 1⅓ art. corn. (Signed), Pete(   ), sitologus.'

1. Ἔτους ε: see note on 12. 1.

**16.** (G. 138). ·115 × ·087. Second to first century B.C.

*Ἔτους λ̣ Παῦνι κγ̅ με(μέτρηκεν) εἰς τὸν ἐν Διὸς πόλ(ει)*
*τῆι με(γάλη) θη(σαυρὸν) ἐ̣π̣ι̣γ̣ρ̣α̣(φῆς) ε̣ἰ̣ς̣ τ̣ὸ̣ λ̣L Σελοῦλις Λο̣λ̣ή̣νιος,*
*τῶι δὲ πρότερον γρα(φέντι) μὴ χρή(ση), τῶι δὲ ἐν τῶι κθL*
*εἰς τὴν ἐπιγρα(φὴν) τοῦ αὐτοῦ L εἰς πλήρ̣ω̣σ̣ι̣ν̣ Σελού(λεως) μὴ χρήσηι,*
*⁊ δέκα τρεῖς ∠δ´ / ⁊ ιγ∠δ´. Ἀπ̣ο̣λ̣λ̣(ώνιος ?).*

Two lines demotic, mainly effaced.

'Year 30, Pauni 23. Seloulis son of Lolenis has paid into the granary at Diospolis Magna for the epigraphe for the thirtieth year—the receipt previously given is not to be used, nor that given in the twenty-ninth year for the epigraphe of the same year for the balance due from Seloulis—thirteen and three-quarters artabae of corn = 13¾ art. corn. (Signed), Apollonios.'

3. τῶι δὲ πρότερον γρα(φέντι) μὴ χρή(ση) κτλ.: the prohibition to use a former receipt—i.e. the cancellation of a receipt by a subsequent one—is found on several ostraca (G. O. 351, 1026, 1496, and 1526, and no. 25 of this collection). It is

discussed by Wilcken (*Ostr.* i, p. 78), and Grenfell and Hunt have treated of the similar formula on papyri (*Fayûm Towns*, p. 181). The present instance is exceptional, as in it two previous receipts are cancelled by a single one.

4. εἰς πλήρωσιν Σελού(λεως): this phrase is explained by G. O. 464, which contains a receipt for τέλος ἡπητῶν specified as λοιπαὶ δραχμαὶ δύο/ ⊢β εἰς πλήρωσιν—i.e. it was the payment of the balance owing to complete the tax; though it is not clear in this instance why a receipt for a payment towards the ἐπιγραφή of the thirtieth year should cancel one for the balance of that of the twenty-ninth year, unless it had been proved that the amount paid as balance brought the total payment above the amount due for the twenty-ninth year, and so could be credited towards the payments for the next year.

## (*c*) *Unspecified purposes.*

A considerable proportion of the Ptolemaic receipts for payments of corn from Thebes do not specify the tax or other purpose for which these payments were made. It is probable that many, if not all, of these refer to rent for the royal domain-land, which, as suggested by Grenfell and Hunt (*Tebtunis Papyri*, i, p. 40), most likely accounted for the bulk of the corn received by the government. In this case the receipts would presumably be given by the sitologi at the royal granaries direct to the holders of the land. Wilcken (*Ostr.* i, p. 99) is of opinion that the receipts were addressed to the tax-collectors. But the receipts for corn, with a very similar formula, of the Roman period were clearly, as Wilcken admits, made out to the actual taxpayers; and it is rather against his theory that receipts occur addressed to the same person over a long series of years (e.g. nos. 18, 19, 20, and 21, covering ten years). The position of the landholders in regard to μετρήματα εἰς θησαυρόν is shown for a later date by no. 133. There is, indeed, no definite evidence that any of the payments of corn into the royal granaries, whether for taxes in kind or for rents of royal domain-land, were farmed or made through collectors. The group of receipts given to Pikos, the son of Permamis, for ἐπιγραφή during a period of 18 years (nos. 12 to 15) do not suggest that he was a tax-farmer. Further, the amounts paid in are not such as would be likely to be passed on to the granaries by collectors; it would not, at any rate, seem reasonable that a collector should go round to the granary with half an artaba which he had happened to receive: he would be much more likely to wait till he had accumulated rather more. The formula of cancellation (cf. note on 16. 3) also distinctly suggests that the receipt was to the actual taxpayer; there would be little point in cancelling a receipt to a collector; and the words *εἰς πλήρωσιν Σελούλεως* added to the description of the receipt cancelled in no. 16 show that this receipt had been given to the person liable for the tax, to whom the new receipt also was addressed.

**17.** (G. 125). ·090 × ·102. Latter part of third century B.C.

*Lιγ Φαρμοῦθι λ̄ εἰς τὸν κατὰ Διὸς*
*πόλιν* [[. . . . .]] *Ἀμενώθης Ἀμενώ-*
*θου καὶ Ψεμμῖνις Πετεμίνιος*
*εἰς τὸ ιγL διὰ Καλλίου πυρῶν*
*νη μόνον.*

'Year 13, Pharmouthi 30. Amenothes son of Amenothes and Pseminis son of Peteminis (have paid) into (the granary) at Diospolis for the thirteenth year through Kallias 58 (artabae) of corn only.'

1. Lιγ: probably the thirteenth year of Euergetes I or of Philopator.
2. [[. . . . .]]: the cancelled word may have been *θησαυρόν*, but it has been thoroughly erased, and it does not appear why, if it was this word, it should have been struck out.

**18.** (G. 106). ·084 × ·087. 123 B.C.

*Ἔτους μζ Παῦ(νι) ε̄ με(μέτρηκε)*
*μζL Μεμ(νονείων) Φῖβις Ψεμώ(νθεως)*
*πέντε / ⳨ ε.* *Π̣ι̣ν̣ε̣(  ).*

'Year 47, Pauni 5. Phibis son of Psemmonthes has paid for the forty-seventh year in the Memnonia five (artabae of corn) = 5 art. corn. (Signed), Pine(  ) (?).'

**19.** (G. 107). ·058 × ·073 (chipped on right). 115 B.C.

*Ἔτους β Ἐπεὶφ ι̅θ̅ με(μέτρηκεν) αL* [[·]]
*Φῖβις Ψεμμώνθεως πυροῦ*
*μίαν ἥμισυ ιβʹ / ⳨ α∠ιβʹ.* ·[

'Year 2, Epeiph 19. Phibis son of Psemmonthes has paid for the first year one and seven-twelfths (artabae) of corn = $1\frac{7}{12}$ art. corn.'

1. Ἔτους β: there can be little doubt that, as the forty-seventh year of no. 18 must be of Euergetes II, the second year of this ostracon, a receipt addressed to the same man as no. 18, is of the following reign of Soter II.
3. The signature at the end of the line is almost entirely broken away.

**20.** (G. 117). ·060 × ·099. 115 B.C.

*Ἔτους β Μεσορὴ ιϛ*
*με(μέτρηκε) βL Μεμ(νονείων) Φῖβις Ψεμμώ(νθεως)*
*ϡ μίαν β′ / ϡ αβ′. Ἀμμώ(νιος).*

'Year 2, Mesore 16. Phibis son of Psemmonthes has paid for the second year in the Memnonia one and two-thirds artabae of corn = $1\frac{2}{3}$ art. corn. (Signed), Ammonios.'

1. Ἔτους β: see note on 19. 1.
3. μίαν β′: it may be observed that the payment made by Phibis for the second year—$1\frac{2}{3}$ artabae of corn—was almost identical in amount with the belated payment for the first year—$1\frac{7}{12}$ artabae—made twenty-seven days previously (no. 19). On the other hand, in the forty-seventh year he paid 5 artabae (no. 18), and in the fourth he with others paid $5\frac{1}{2}$ (no. 21). The explanation of the variations may be that the payments were instalments; or, if it be accepted that they represent rent of domain-land, the amount cultivated may have varied from year to year.

**21.** (G. 108). ·069 × ·077. 113 B.C.

*Ἔτους δ Παχὼν ᾱ*
*με(μετρήκασιν) δL ἐξ ἀν(τιδιαγραφῆς) Μεμ(νονείων) Φῖβις*
*τοῦ Φίβιος*
*Ψεμμώ(νθεως) καὶ οἱ λοιπ(οὶ) πέντε ιβ′*
*/ ειβ′.*
P-hb s P-sř-Mnt sw $5\frac{1}{12}$

'Year 4, Pachon 1. Phibis son of Psemmonthes and others, sons of Phibis, have paid for the fourth year . . . . . . . . . . . . . . . . (?) in the Memnonia five and one-twelfth (artabae of corn) = $5\frac{1}{12}$. Phibis son of Psemmonthes $5\frac{1}{12}$ (art.) of corn.'

1. Ἔτους δ: see note on 19. 1.
2. ἐξ ἀν(τιδιαγραφῆς): this phrase occurs on Ptolemaic ostraca in reference to payments both in money (G. O. 1518) and in kind (G. O. 713, 742, 1509, 1533); but its meaning remains obscure.

**22.** (G. 133). ·074 × ·070 (chipped at edges). Second century B.C.

*? L ι]ϛ Φαρμοῦθι ᾱ με(μετρήκασιν) εἰς τὸν ἐ[ν*
*Διὸς] πό(λει) τῇ με(γάλῃ) θησαυρὸν Ἑρμίας Πτολεμαί[ου*
*καὶ .]αῦσις Ψεναμούνιος κριθ(ῆς) ἑ[ξήκον-*

*τα ἑ]ξ ἥμισυ τρίτον ιβʹ / κρ[ιθ(ῆς) ξϛ∠γʹιβʹ.*
*Ἀντίοχος.*
Ns-p-mt a yt (?) 66$\frac{5}{6}$ . .
[P]-šr-Mn a yt (?) 66$\frac{5}{6}$ . .
. . . . . . 66$\frac{5}{6}$ $\frac{1}{12}$

'Year 17 (?), Pharmouthi 1. Hermias son of Ptolemaios and [ ]ausis son of Psenamounis have paid into the granary at Diospolis Magna sixty-six and eleven-twelfths (artabae) of barley = 66$\frac{11}{12}$ (art.) barley. (Signed), Antiochos.

Estimetis for barley 66$\frac{11}{12}$ (?).
Psemminis for barley 66$\frac{11}{12}$ (?).
[ ] 66$\frac{11}{12}$.'

**23.** (G. 112). ·099 × ·105. 155 or 144 B.C.

*Lκϛ Ἐπεὶφ ιε με(μέτρηκε) κϛL Μεμ(νονείων)*
*Χεσθώτης Π̣α . . . χ̣ί̣μου*
(2 h.) *δι' Ἀπολλωνίου τοῦ Θέωνος*
(1 h.) *⳨ ἐννέα γʹιβʹ / θγʹιβʹ. Ἀ̣π̣ο̣λ̣λ̣ώ̣ν̣ι̣ο̣ς̣.*
*Ἀπολλώνιος ⳨ θγʹιβʹ / θγʹιβʹ.*
(3 h.) *Ἁρσιῆσις ⳨ θγʹιβʹ / θγʹιβʹ.*
sw 9$\frac{1}{3}$ $\frac{1}{12}$
ḥsp 26 3-šm ss 15 sw 9$\frac{1}{3}$ $\frac{1}{12}$

'Year 26, Epeiph 15. Chesthotes son of Pa . . . chimos has paid for the twenty-sixth year in the Memnonia through Apollonios son of Theon nine and five-twelfths artabae of corn = 9$\frac{5}{12}$. (Signed), Apollonios. (Countersigned), Apollonios, 9$\frac{5}{12}$ art. corn = 9$\frac{5}{12}$. (Countersigned), Harsiesis, 9$\frac{5}{12}$ art. corn = 9$\frac{5}{12}$.

9$\frac{5}{12}$ (art.) of corn. Year 26, Epeiph 15, 9$\frac{5}{12}$ (art.) of corn.'

3. This line has been inserted in a different hand from that of the body of the receipt. Apollonios, the son of Theon, who made the payment on behalf of Chesthotes, appears five days later as paying in corn on his own account (no. 24).

**24.** (G. 105). ·135 × ·092. 155 or 144 B.C.

*Ἔτους κϛ Ἐπεὶφ κ̄ με(μέτρηκε)*
*κϛ∟ Μεμ(νονείων) Ἀπολλώνιος*
*Θέωνος πυροῦ δέκα*
*ἑπτὰ ∠ιβʹ / ιζ∠ιβʹ. Ἡλιόδωρος.*
*Ἀρσιῆσις ⳨ ιζ∠ιβʹ.*
sw $17\frac{1}{2}\ \frac{1}{12}$
ḥsp 26 3-šm sw $17\frac{1}{2}\ \frac{1}{12}$

'Year 26, Epeiph 20. Apollonios son of Theon has paid for the twenty-sixth year in the Memnonia seventeen and seven-twelfths (artabae) of corn = $17\frac{7}{12}$. (Signed), Heliodoros. (Countersigned), Harsiesis, $17\frac{7}{12}$ art. corn. $17\frac{7}{12}$ (art.) of corn. Year 26, Epeiph, $17\frac{7}{12}$ (art.) of corn.'

5. Ἀρσιῆσις: the sitologus who signs this receipt is the same who signs no. 23 of five days earlier, though the subordinate clerks are different—in this instance Heliodoros, in the earlier Apollonios. Possibly it is the same Harsiesis who signs G. O. 732 of the twenty-eighth year as sitologus, with Antiochos and Apollonios as clerks, and no. 26 of the thirty-third year with Antiochos as clerk.

**25.** (G. 118). ·073 × ·079. 149 or 138 B.C.

*Ἔτους λβ Παῦνι ᾱ με(μέτρηκε) λβ∟*
*Μεμ(νονείων) Ἀρυώθης Ψεμμώ(νθου)*
*⳨ ὀκτὼ βʹ / ηβʹ. Ἡρα(κλείδης).*
*τῶι δὲ (πρότερον) γρα(φέντι) μὴι χρήσῃ.*
*Ἑρμίας ⳨ ηβʹ.*
ḥsp 32 sw $8\frac{1}{4}$ (?)
Ḥtr (?)

'Year 32, Pauni 1. Haruothes son of Psemmonthes has paid for the thirty-second year in the Memnonia eight and two-thirds artabae of corn = $8\frac{2}{3}$. (Signed), Herakleides. The receipt previously given is not to be used. (Countersigned), Hermias, $8\frac{2}{3}$ art. corn.
Year 32, $8\frac{1}{4}$ (?) (art.) of corn. (Signed), Hatres.'

2. Ἀρυώθης Ψεμμώ(νθου): the same man appears as paying in $2\frac{1}{4}$ artabae of corn on Pauni 30 of the twenty-ninth year in an ostracon of this collection (G. 114) not published here.

4. (πρότερον): written ᾱ. For the formula see note on 16. 3.

7. Ḥtr: it is noticeable that, as a rule, when a demotic docket is added to a receipt and signed by a clerk, this clerk is not the same as the one signing the Greek receipt; cf. nos. 22 and 26, and, in the case of a bank-receipt, no. 8.

**26.** (G. 111). ·117 × ·085. 148 or 137 B.C.

Lλγ Ἐπεὶφ ιε̄ με(μέτρηκε) λγL Με(μνονείων)
Ὧρος Ψεμμίνιος ⳨ μίαν
/ ⳨ α. Ἀντίοχος.
sh Thwt-stm s Pa-mnt a sw 1
Ἁρσιῆσις ⳨ α.
ις̄ ὁ αὐτὸς ⳨ ἥμισυ / ⳨ ∠.
Ἀντίοχος.
sh Thwt-stm s Pa-mnt a sw ½

'Year 33, Epeiph 15. Horos son of Psemminis has paid for the thirty-third year in the Memnonia one artaba of corn = 1 art. corn. (Signed), Antiochos. (Countersigned), Written by Thotsutmis for 1 artaba. (Countersigned), Harsiesis, 1 art. corn.

(Epeiph) 16. The same man (has paid) half an artaba of corn = ½ art. corn. (Signed), Antiochos. (Countersigned), Written by Thotsutmis for ½ artaba.'

5. Ἁρσιῆσις: see note on 24. 5.

**27.** (G. 124). ·087 × ·125. 128 B.C.

Ἔτους μβ Φαμενὼθ ιε̄ με(μέτρηκεν) εἰς τὸν
ἐν Διὸς πό(λει) τῆι με(γάλῃ) θη(σαυρὸν) μβL ὑπὲρ τόπ(ου) Στράτων
Μηνοδώρου πυροῦ ἑξήκοντα τέσσαρες
ἥμισυ / ⳨ ξδ∠.
ιη̄ ὁ αὐτὸς ἄλλας ⳨ δέκα ὀκτὼ / ⳨ ιη.

'Year 42, Phamenoth 15. Straton son of Menodoros has paid into the granary at Diospolis Magna for the forty-second year for the district sixty-four and a half (artabae) of corn = 64½ art. corn.

(Phamenoth) 18. The same man (has paid) eighteen artabae of corn more = 18 art. corn.'

2. ὑπὲρ τόπ(ου): this phrase, which is found frequently in Ptolemaic receipts for payments in kind, is explained by Wilcken (*Ostr.* i, p. 306) as the equivalent of ὑπὲρ τοπαρχίας.

Στράτων Μηνοδώρου: the same payer occurs in G. O. 749, a receipt for 20 artabae of corn dated Pharmouthi 22 in the fortieth year.

## III. Miscellaneous Receipts.

### (*a*) Ἐκφόριον.

As the term ἐκφόριον was used commonly for rent of any kind, receipts specifying this may be of a purely private nature (cf. Wilcken, *Ostr.* i, p. 185). No. 29, though it does not include the word ἐκφόριον, may be placed under this head, as it clearly refers to a payment of rent.

**28.** (G. 131). ·086 × ·095. Second to first century B.C.

Lιβ Φαρμοῦθι ᾱ ἐκφορίου τοῦ ιβL
Ψεναμοῦνις Σινᾶτος κριθ(ῆς) κ. × × ×
p šm ḥsp 12 n (?) P-šr-'mn . . . . . yt (?) 20
sẖ Hry 4-pr 1

'Year 12, Pharmouthi 1. Psenamounis son of Sinas (has paid) for rent of the twelfth year 20 (artabae ?) of barley.

The rent year 12 of (?) Psenamounis 20 . . . . . . . barley (?). Written by Erieus, Pharmouthi 1.'

**29.** (G. 16). ·100 × ·061. Possibly 88–87 B.C.

Σαραπίω⟨ν⟩ Σελούλει χα-
ίρειν. Ἀπέχω παρ⟨ὰ⟩
σοῦ τοῦ λαL
τὸν πυρὸν τῶν
γῶν καὶ οὐθὲ⟨ν⟩ σοὶ
ἐνκαλῶ.

'Sarapion to Seloulis, greeting. I have received from you for the thirty-first year the corn in respect of the lands, and I make no claim against you.'

3. λαL: the handwriting would suit the thirty-first year of Soter II.

### (*b*) Ἐπιδέκατον.

The word ἐπιδέκατον, as has been shown by Grenfell and Hunt (*Hibeh Papyri*, i, p. 171), means an 'extra tenth' in connexion with fines. But in the present instance there is no suggestion of a fine; and it would seem probable that the receipt is for a tithe simply. It is given by the προστάται of Philae, who were certainly temple officials (see Otto, *Priester u. Tempel*, ii, p. 75, note 1): in a series of ostraca dated in the reign of Nero (G. O. 412–18, 420, 421) Psenamounis the son of Pekusis bears the titles of προστάτης τοῦ θεοῦ and φεννῆσις, and gives receipts for the λογεία Ἴσιδος, which facts mark him as the representative of the temples of Isis and her associated gods at Philae, who collected dues for them at Thebes (see Otto, *op. cit.* i, p. 362. It does not appear necessary to suppose with Wilcken (*Archiv für Papyrusf.* iv, pp. 251, 267) that these collections were made by a subordinate temple of Isis at Hermonthis—a sort of chapel of ease to Philae—though this explanation is possible). The ἐπιδέκατον may be another form of the later λογεία, derived from lands, as is suggested by the addition of a place-name.

**30.** (G. 130). ·117 × ·105. 87 B.C. (?).

'Εριεὺς 'Ηρακλείδου
καὶ Ὧρος καὶ Πικῶς ἀμ-
φότεροι 'Εριέως προσ-
τάται Φίλων στρατη( )
Πικῶς Περμάμιος χαίρειν.
'Απέχομεν παρὰ σοῦ τὸ ἐπιδέκατον τῆς 'Ιβιωνιτοπ(όλεως ?)
τοῦ κθ∟. Π̣ρα(κτορείου ?) τοῦ βα(σιλι)-
κοῦ (?) ∟̣λ̣ Φ̣α̣μ̣ενὼθ α̅.

5. l. Πικῶτι.

'Erieus son of Herakleides and Horos and Pikos sons of Erieus, assistant priests of Philae . . . . , to Pikos son of Permamis greeting. We have received from you the tithe of Ibionitopolis (?) for the twenty-ninth year. At the royal tax-office (?), year 30, Phamenoth 1.'

4. στρατη( ): the meaning of this contraction is obscure: presumably it relates to the στρατηγός in some way.
7. 'Ιβιωνιτοπ(όλεως): this seems the natural resolution of the contraction.
8. Πρα(κτορείου) τοῦ βα(σιλι)κοῦ: this is suggested by Dr. Hunt as a possible explanation of the text πρ< του β<κου; for the contraction β<κου cf. P. Amh. 35, 55.
9. ∟λ: see note on 12. 1.

(*c*) 'Οφειλήματα.

This ostracon may refer either to public or to private debts: more probably perhaps the former.

**31.** (G. 137). ·106 × ·049. Latter part of third century B.C.

*Lι Ἁθὺρ ζ̄ εἰς τὰ*
*ὀφειλήματα τοῦ θL*
*Ἀθηνίων πυρ(οῦ) γβ΄.*
’tnyn
sw $3\frac{2}{3}$ P . . .
ḥsp . . . . . .

‘Year 10, Hathur 7. Athenion has paid for debts of the ninth year $3\frac{2}{3}$ (artabae) of corn.

Athenion: $3\frac{2}{3}$ (art.) of corn. Year . . . .’

## B. ROMAN

### I. Receipts for Taxes paid in Money.

(*a*) $A\iota^{\kappa}$.

It seems desirable to treat the ostraca in which the symbol $\alpha\iota^{\kappa}$ occurs separately, as Wilcken (*Ostr.* i, p. 132) has regarded this symbol as the name of a tax. There is, however, considerable reason to take a different view. The symbol is always used in immediate sequence to a stated sum of money, and is followed by a second sum slightly less than the previous one, e.g. ϛδ $\alpha\iota^{\kappa}$ ϛγϝc. If it introduced a fresh payment, it should be preceded by *ὁμοίως*, according to the general rule observed in ostraca giving a series of payments (cf. nos. 32–6). Commonly, further, the symbol ϛ is omitted before the second sum, and the entry runs ϛδ $\alpha\iota^{\kappa}$ γϝc. The second sum also bears approximately the same proportion to the first in all instances, the normal decrease being that in the instance cited—one and a half obols in four drachmae. It would appear therefore that the second sum is a restatement of the first with the omission of a fixed charge or discount. The payments in connexion with which $\alpha\iota^{\kappa}$ occurs are usually for *χωματικόν* or, more rarely, *λαογραφία*, during a period extending from the fourth year of Claudius to the second of Antoninus Pius. During this same period another formula is found in receipts for these taxes—a sum is stated with the addition *καὶ τὰ τούτων προσδιαγραφόμενα*, sometimes with the further words *ἐξ*–c, which Wilcken has lately explained (*Archiv für Papyrusforschung*, iv, p. 146) on the basis of the fuller phrase *ὡς τοῦ ἑνὸς στατῆρος ἐκ*–c of a Strasburg ostracon as meaning an additional charge of 1½ obols to the stater of four drachmae. Another rate for the *προσδιαγραφόμενα*—one-tenth—is found in connexion with the naubion (*Tebtunis Papyri*, ii, App. I). The two formulae—$\alpha\iota^{\kappa}$ and *καὶ προσδιαγραφόμενα*—never occur together; but as they both relate to a charge of the same proportion to the sum paid, so far as the ostraca show, it seems clear that they are two separate ways of stating the same transaction: when a payment was made the payer might either add to the amount on account of the tax a sum of 1½ obols for each stater, in which case he would get a receipt for the amount of the tax *καὶ προσδιαγραφόμενα*, or he might have a deduction made from what he actually paid at a similar rate, when the receipt would be for the sum paid *αιᵏ* this sum less the deduction. Under these circumstances the meaning of *αιᵏ* would appear to be *αἲ καί*, treated as indeclinable.

It is still, however, not clear why the extra payment or alternative deduction should have been required in the case of certain taxes only. But the charge of 1½ obols to a stater is approximately the same as that found in cases of conversion of copper into silver. In the Ptolemaic period a silver stater was reckoned as the equivalent of 26¼ obols copper for the purposes of certain taxes, in the payment of which copper was only accepted at a discount. In the early part of the first century A.D. the rate of exchange had fallen, as appears from a case of conversion of copper into silver at 26 obols to the stater (P. Tebt. 401). In the ostraca now under consideration the rate is practically 25½ obols to the stater. The discount on copper seems to have been about the same at Pergamon in the second century A.D., viz. one-eighteenth.

No clear distinction can yet be drawn, either for the Ptolemaic or for the Roman period, between taxes for which payment could be made at par and those for which it was subject to a discount. As has already been noted, on the ostraca the deduction is made most commonly in payments for *χωματικόν*—sometimes (e.g. G. O. 1379) in a receipt given for this tax alone; but more usually a series of payments for *λαογραφία*, *ὀψώνιον φυλάκων*, or other taxes is followed by an entry or two for *χωματικόν*, from which alone the deduction is made (e.g. nos. 32, 33, 34). Occasionally, however, the amount reduced is for *λαογραφία*, in two instances (nos. 37 and 39) through a series of payments. In one ostracon (G. O. 1282) a reduction of uncertain proportions seems to be made from a payment for *τέλος ἠπητῶν*, and in another (no. 40) the tax concerned is *ἐνκ(ύκλιον?)*.

The two formulae—that with *αἲ καί* and that with *καὶ προσδιαγραφόμενα*—may have been local variants. Wilcken (*Ostr.* i, pp. 133 and 287) has pointed out that the great majority of his ostraca in which the former is used come from the district *Νότος καὶ Λίψ*, while those with the latter are from *Χάραξ*, *Ὠφιεῖον*, and *Ἀγοραὶ βορρᾶ*: and from the examples here published it would appear that the usage of *Μεμνόνεια* was the former. In a number of instances the precise district is omitted: but all examples of either formula on ostraca come from the neighbourhood of Thebes; and, so far as our present information goes, the cases may be grouped as follows:

| | | |
|---|---|---|
| *αἶ καί* | : Ἆφις (?) | : χωματικόν. |
| | Μεμνόνεια | : χωματικόν, λαογραφία, ἐγκύκλιον (?). |
| | Νότος | : χωματικόν. |
| | Νότος καὶ Λίψ | : χωματικόν, λαογραφία. |
| | Φωτρ(     ) | : χωματικόν. |
| *προσδιαγραφόμενα*: | Ἀγοραὶ βορρᾶ | : χωματικόν, λαογραφία, βαλανικόν. |
| | Ἀγοραὶ νότου | : λαογραφία. |
| | Ἄνω τοπαρχία | : φοινικώνων. |
| | Νότος | : λαογραφία, βαλανικόν. |
| | Νότος καὶ Λίψ | : χωματικόν (once). |
| | Χάραξ | : χωματικόν, λαογραφία, βαλανικόν. |
| | Ὠφιεῖον | : λαογραφία, γεωμετρία. |

But, even during the period when these formulae were in use, ostraca occur relating to the above-mentioned localities and taxes in which there is no note of any addition or subtraction.

In illustration, a few examples of the use of *αἶ καί* may be given here instead of under the headings of the taxes to which they should more strictly be referred.

**32.** (G. 263). ·112 × ·137. 68 A.D.

*Διέγρα(ψεν) Ψεμμώ(νθης) Πατεφμόι(τος) μη(τρὸς) Ταχούλ(εως)*
*Παμούνι(ος) ὑπ(ὲρ) λαογ(ραφίας) Μεμνο(νείων) ιδ⟋ ⟋η. Lιδ Νέρωνος*
*τοῦ κυρίου Μεχ(εὶρ) κ̅ϛ̅. Ὁμο(ίως) Φαμ(ενὼθ) κ̅ε̅ ⟋δ.*
*Ὁμο(ίως) Φαρμοῦ(θι) κ̅ ⟋δ. Ὁμο(ίως) Παχ(ὼν) κ̅γ̅ ⟋δ. Ὁμο(ίως)*
*Παῦν(ι) κ̅θ̅ ⟋δ. Ὁμο(ίως) α⟋ Μεσ(ορὴ) ε̅ ὑπ(ὲρ) χω(ματικοῦ) α⟋*
*⟋γ- αἶ κ(αὶ) β𐅵c.*

'Psemmonthes son of Patephmois and Tachoulis daughter of Pamounis has paid for poll-tax in the Memnonia for the fourteenth year 8 dr. Year 14 of Nero our lord, Mecheir 26. Likewise on Phamenoth 25, 4 dr. Likewise on Pharmouthi 20, 4 dr. Likewise on Pachon 23, 4 dr. Likewise on Pauni 29, 4 dr. Likewise in the first year, on Mesore 5, for dyke-tax for the first year 3 dr. 1 obol, reckoned as 2 (dr.) 5½ obols.'

5. α∫ : i.e. the first year of Galba. It would appear that the writer of this receipt had heard of the death of Nero (June 9, 68) by July 29. But G. O. 1399, written ten days later, is still dated under Nero.

**33.** (G. 273). ·115 × ·109. 70 A.D.

*Διέγρ(αψεν) Πασῆμις Ψεναμού(νιος) Πατφ(άους) ὑπ(ὲρ) λαο(γραφίας) Φωτρ( ) β∫ ∫ιβ. Lβ Οὐεσπασιανοῦ τοῦ κυρίου Φαρμο(ῦθι) β̄. Ὁμο(ίως) Παχὼ(ν) κ̄γ̄ ∫η. Ὁμο(ίως) Ἐπεὶφ β̄ ∫δ. Ὁμο(ίως) γ∫ Θὼθ γ̄ χω(ματικοῦ) ∫β– αἳ κ(αὶ) β.*

'Pasemis son of Psenamounis son of Patphaes has paid for poll-tax in Photr( ) for the second year 12 dr. Year 2 of Vespasianus our lord, Pharmouthi 2. Likewise on Pachon 23, 8 dr. Likewise on Epeiph 2, 4 dr. Likewise in the third year, on Thoth 3, for dyke-tax 2 dr. 1 obol, reckoned as 2 (dr.).'

**34.** (G. 422). ·104 × ·115. 109 A.D.

*Πετοσῖρις πράκτωρ ἀργ(υρικῶν) Μεμνο(νείων) Φθουμώ(νθῃ) Χεμσν(εῦτος) σκ(οπέλων) Μεμ(νονείων) ιβ∫ ∫αƒ. Lιβ Τραιανοῦ Καίσαρος τοῦ κυρίου Φαμ(ενὼθ) ᾱ. Ὁμοίως Φαμ(ενὼθ) ε̄ ∫δ. Ὁμοίως Φαρμ(οῦθι) ι̅δ̅ ∫δ. Ὁμοίως Παχὼν ϛ̄ ∫δ. Ὁμοίως κ̅β̅ ∫δ. Ἄλλ(ας) Ἐπεὶφ δ̄ βαλ(ανικοῦ) ∫δ. Ὁμοίως ιγ∫ Θὼθ κ̅β̅ χω(ματικοῦ) ∫δ αἳ κ(αὶ) γƒc. Ὁμοίως Τῦβι δ̄ ∫βƒcχ αἳ κ(αὶ) βƒχ.*

'Petosiris, collector of money-taxes of the Memnonia, to Phthoumonthes son of Chemsneus. (I have received) for guard-tax in the Memnonia for the twelfth year 1 dr. 3 obols. Year 12 of Trajanus Caesar our lord,

Phamenoth 1. Likewise on Phamenoth 5, 4 dr. Likewise on Pharmouthi 14, 4 dr. Likewise on Pachon 6, 4 dr. Likewise on (Pachon) 22, 4 dr. Also on Epeiph 4, for bath-tax 4 dr. Likewise in the thirteenth year, on Thoth 22, for dyke-tax 4 dr., reckoned as 3 (dr.) 4½ obols. Likewise on Tubi 4, 2 dr. 5 obols 5 chalki, reckoned as 2 (dr.) 4 obols 1 chalkus.'

1. Πετοσῖρις: the same *πράκτωρ* appears in G. O. 1613, which is a receipt for payments of *λαογραφία* and *χωματικόν* from March 16 to December 3, 109, while this one covers a period from February 25 to December 30 of the same year. From no. 82 it appears that Petosiris was still in office in the fourteenth year of Trajan, but had retired before the seventeenth year.

2. Φθουμώ(νθη): the names of the taxpayers are usually abbreviated in the receipts given by the collectors of the Memnonia during the reigns of Trajan and Hadrian. It has been assumed that they should be restored in the dative, and that the formula is a summary variant of that more commonly found elsewhere, which would run in this case Πετοσῖρις . . . *Φθουμώνθῃ χαίρειν. Ἔσχον παρὰ σοῦ ὑπὲρ σκοπέλων . . ϛαϛ.*

4. Ὁμοίως Φαμ(ενὼθ) ε̄ ϛδ: the objects of this and the three following payments are not specified, and at first sight they would appear, like the preceding one, to be for *σκοπέλων*. But this would give an unusually high total for this tax, and it is more probable that the sums were actually paid for *λαογραφία*.

**35.** (G. 228). ·133 × ·111. 110 A.D.

*Πετοσῖρις καὶ Πασῆμις πράκ(τορες) ἀργ(υρικῶν) Με(μνονείων) Σαχομνεὺς*
*Παμώνθ(ου) λαο(γραφίας) ιγϛ Με(μνονείων) ϛη. Lιγ Τραιανοῦ*
*Καίσαρος τοῦ κυρίου Φαμ(ενὼ)θ γ̄. Ὁμοίως Φαρμ(οῦθι)*
*η̄ ϛδ. Ὁμοίως Παχὼν ᾱ ϛδ.*
*Ὁμοίως ιϛ̄ ϛδ. Ὁμοίως χω(ματικοῦ) $\chi^{\beta}$ αἰ κ(αὶ) $\chi^{a}$.*

1. l. Σαχομνεῖ.

'Petosiris and Pasemis, collectors of money-taxes of the Memnonia, to Sachomneus son of Pamonthes. (We have received) for poll-tax for the thirteenth year in the Memnonia 8 dr. Year 13 of Trajanus Caesar our lord, Phamenoth 3. Likewise on Pharmouthi 8, 4 dr. Likewise on Pachon 1, 4 dr. Likewise on (Pachon) 16, 4 dr. Likewise for dyke-tax 2 chalki, reckoned as 1 chalkus.'

**36.** (G. 231). ·116 × ·157 (broken above on left). 113 A.D.

'Ερ]ιεὺς Παμώ(νθου) πράκ(τωρ) ἀργ(υρικῶν) Μεμνο(νείων) δι(ὰ) Ὥρ(ου) βο(ηθοῦ)
Πετεχώ(νσει) Φθομώ(νθου) Ἁτρήους ὑπ(ὲρ) λαο(γραφίας) Μεμνο(νείων) ιϛ∫
δραχ(μὰς) τέσερας / ∫δ. ∟ιϛ Τραιανοῦ τοῦ κυρίου
Φαρμο(ῦθι) κη̅. Παχὼ(ν) ιθ̅ δραχ(μὰς) τέσερας / ∫δ. Μεσο(ρὴ) ϛ̅
δραχ(μὰς) δύο / ∫β. Ὁμοίως ιε̅ δραχ(μὰς) δύο / ∫β, καὶ ὑπ(ὲρ) ποταμὸν φυλ(ακῆς) δραχ(μὰς) δύο / ∫β. ιζ∫ Φαῶφι κα̅ χω(ματικοῦ) ∫δ αἳ κ(αὶ) γfc.
Ἁθὺρ ιη̅ χω(ματικοῦ) ∫ϛ = $\chi^{\beta}$ αἳ κ(αὶ) ∫ϛ.

'Erieus son of Pamonthes, collector of money-taxes of the Memnonia, through Horos his assistant, to Petechonsis son of Phthomonthes son of Hatres. (I have received) for poll-tax in the Memnonia for the sixteenth year four drachmae = 4 dr. Year 16 of Trajanus our lord, Pharmouthi 28. Pachon 19, four drachmae = 4 dr. Mesore 6, two drachmae = 2 dr. Likewise on (Mesore) 15, two drachmae = 2 dr.: and for river-police two drachmae = 2 dr. Year 17, Phaophi 21, for dyke-tax 4 dr., reckoned as 3 (dr.) 4½ obols. Hathur 18, for dyke-tax 6 dr. 2 obols 2 chalki, reckoned as 6 dr.'

1. 'Εριεὺς Παμώ(νθου): this πράκτωρ occurs in several receipts of this collection (cf. nos. 37, 38, 99, with G. 217 and G. 417, not published here). He employed various βοηθοί, but the receipts are all written in the same hand, presumably that of Erieus. One receipt (G. 217) is to the same taxpayer as the present one, and is also for payments of λαογραφία of the sixteenth year, ending on Pharmouthi 23, five days before the first payment recorded on this one. The two must therefore clearly be taken together (see p. 119).

3 and 4. l. τέσσαρας. Erieus habitually misspelt this word.

4. Μεσο(ρὴ): from this point the entries, though in the same hand, are written with a different ink and pen.

5–6. l. ποταμῶν. For the term cf. G. O. 440.

7. The entry on this line is again in a changed ink and pen.

**37.** (G. 251). ·204 × ·170. 113–14 A.D.

'Εριεὺς Παμώ(νθου) πράκ(τωρ) ἀργ(υρικῶν) Μεμνο(νείων) δι(ὰ) Ὥρ(ου) β(οηθοῦ)
Ψεναμοῦνις Πατφαή(ους) Ψενθυ̣ν̣τασή(μιος) ὑπ(ὲρ)
λ(αογραφίας) Μεμνο(νείων) ιζ∫ ∫βc$\chi^{\beta}$ αἳ κα(ὶ) ∫β. ∟ιζ Τραιανοῦ

τοῦ κυρίου Φαῶφι δ̄. Ἁθὺρ ῑᾱ ϛβϲχ$^{\beta}$ αἰ κ(αὶ)
ϛβ. Χοι(ὰκ) ῑᾱ ϛβϲχ$^{\beta}$ αἰ κ(αὶ) ϛβ. Τῦβι ϛ̄ ϛβϲχ$^{\beta}$
αἰ κ(αὶ) ϛβ. Μεχεὶρ ε̄ ϛβϲχ$^{\beta}$ αἰ κ(αὶ) ϛβ. Φαμ(ενὼθ) ϛ̄ ϛβϲχ$^{\beta}$
αἰ κ(αὶ) ϛβ. Φαρμ(οῦθι) ζ̄ ϛβϲχ$^{\beta}$ β. [[Παχ]] ϛ–. Παχὼν
γ̄ ϛβϲχ$^{\beta}$ αἰ κ(αὶ) β. Παῦν(ι) δ̄ ϛβϲχ$^{\beta}$ αἰ κ(αὶ) β.
Ἐ(πεὶ)φ ϛ̄ ϛβϲχ$^{\beta}$ αἰ κ(αὶ) ϛβ. Μεσο(ρὴ) ϛ̄ ϛβϲχ$^{\beta}$ αἰ κ(αὶ)
ϛβ. Θὼθ γ̄ ϛβϲχ$^{\beta}$ αἰ κ(αὶ) ϛβ.

2. l. Ψεναμούνει.

'Erieus son of Pamonthes, collector of money-taxes of the Memnonia, through Horos his assistant, to Psenamounis son of Patphaes son of Psenthuntasemis. (I have received) for poll-tax in the Memnonia for the seventeenth year 2 dr. 6 chalki, reckoned as 2 dr. Year 17 of Trajanus our lord, Phaophi 4. Hathur 11, 2 dr. 6 chalki, reckoned as 2 dr. Choiak 11, 2 dr. 6 chalki, reckoned as 2 dr. Tubi 6, 2 dr. 6 chalki, reckoned as 2 dr. Mecheir 5, 2 dr. 6 chalki, reckoned as 2 dr. Phamenoth 6, 2 dr. 6 chalki, reckoned as 2 dr. Pharmouthi 7, 2 dr. 6 chalki, (reckoned as) 2 (dr.). Pachon 3, 2 dr. 6 chalki, reckoned as 2 (dr.). Pauni 4, 2 dr. 6 chalki, reckoned as 2 (dr.). Epeiph 6, 2 dr. 6 chalki, reckoned as 2 dr. Mesore 6, 2 dr. 6 chalki, reckoned as 2 dr. Thoth 3, 2 dr. 6 chalki, reckoned as 2 dr.'

1. Ἐριεύς: cf. note on 36. 1.

7. [[Παχ]] ϛ–: there has been a blunder here, partly corrected; perhaps the writer, after entering Παχ(ὼν) as the beginning of the next item, realized that he had omitted αἰ κ(αὶ) ϛ before the preceding β, and erased Παχ(ὼν), adding ϛ. He has, however, left out ϛ after αἰ κ(αὶ) in both entries on the next line.

**38.** (G. 216). ·063 × ·135 (chipped on right). 114 A.D.

Ἐριεὺς Παμώ(νθου) πράκ(τωρ) ἀργ(υρικῶν) Μεμν(ονείων)
δι(ὰ) Φθομ(ώνθου) Ψωμμώ(νθῃ) Πατφεῦτο(ς) ὑπ(ὲρ) λαο(γραφίας) Μεμ[ν(ονείων)
δραχμὰς τέσερας / ϛδ. Ŀιζ Τραιαν[οῦ
Καίσαρος τοῦ κυρίου Παχὼν η̄. Ἄλ(λο) ϛδ [
Παῦν(ι) ᾱ δραχμ(ὰς) τέσερες / ϛδ. ιηϛ Ἁθὺ[ρ . .
χω(ματικοῦ) ϛδ αἰ κ(αὶ) ϛγϟc. Τῦβι δ̄ [. . . . . .

'Erieus son of Pamonthes, collector of money-taxes of the Memnonia, through Phthomonthes, to Psommonthes son of Patpheus. (I have received) for poll-tax in the Memnonia four drachmae=4 dr. Year 17 of Trajanus Caesar our lord, Pachon 8. Also 4 dr. . . . . . Pauni 1, four drachmae=4 dr. Year 18, Hathur . . for dyke-tax 4 dr., reckoned as 3 dr. 4½ obols. Tubi 4 . . . .'

3 and 5. l. *τέσσαρας*: cf. note on 36. 3 and 4.

**39.** (G. 275). ·084 × ·131. 126 A.D.

*Ψανσνῶς πράκ(τωρ) ἀργ(υρικῶν) Μεμ(νονείων) δι(ὰ) Φμ(όιτος) γρα(μματέως) Πετεαρουήριος Ἀσκλᾶτο(ς) δι(ὰ) Πρεμτώ(του). Ἔσχ(ον) ὑπ(ὲρ) λαο(γραφίας) ι∫ ∫δ αἳ κ(αὶ) γϝc. Lια Ἀδριανοῦ Καίσαρος τοῦ κυρίου Ἀθὺρ δ̄. Χο(ιὰκ) θ̄ λαο(γραφίας) ∫δ αἳ κ(αὶ) γϝc.*

2. l. Πετεαρουήρει.

'Psansnos, collector of money-taxes of the Memnonia, through Phmois his clerk, to Petearoueris son of Asklas through Premtotes. I have received for poll-tax for the tenth year 4 dr., reckoned as 3 (dr.) 4½ obols. Year 11 of Hadrianus Caesar our lord, Hathur 4. Choiak 9, for poll-tax 4 dr., reckoned as 3 (dr.) 4½ obols.'

**40.** (G. 226). ·086 × ·105. 138 A.D.

*Ἱέραξ καὶ Ποριεύθ(ης) πράκ(τορες) ἀργ(υρικῶν) Μεμν(ονείων) δι(ὰ) Ψενσενπάο(υς) γρα(μματέως) Σενπασήμ(ει) Παήρι(ος). Εσχ(ομεν) ὑπ(ὲρ) ἐνκ(υκλίου) κλ(ηρονομιῶν ?) α∫ ∫αϝ. Lβ Ἀντωνίνου Καίσαρος τοῦ κυρίου Φαῶ(φι) ζ̄. Ὁμ(οίως) Φαῶ(φι) ιθ̄ ὑπ(ὲρ) ἐνκ(υκλίου) κλ(ηρονομιῶν ?) ∫α αἳ κ(αὶ) ϝc.*

'Hierax and Porieuthes, collectors of money-taxes of the Memnonia, through Psensenpaes their clerk, to Senpasemis daughter of Paeris. We have received for the fee on inheritances (?) for the first year 1 dr. 4 obols. Year 2 of Antoninus Caesar our lord, Phaophi 7. Likewise on Phaophi 19 for the fee on inheritances (?) 1 dr., reckoned as 5½ obols.'

3 and 5. κλ(ηρονομιῶν): this is suggested as a possible expansion of the abbreviation κ^λ, as κληρονομίαι were a likely subject for ἐγκύκλιον; see note below, p. 114.

4. ὁμ(οίως): written $\frac{\ }{o}$.

(*b*) Ἁλική.

The receipts on Theban ostraca for salt-tax previously published have all been of Ptolemaic period (cf. Wilcken, *Ostr.* i, p. 141); but the existence of the tax in Roman times is shown by papyri (e. g. P. Fay. 42 (a), 192, 341, of the second century A.D., P. Tebt. 482 of the reign of Augustus). It is not clear in what manner the tax was levied; but it appears to have been collected with other money-taxes by the πράκτορες. The suggestion of Wilcken (*l. c.*) that the consumers of salt—i. e. practically all inhabitants—paid an annual sum to the state in recognition of the royal monopoly, in addition to buying their salt from the retailers, is not in accordance with any of the known principles of Egyptian tax-collection: a more probable supposition is that it was paid by the dealers for the right to sell salt. It is fairly clear that the tax was accounted a yearly one; and the receipts are mostly for small sums, though of very varying amounts.

**41.** (G. 291). ·097 × ·099. 64–5 A.D.

Πικῶς Παμώνθ(ου) καὶ μέτοχοι
Σενφαήριος χαί(ρειν). Ἀπεσχή(καμεν) ἁλὸς
δραχ(μὰς) τέσαρας / 𐅵δ τοῦ ιαʃ Νέρων(ος)
τοῦ κυρίου.

2. l. Σενφαήρει.

'Pikos son of Pamonthes and his colleagues to Senphaeris, greeting. We have received for salt four drachmae = 4 dr., for the eleventh year of Nero our lord.'

(*c*) Ἀνδ(ριάντων ?).

There are three Theban receipts published by Wilcken (G. O. 559, 603, 604) for μερισμὸς αν^δ; and he offers no explanation of the contracted word. It would appear possible that the levy was one ὑπὲρ ἀνδριάντων, which he recognizes in G. O. 1430 from Thebes and a long series of ostraca from Elephantine. In the latter the full particulars given admit of no doubt as to the purpose of the tax; and it is commonly described as a *μερισμός* and collected in small amounts, as in the examples from Thebes. It may be due to chance only, but the three receipts of Wilcken and the one here published belong to two years only—the eighteenth of Hadrian and the fifth of Antoninus Pius—which suggests that the tax was a casual one at Thebes, as at Elephantine. The receipts for the eighteenth year of Hadrian may perhaps be taken as representing a collection for a rather belated statue of the emperor, put up to celebrate his visit to Thebes over two years previously; but it is difficult to suggest an occasion for the erection of a statue of Antoninus Pius in his fifth year, unless it was an even more belated record of the completion of a Sothic period in 138 A.D. (It may be noted that the Phoenix, which occurs as a type on Alexandrian coins of the second year of Antoninus, doubtless with reference to the Sothic celebration of that year, is used again on coins of the sixth year.) In one case—G. O. 603—the tax is said to have been levied on land, the receipt being for $5\frac{1}{2}$ obols on $30\frac{1}{16}$ arourae, which shows a very low rate per aroura, much below that of any known land-tax.

**42.** (G. 246). ·053 × ·077. 133 A.D.

*Πασῆ(μις) καὶ Ἀπίων ἀπαιτ(ηταὶ) μερισμ(οῦ)*
*ἀνδ(ριάντων ?) Ἀγο(ρῶν) δ̣ Νό(του) [[. . .]] Πετερμού(θη̣)*
*Φαή(ριος). Ἔσχ(ομεν) κέρμ(ατος) ὀ̣β̣ο̣λ̣(οὺς) τέσσαρ(ας)*
*κέρμ(ατος) ὀβολ(οὺς) δ. ∟ιη Ἀδριανοῦ Καίσαρος*
*Θὼθ κη̄.*
(2 h.) *Ἀπίων σεσημ(είωμαι).*

'Pasemis and Apion, collectors of the rate for statues (?) in the fourth district of Agorai South, to Petermouthes son of Phaeris. We have received four obols in copper = 4 obols in copper. Year 18 of Hadrianus Caesar, Thoth 28. Signed, Apion.'

2. Ἀγο(ρῶν) δ̣ Νό(του): see note on 125. 3.
3. *κέρμ(ατος)*: the term *κέρμα* was probably used to denote the copper (or bronze) coinage of Alexandria of the first and second centuries A.D., which supplied the needs of Egypt for any change less than a tetradrachm.

### (*d*) *Βαλανικόν*.

Receipts for *βαλανικόν* are among the commonest of those found on Theban ostraca; but in spite of their number it is still obscure how the tax was assessed or collected: and the additional information given by those published here does not agree with the conclusions previously formed by Wilcken (*Ostr.* i, pp. 165 ff.). It has already been mentioned (p. 71) that his supposition, that the tax was introduced by Augustus into Egypt, has been found to be wrong; and it now appears that the tax might be reckoned in monthly payments (no. 47). As a general rule, however, the payments for bath-tax are entered as adjuncts to other taxes, usually *λαογραφία* and *χωματικόν*; and the amounts of the receipts in the first century A.D. may explain the reason for this. The normal forms of statement are either *λαογραφία* 10 drachmae, *βαλανικόν* 1 dr. 1½ obols, *καὶ προσδιαγραφόμενα*, or *χωματικόν* 6 dr. 4 obols, *βαλανικόν* 4 (later 4½) obols, *καὶ προσδιαγραφόμενα*. It is probable that at this period the fixed rates for *λαογραφία* and *χωματικόν* in most regions of Thebes were 10 drachmae and 6 dr. 4 obols respectively, though the evidence with regard to *λαογραφία* is not very definite (see p. 118). There was always, during the Roman rule in Egypt, a dearth of small change in the country; a disproportionately large part of the coinage in circulation consisted of tetradrachms, and consequently as many payments as possible were made in coins of this denomination. A man desiring to pay his 10 drachmae as *λαογραφία* for a year would accordingly hand in three tetradrachms; and, instead of receiving any change, he would have the balance credited to his *βαλανικόν*, after the *προσδιαγραφόμενα* had been written off at the rate of 1½ obols to the tetradrachm. Similarly, in the case of a year's *χωματικόν* he would pay in two tetradrachms; though in the latter class of transactions the payers seem to have lost an obol or half an obol, as the 6 dr. 4 obols for *χωματικόν* and 3 obols for *προσδιαγραφόμενα* on two tetradrachms should have left 5 obols for *βαλανικόν*, whereas only 4 or 4½ are credited. It might be supposed that the total amount due for the year was made up by the two balances—as the same man occurs paying in both forms in the same year (nos. 49 and 50), and 1 dr. 1½ obols and 4½ obols at any rate make up a round sum—but other instances of higher payments for *βαλανικόν* alone conflict with this idea. Possibly these sums were taken as convenient instalments and the remainder of the tax due was collected later: the latter may be referred to in the receipts for *τὸ πρόλοιπον τοῦ βαλανικοῦ* of G. O. 1032, 1033, 1035, 1036, 1037; the only two of these which are exactly dated are at the end of the year for which the tax was due or the beginning of the next.

The amounts, however, for which receipts are given, even in the same year and place, or to the same individual, do not show any definite basis: it may be remarked that in one instance (no. 47) the sum is much higher than anything noted by Wilcken; but in no case do they approach what appears to have been the regular payment at Tentyra in the reign of Tiberius—40 drachmae a year—as shown by a series of demotic ostraca, an account of which I hope to publish shortly.

**43.** (G. 83). ·104 × ·095. 76 A.D.

*Διαγεγρά(φηκε) Ψεναμοῦ[ν]ις*
*Ἁρφμόιτος ὑπ(ὲρ) χω(ματικοῦ) Ἀγ(ορῶν) Βο(ρρᾶ) η* L
*ʕς ϝ βα(λανικοῦ) ϝc / καὶ π(ροσδιαγραφόμενα).* L *η Οὐεσ-*
*πασιανοῦ τοῦ κυρίου*
*Ἐπεὶφ λγ̄. Ἀπίω(ν) σεση(μείωμαι).*

'Psenamounis son of Harphmois has paid for dyke-tax in Agorai North for the eighth year 6 dr. 4 obols, for bath-tax 4½ obols, with the extra charges. Year 8 of Vespasianus our lord, Epeiph 33. Signed, Apion.'

3. ϝc /: the writer has omitted to enter the total amount.
5. Ἐπεὶφ λγ̄: for suggested explanations of this peculiar style of dating see Wilcken, *Ostr.* i, p. 813.

**44.** (G. 269). ·090 × ·104. 78 A.D.

*Θέων καὶ μέτ(οχοι) τελ(ῶναι) θησ(αυροῦ) ἱερ(ῶν) Μαιεύρι*
*Ἁρφμόι(τος) καὶ Ψεναμο(ύνει) ἀδελ(φῷ) χαί(ρειν). Ἔσχ(ομεν)*
*τὸ βαλ(ανικὸν) τοῦ ι* L *Οὐεσπασιανοῦ*
*τοῦ κυρίου Παχὼν ᾱ.*

'Theon and his colleagues, farmers of the granary of the temples, to Maieuris son of Harphmois and Psenamounis his brother, greeting. We have received the bath-tax for the tenth year of Vespasianus our lord; Pachon 1.'

**45.** (G. 252). ·078 × ·109. 80 A.D.

*Διέγρα(ψε) Μαιεῦρις*
*Ἁρφμόιτος ὑπ(ὲρ) λαο(γραφίας) Ἀγο(ρῶν) Βο(ρρᾶ)*

βL [ϛ] δέκα βαλ(ανικοῦ) α–c / ια–c καὶ προ(σδιαγραφόμενα).
Lβ Ṭ[ίτο]υ τοῦ κυρίου
Μεχ(εὶρ) λ̅ λ̅δ̅. Ἡρạḳ(λείδης) σε(σημείωμαι)
(An illegible line of demotic.)

'Maieuris son of Harphmois has paid for poll-tax in Agorai North for the second year ten dr., for bath-tax 1 (dr.) 1½ obols = 11 (dr.) 1½ obols, with the extra charges. Year 2 of Titus our lord, Mecheir 30–34. Signed, Herakleides.'

4. Ṭ[ίτο]υ: the name, which is almost rubbed out, might be Δομιτιανοῦ in a very abbreviated form, but the traces of the first letter look like T.

5. Μεχ(εὶρ) λ̅ λ̅δ̅: for an explanation of the peculiar system of dating by 30 followed by a second number for the days of a month see Wilcken, *Ostr.* i, p. 813. In the instances cited by him, however, the series runs from λ̅α̅ to λ̅λ̅: here the second number exceeds 30.

**46.** (G. 264). ·060 × ·088. 80 A.D.

Ἀπολλῶς καὶ μέ(τοχοι) τελ(ῶναι)
θησ(αυροῦ) ἱε(ρῶν) Ὥρῳ 'Οσορουήρ(ιος)
καὶ 'Οσορουή(ρει) υἱ(ῷ) χα(ίρειν). Ἀπέχο(μεν) τὸ
βαλ(ανικὸν) τοῦ βL Τίτου Καίσαρος
τοῦ κυρίου Παῦνι κ̅η̅.

'Apollos and his colleagues, farmers of the granary of the temples, to Horos son of Osoroueris and Osoroueris his son, greeting. We have received the bath-tax for the second year of Titus Caesar our lord; Pauni 28.'

**47.** (G. 245). ·097 × ·106. 82 A.D.

Διαγεγρ(άφηκε) Μαιεῦρις Ἁρφμόι(τος)
ὑπ(ὲρ) βαλ(ανικοῦ) Ἀγο(ρῶν) βο(ρρᾶ) εἰς ἀρί(θμησιν) Μεχ(εὶρ) αϛ
καὶ εἰς ἀρί(θμησιν) Φαμ(ενὼθ) δρ(αχμὰς) ἓξ κ(αὶ) δέκα / ϛις
καὶ προ(σδιαγραφόμενα). La Δομιτιανοῦ
τοῦ κυρίου Μεσ(ορὴ) λ̅α̅.
Ἀμ(      ) σεση(μείωμαι).

'Maieuris son of Harphmois has paid for bath-tax in Agorai North on account of Mecheir of the first year and on account of Phamenoth sixteen drachmae = 16 dr., with the extra charges. Year 1 of Domitianus our lord, Mesore 31. Signed, Am.......'

5. Μεσ(ορὴ) $\overline{λα}$: see note on 45. 5. This instance rather militates against Wilcken's suggested explanation (*l.c.*, p. 815) of e.g. Μεσορὴ $\overline{λα}$ as equivalent to Θὼθ ᾱ εἰς ἀρίθμησιν Μεσορή, since here the payment is not εἰς ἀρίθμησιν Μεσορή, but εἰς ἀρίθμησιν Μεχεὶρ καὶ Φαμενώθ.

**48.** (G. 297). ·080 × ·070 (chipped on right). 82 A.D.

*Διαγ(εγράφηκε) Μαιεῦρ(ις) Ἁρφμόι[τ(ος)*
*ὑπ(ὲρ) χω(ματικοῦ) Ἀγο(ρῶν) βο(ρρᾶ) γ𐅵 𐅵ϛ̣[𐅶 (?)*
*βαλ(ανικοῦ) 𐅶 κ(αὶ) πρ(οσδιαγραφόμενα). ∟γ Δ(ομιτ)ι̣α̣ν̣[οῦ*
*τοῦ κ(υ)ρίου Ἐπεὶφ*
*$\overline{κθ}$. Α( ) σ(εσημείωμαι).*

'Maieuris son of Harphmois has paid for dyke-tax in Agorai North for the third year 6 dr. [4 obols?], for bath-tax 3 obols, with the extra charges. Year 3 of Domitianus our lord, Epeiph 29. Signed, A.......'

**49.** (G. 68). ·110 × ·089. 85 A.D.

*Διαγεγρά(φηκε) Ψεναμο⟨ῦ⟩νις*
*Ἀροφμόιτος Μαείριος*
*ὑπ(ὲρ) λαο(γραφίας)*
*Ἀγορὰ βο(ρρᾶ) ε∟ 𐅵ι βαλ(ανικοῦ) α–c*
*/ 𐅵ια-c καὶ τὰ προ(σδιαγραφόμενα). ∟ε Δομι-*
*τιανοῦ τοῦ κυρίου Μεχεὶρ*
*$\overline{λε}$. Πτολ(εμαῖος) σεση(μείωμαι).*

2. l. Ἁρφμόιτος Μαιεύριος. 4. l. Ἀγορῶν.

'Psenamounis son of Harphmois son of Maieuris has paid for poll-tax in Agorai North for the fifth year 10 dr., for bath-tax 1 (dr.) 1½ obols = 11 dr. 1½ obols, with the extra charges. Year 5 of Domitianus our lord, Mecheir 35. Signed, Ptolemaios.'

**50.** (G. 293). ·079 × ·096. 85 A.D.

*Διαγεγρά(φηκε) Ψεναμο(ῦνις) Ἁρφμόιτο(ς) Μαι-*
*εύριο(ς) ὑπ(ὲρ) χω(ματικοῦ) Ἀγο(ρῶν) βο(ρρᾶ) ε*L ϛ ἓξ ϝ
*βαλ(ανικοῦ)* ϝc / ϛζ = c *καὶ προ(σδιαγραφόμενα).* Lε *Δομ(ιτιαν)οῦ*
*τοῦ κυρίου Ἐπεὶφ η̄.*

'Psenamounis son of Harphmois son of Maieuris has paid for dyke-tax in Agorai North for the fifth year six dr. 4 obols, for bath-tax 4½ obols = 7 dr. 2½ obols, with the extra charges. Year 5 of Domitianus our lord, Epeiph 8.'

**51.** (G. 274). ·089 × ·105. 119 A.D.

*Θέων πράκ(τωρ) ἀργ(υρικῶν) Φμόις*
*Ἀμμωνίο(υ) Ἀπολλωνίο(υ). Ἔσχ(ον) ὑπ(ὲρ) χω(ματικοῦ)*
*καὶ βαλ(ανικοῦ) Νό(του) γϛ ῥυπ(αρὰς)* ϛ ζϝχ^β / *ῥυπ(αραὶ)* ϛ ζϝχ^β.
Lδ *Ἁδρια(νοῦ) Καίσ(αρος) τ(οῦ) κυρίου Ἁθὺρ ιθ̄.*
*Εὐδ̣ . . . ς σεση(μείωμαι).*

1. l. Φμόιτι.

'Theon, collector of money-taxes, to Phmois son of Ammonios son of Apollonios. I have received for dyke-tax and bath-tax in the South district for the third year 7 bad dr. 4 obols 2 chalki = 7 bad dr. 4 obols 2 chalki. Year 4 of Hadrianus Caesar our lord, Hathur 19. Signed, Eud . . . s.'

3. ῥυπ(αρὰς): the term ῥυπαρός occurs not infrequently in statements of payments in the Roman period, most commonly in the latter half of the first and early half of the second centuries. It does not appear to refer to any distinct class of coins—all Roman tetradrachms of Alexandria might have been called ῥυπαρά—and probably was a term of account, like the 'bad' piastre of some Turkish towns, e.g. Smyrna.

**52.** (G. 87). ·085 × ·095. 140 A.D.

*Παμώ(νθης) καὶ Ποριε(ύθης) ἀπαιτ(ηταὶ) μερισμ(οῦ)*
*βαλ(ανείων) Κωμ(ῶν) Ὥρ(ῳ) Ψεντφο(ῦτος) Ψενμίνιο(ς).*
*Ἔσχ(ομεν)* ϛα *ὀβ(ολοὺς) β.* Lδ *Ἀντωνίνου*
*Καίσαρος τοῦ κυρίου μην(ὸς) Ἁδριανοῦ*
*η̄.*

'Pamonthes and Porieuthes, collectors of the rate for baths in the Villages, to Horos son of Psentphous son of Psenminis. We have received 1 dr. 2 obols. Year 4 of Antoninus Caesar our lord, month Hadrianus 8.'

**53.** (G. 230). ·134 × ·121. 160 A.D.

*Πλῆνις καὶ Ῥοῦφος πράκ(τορες) ἀργ(υρικῶν) Μ(εμνονείων) διὰ*
*Αὐ̣φο(  ) βοη(θοῦ) Παῆρις Παῆρις Ψενο(σίριος ?). Ἔσχ(ομεν) ὑπ(ὲρ)*
*λαογ(ραφίας) καὶ βαλ(ανικοῦ) κγ∫ ∫ιϛ. ∟κγ Ἀντωνίνου*
*τοῦ κυρίου Φαρμ(οῦθι) ιε̅.*
*Ὁμ(οίως) Παχὼ(ν) ια̅ ∫δ. Ὁμ(οίως) Ἐπ(εὶ)φ ια̅ ∫δ.*

2. l. Παήρει Παήριος.

'Plenis and Rufus, collectors of money-taxes of the Memnonia, through Aupho(  ) their assistant, to Paeris son of Paeris son of Psenosiris (?). We have received for poll-tax and bath-tax of the twenty-third year 16 dr. Year 23 of Antoninus our lord, Pharmouthi 15. Likewise on Pachon 11, 4 dr. Likewise on Epeiph 11, 4 dr.'

**54.** (G. 237). ·092 × ·104. 189–90 A.D.

*Ὠριγέ(νης) κ(αὶ) μ(έτοχοι) ἐπιτ(ηρηταὶ) τέλ(ους)*
*θησ(αυροῦ) Πετεμ(ενώφει) Σενπετεμ(ενώφιος).*
*Ἐσχήκ(αμεν) τὸ βαλ(ανικὸν) τοῦ λ∫.*

'Origenes and his colleagues, supervisors of the tax of the granary, to Petemenophis son of Senpetemenophis. We have received the bath-tax for the thirtieth year.'

2. Πετεμ(ενώφει) Σενπετεμ(ενώφιος): the abbreviated names are restored on the assumption that the taxpayer is the same man who appears in nos. 60 and 61 of this same year.

3. λ∫: the thirtieth year must be of Commodus, as the hand is clearly a late second century one.

**55.** (G. 265). ·059 × ·074. 190–1 A.D.

*Παμώνθ(ης) κ(αὶ) μ(έτοχοι) ἐπι(τηρηταὶ) τέλ(ους)*
*θησ(αυροῦ) ἱερ(ῶν) Ἐσουή(ρει) σὺν υἱ(ῷ)*

*Πετοσ(ίρει). Ἔσχομ(εν) τὸ βαλ(ανικὸν)*
*τοῦ λα∫⸎*

'Pamonthes and his colleagues, supervisors of the tax of the granary of the temples, to Esoueris and his son Petosiris. We have received the bath-tax for the thirty-first year.'

4. λα∫: see note on 54. 3.

**[See also no. 34 for another receipt for *βαλανικόν*.]**

(e) *Γερδιακόν.*

The information to be obtained from these ostraca on the subject of the tax on weavers does not add much to that already summarized by Wilcken (*Ostr.* i, p. 172). The facts that the tax is usually stated to be for a particular month, and that it is usually paid at the close of that month or shortly after, suggest strongly that it was regarded as accruing from month to month, at any rate at Thebes (though the evidence of papyri—e.g. P. Oxy. 288, P. Fay. 48—does not show the same principle in other districts). Wherever we have more than one receipt given to the same individual (e.g. nos. 59 and 62, 60 and 61) he always appears as paying at the same monthly rate, though for different individuals the rates vary from 2 to 10 drachmae a month; which looks as if the assessment was based in some way on the extent of the business activities of the taxpayer in each case.

It may be noted that the receipts down to the end of the reign of Marcus Aurelius were always given by *τελῶναι*, with the exception of two (G. O. 574 and no. 56) given by Erieus *καὶ μέτοχοι ἐπιτηρηταί* in the nineteenth and twentieth years of Hadrian, whereas afterwards they were regularly given by *ἐπιτηρηταί*, with one exception (no. 64) given by Asklas *καὶ μέτοχοι τελῶναι* in the reign of Pertinax.

**56.** (G. 299). ·077 × ·063. 136 A.D.

*Ἐριεὺς καὶ μέτοχ(οι) ἐπιτηρητ(αὶ)*
*τέλους γερδίων Νεφερῶ̣ς̣*
*Ψεμμώνθου. Ἔσχομ(εν) παρὰ*
*σοῦ δραχ(μὰς) τέσσαρας.*

Lκ Ἀδριανοῦ τοῦ
κυρίου Φαμενὼθ ιη̅.

2. l. Νεφερῶτι.

'Erieus and his colleagues, supervisors of the tax on weavers, to Nepheros son of Psemmonthes. We have received from you four drachmae. Year 20 of Hadrianus our lord, Phamenoth 18.'

**57.** (G. 99). ·066 × ·105 (surface chipped). 156 A.D.

Ὧρος καὶ μέτοχ(οι) τελ(ῶναι) γερδ(ιακοῦ) Ψεναμεούνιος
Φαήριος. Ἀπέσχ[ο]με[ν π]α[ρ]ὰ σοῦ τέλ(ος) Ἀθὺρ
καὶ Ἀδριανοῦ [ιθL] δραχ(μὰς) ὀκτὼ
/ ϛη. Lιθ Ἀντωνίνου Καίσ[αρος]
τοῦ κυρίου Τῦβι ιη̅

1. l. Ψεναμοῦνει.

'Horos and his colleagues, farmers of the weaving-tax, to Psenamounis son of Phaeris. We have received from you the tax for Hathur and Hadrianus of the nineteenth year, eight drachmae = 8 dr. Year 19 of Antoninus Caesar our lord, Tubi 18.'

**58.** (G. 215). ·073 × ·089. 167 A.D.

Ποριεύθης καὶ μ(έτοχοι) τελ(ῶναι) γερδ(ιακοῦ) τέλ(ους) ηϛ
Λελοῦς Σεναμενρώσι(ος). Ἔσχ(ομεν) πα-
ρὰ σοῦ ὑ̣π̣(ὲρ) τέλ(ους) μηνῶ(ν) Θὼθ κ(αὶ)
Φαῶφι τ(οῦ) αὐ(τοῦ) ϛ ϛ ὀκτὼ / ϛη. Lη Ἀντω(νίνου)
κ(αὶ) Οὐήρου τῶν κυρίων Σεβαστῶ[ν
Ἀθὺρ ιϛ̅.

2. l. Λελοῦτι.

'Porieuthes and his colleagues, farmers of the weaving-tax of the eighth year, to Lelous son of Senamenrosis. We have received from you for the tax of the months Thoth and Phaophi of the said year eight dr. = 8 dr. Year 8 of Antoninus and Verus our lords Augusti, Hathur 16.'

**59.** (G. 278). ·081 × ·083. 189 A.D.

*Πορειεύθης καὶ μέτοχ(οι)*
*ἐπιτ(ηρηταὶ) τέλ(ους) γερδ(ίων) Περμάμει*
*Φθουμίνι(ος). Ἔσχ(ομεν) ὑπ(ὲρ) τέλ(ους)*
*Ἀθὺρ ϛη.* Lλ∕
*Ἀθὺρ ιγ.*

'Porieuthes and his colleagues, supervisors of the tax on weavers, to Permamis son of Phthouminis. We have received for the tax of Hathur 8 dr. Year 30, Hathur 13.'

2. Περμάμει: the same payer occurs on no. 62 of the thirty-second year.

4. Lλ∕: the thirtieth year must be of Commodus, as the hand is a late second century one. The bad habit of omitting the name of the reigning emperor in dates seems to have arisen at Thebes, as elsewhere, about this time.

**60.** (G. 80). ·068 × ·124. 191 A.D.

*Πρεμαῶς καὶ μ(έτοχοι) ἐπιτη(ρηταὶ) τέλ(ους) γερδ(ίων)*
*Πετεμ(ενώφει) Σενπετεμ(ενώφιος) χα(ίρειν).*
*Ἔσχομ(εν) ὑπ(ὲρ) τέλ(ους) μη(νὸς) Φαμ(ενὼθ) τοῦ λαϛ*
*ϛη / ϛη.*
Lλα∕ *Φαρμ(οῦθι) ϛ̄.*

'Premaos and his colleagues, supervisors of the tax on weavers, to Petemenophis son of Senpetemenophis, greeting. We have received for the tax of the month Phamenoth of the thirty-first year 8 dr. = 8 dr. Year 31, Pharmouthi 6.'

1. Πρεμαῶς: this collector occurs also in G. O. 664 and no. 61, of the same year; in no. 63, of the thirty-second year; and in G. O. 1073, and two unpublished ostraca of this collection (G. 85 and G. 292) of the third year of Severus.

2. Πετεμ(ενώφει) Σενπετεμ(ενώφιος): these names are completed from two other receipts for the same tax, not published here, on which they are written out more fully (G. 84 and G. 292, of the second and third years of Severus). The same payer occurs on the next ostracon.

5. Lλα∕: see note on 59. 4.

**61**. (G. 220). ·079 × ·090. 191 A.D.

*Πρεμαῶς καὶ μ(έτοχοι) ἐπιτη(ρηταὶ)*
*γερδ(ιακοῦ) Πετεμ(ενώφει) Σενπετεμ(ενώφιος)*
*χα(ίρειν). Ἔσχομ(εν) ὑπ(ὲρ) τέλ(ους) μη(νὸς)*
*Φαρμ(οῦθι) ϛη / ϛη*
*Lλα⸗ Παχὼ(ν) β̄.*

'Premaos and his colleagues, supervisors of the weaving-tax, to Petemenophis son of Senpetemenophis, greeting. We have received for the tax of the month Pharmouthi 8 dr. = 8 dr. Year 31, Pachon 2.'

1. Πρεμαῶς: see note on 60. 1.
2. Πετεμ(ενώφει): see note on 60. 2.
5. Lλα⸗: see note on 59. 4.

**62**. (G. 284). ·048 × ·060. 191 A.D.

*Ψανσνῶ(ς) καὶ μέτοχ(οι)*
*ἐπιτ(ηρηταὶ) τέλ(ους) γερδ(ίων)*
*Περμ(άμει) Φθουμ(ίνιος).*
*Ἔσχ(ομεν) ὑπ(ὲρ) Ἀθὺρ ϛη.*
*Lλβ⸗ Ἀθὺρ ᾱ.*

'Psansnos and his colleagues, supervisors of the tax on weavers, to Permamis son of Phthouminis. We have received for Hathur 8 dr. Year 32, Hathur 1.'

3. Περμ(άμει): see note on 59. 2.
5. Lλβ⸗: see note on 59. 4.

**63**. (G. 420). ·076 × ·073. 192 A.D.

*Πρεμαῶς καὶ*
*μέτοχ(οι) ἐπιτη(ρηταὶ)*
*τέλ(ους) γερδ(ίων).*
*Ἔσχ(ομεν) παρὰ σοῦ*
*ὑπ(ὲρ) Μεχεὶρ*
*ϛδ. Lλβ⸗*
*Μεχεὶρ*
*λ̄.*

'Premaos and his colleagues, supervisors of the tax on weavers. We have received from you for Mecheir 4 dr. Year 32, Mecheir 30.'

1. Πρεμαώς: see note on 60. 1.
4. παρὰ σοῦ: the name of the payer of the tax is not given.
6. Lλβ∻: see note on 59. 4.

**64.** (G. 294). ·078 × ·103. 193 A.D.

*Ἀσκλᾶς καὶ μέτοχ(οι)*
*τελ(ῶναι) γερδ(ιακοῦ) Πετεμενώφι Φθου-*
*μίνιος. Ἔσχ(ομεν) παρὰ σοῦ ὑπ(ὲρ) μη(νὸς)*
*Παχὼν τὸ καθῆκον τ(έλος).*
*Lα Πουβλίου Ἑλουίου*
*Περτίνακος Σεβαστοῦ*
*Παχὼν λ̄.*

'Asklas and his colleagues, farmers of the weaving-tax, to Petemenophis son of Phthouminis. We have received from you for the month Pachon the appointed tax. Year 1 of Publius Helvius Pertinax Augustus, Pachon 30.'

2. l. Πετεμενώφει: the same payer occurs in G. 85 (not published) of year 3, presumably of Severus.

7. Παχὼν λ̄: on this date (May 25) Pertinax had been dead for nearly two months.

**65.** (G. 82). ·048 × ·076. 197 A.D.

*Νεφερῶς πρ(εσβύτερος) Φθουμί(νιος) καὶ μ(έτοχοι) ἐπιτη(ρηταὶ)*
*τέλ(ους) γερδ(ίων) τοῦ ε∕ ὀνόμ(ατος) Πεμσ(αοῦς).*
*Ἔσχ(ομεν) παρὰ σ(οῦ) τὸ τέλ(ος) μη(νὸς) Τῦβι ϛβ.*
*Lε Μεχ(εὶρ) ϛ̄.*

'Nepheros the elder, son of Phthouminis, and his colleagues, supervisors of the tax on weavers of the fifth year, in respect of Pemsaos. We have received from you the tax for the month Tubi, 2 dr. Year 5, Mecheir 6.'

1. Νεφερῶς: this collector also occurs in G. 84 (unpublished) of the second year; in G. O. 1332 of the fifth year; in no. 68 of the sixth year; and possibly in no. 69 of the seventh year. These years are practically fixed as of Severus, since G. 84 is a receipt to the same payer as nos. 60 and 61 of the thirty-first year of Commodus.

**66.** (G. 86). ·069 × ·072. 197 A.D.

*Πορούσιος κ(αὶ) μ(έτοχοι) ἐπ(ιτηρηταὶ) τέλ(ους) γερδί(ων) τοῦ ε∫ ὀνό(ματος) Πετεμ(ενώφιος ?). Ἐσχήκ(αμεν) παρὰ σ(οῦ) τὸ τέλ(ος) μηνὸς Παχὼν τοῦ ε∫ ∫δ.*

*Lε∫ Παχὼν λ̄.*

'Porousios and his colleagues, supervisors of the tax on weavers of the fifth year, in respect of Petemenophis. We have received from you the tax for the month Pachon of the fifth year, 4 dr. Year 5, Pachon 30.'

1. ε∫ : the fifth year may be taken to be of Severus, as the handwriting suggests this rather than the next fifth year in Egyptian dating—that of Elagabalus (who was indeed dead three months before Pachon 30 of his fifth year, but this would not be decisive against such a date at Thebes); also the Πετεμ( ) of l. 2 may be identical with the Πετεμενῶφις of no. 69 who got a receipt in the seventh year from Νεφερῶς, who was collecting in the early years of Severus (see note on 65. 1); but Πετεμενῶφις seems to have been such a favourite name at this period among the Theban weavers that the identity cannot safely be accepted.

**67.** (G. 72). ·085 × ·086. Possibly 197 A.D.

*Μιῦσις Ξένωνος ἐπιτηρη(τὴς)*
*τέλ(ους) γερδίων Πετσεν( ) Πετεμ(ενώφιος ?) χαί(ρειν).*
*Ἔσχ(ον) παρὰ σοῦ ὑπ(ὲρ) ἀριθ(μήσεως) μην(ὸς)*
*Ἐ(πεὶ)φ τοῦ ε∫ δραχμὰς ὀκτὼ*
*∕ ∫η. Lε∫ Ἐ(πεὶ)φ ιζ̄.*

'Miusis son of Xenon, supervisor of the tax on weavers, to Petsen..... son of Petemenophis, greeting. I have received from you for the account of the month Epeiph of the fifth year eight drachmae = 8 dr. Year 5, Epeiph 17.'

3. ὑπ(ὲρ) ἀριθ(μήσεως) μην(ὸς) Ἐ(πεί)φ: cf. G. O. 660.
4. ε∫ : the fifth year is most likely to be that of Severus, on grounds of handwriting.

**68.** (G. 243). ·079 × ·088. 198 A.D.

*Νεφερῶς πρ(εσβύτερος) Φθουμί(νιος) καὶ μ(έτοχοι) ἐπιτη(ρηταὶ) τέλ(ους) γερδίων τοῦ ϛL ὀνόμ(ατος) Πετεμ(ενώφιος ?) Ἀρβή(χιος).*
*Ἔσχ(ομεν) παρὰ σοῦ ὑπ(ὲρ) τέλ(ους) μη(νὸς) Παῦνι*
*δραχμὰς ἕξ ∕ ∫ϛ.*
*Lϛ∫ Ἐπεὶφ ῑ.*

'Nepheros the elder, son of Phthouminis, and his colleagues, supervisors of the tax on weavers of the sixth year, in respect of Petemenophis son of Harbechis. We have received from you for the tax of the month Pauni six drachmae = 6 dr. Year 6, Epeiph 10.'

2. ϛL: see note on 65. 1 as to the date of Nepheros son of Phthouminis.

**69.** (G. 93). ·077 × ·107 (chipped on left). Possibly 198 A.D.

N]εφερῶς καὶ μ(έτοχοι) ἐπιτηρ(ηταὶ) τέλ(ους) γερδ(ίων).
Ἔ]σχον παρὰ σοῦ ὑπὲρ τέλ(ους) γερδ(ίων) τοῦ
Lζ ὀνόμ(ατος) Πετεμενώφ(ιος) ὑπὲρ
Φαῶφι 𐅵δ καὶ ἀπὸ Ἀθὺρ
δραχ(μὰς) δ / 𐅵δ τοῦ Lζ//.

'Nepheros and his colleagues, supervisors of the tax on weavers. I have received from you for the tax on weavers of the seventh year in respect of Petemenophis for Phaophi 4 dr. and from Hathur 4 drachmae = 4 dr. for the seventh year.'

1. Νεφερῶς: this collector may possibly be the same as the Νεφερῶς πρεσβύτερος Φθουμίνιος who was in office in years 2, 5, and 6 of Severus (see note on 65. 1), although the hand in which the receipt is written is not the same as that of nos. 65 and 68, and the formula is different and considerably confused.

**70.** (G. 211). ·056 × ·082. Early third century A.D.

Βησῶς καὶ μ(έτοχοι) ἐπιτ(ηρηταὶ) τέλ(ους) γερδ(ίων) τοῦ
ϛL ὀνόμ(ατος) Πετεμ(ενώφιος ?). Ἔσχ(ομεν) παρὰ σο(ῦ)
ὑπ(ὲρ) τέλ(ους) μη(νὸς) Θὼθ 𐅵δέκα / 𐅵ι.
Lϛ// Φαῶ(φι) κβ.

'Besos and his colleagues, supervisors of the tax on weavers of the sixth year, in respect of Petemenophis. We have received from you for the tax of the month Thoth ten dr. = 10 dr. Year 6, Phaophi 22.'

2. ϛL: the handwriting of this receipt seems to be of a later date than the sixth year of Septimius Severus, and it more probably belongs to the reign of Severus Alexander or one of his successors.

### (*f*) Γεωμετρία.

It is unfortunately still obscure what the nature of the tax ὑπὲρ γεωμετρίας was—whether it was the ordinary land-tax or a special assessment to cover the survey of land—and it is equally impossible to say at what rate it was levied or how it was assessed. There are many instances of the tax, both on papyri and on ostraca, but the amounts paid vary very widely and do not fall into any apparent system.

**71.** (G. 410). ·055 × ·067 (chipped on left). 67 A.D.

*Διέγρα(ψε) Ψενμῖνις Πετεμ(ίνιος)*
*Πετέχω(ντος) ὑπ(ὲρ) γεο(μετρίας) Ὠφιή(ου) ιγ∫ ∫δέκα*
*/ ∫]ι κ(αὶ) το(ύτων) προ(σδιαγραφόμενα). Lιγ Νέρωνος*
*το]ῦ κυρίου Μεχεὶρ λ̅ϛ̅.*
*]ενων σεση(μείωμαι).*

'Psenminis son of Peteminis son of Petechon has paid for the survey-tax in Ophieion for the thirteenth year ten dr. = 10 dr. and the extra charges on this. Year 13 of Nero our lord, Mecheir 36. Signed, . . enon.'

4. Μεχεὶρ λ̅ϛ̅: see note on 45. 5.

**72.** (G. 412). ·086 × ·088 (chipped on right at top). 161–2 A.D.

*Διέγρ(αψε) Πετεαρουῆρις Φαή[ριος*
*ὑπ(ὲρ) γεωμε(τρίας) Χά(ρακος) α∫ ἀ(ντὶ) Σεμνο(ῦτος) Φαή[ριος*
*ῥυπ(αρὰν) ∫ μίαν / ∫α. Lβ Ἀντωνίνου*
*καὶ Οὐήρου τῶν κυρίων Αὐτοκρατόρων*
*Φαῶ(φι) ζ̄. Κα( ) σ(εσ)η(μείωμαι).*
(2 h.) *Διέγρ(αψε) Σεμνο(ῦς) Φαή(ριος) ἀντὶ Πετεαρο(υήριος)*
*Φαή(ριος) ὑπ(ὲρ) γεωμε(τρίας) Χά(ρακος) ῥυπ(αρὰν) ∫ μίαν*
*/ ∫α. Lγ Ἀν(τωνίνου) καὶ Οὐήρ(ου)*
*τῶν κυρίων Σεβαστῶν*
*Θὼθ κ̄. Γ( ) σ(εσημείωμαι).*

3. ῥυπ(αρὰν): first letter corrected from δ.

'Petearoueris son of Phaeris has paid for the survey-tax in Charax for the first year on behalf of Semnous son of Phaeris one bad dr. = 1 dr. Year 2 of Antoninus and Verus our lords Emperors, Phaophi 7. Signed, Ka....

Semnous son of Phaeris has paid on behalf of Petearoueris son of Phaeris for the survey-tax in Charax one bad dr. = 1 dr. Year 3 of Antoninus and Verus our lords Augusti, Thoth 20. Signed, G . . . . .'

2. ἀ(ντὶ): this seems the probable expansion of the contraction ᾱ, which is written out in full in the second receipt. The two brothers seem to have paid alternately on one another's behalf.

### (*g*) Ἐγκύκλιον.

The one instance in this collection in which a payment for ἐγκύκλιον occurs is printed above as no. 40. The tax is described as ενκ κλ, which I have suggested stands for ἐνκύκλιον κληρονομιῶν; the εἰκοστὴ κληρονομιῶν, which appears in papyri (e.g. B. G. U. 240, 326), might be classified as ἐγκύκλιον, as that term seems to have covered percentages of varying rates payable to the state on contracts and mercantile transactions (Wilcken, *Ostr.* i, p. 182). But on the other hand a sum paid in respect of an inheritance would probably be specifically described as referring to the particular occasion, just as (in G. O. 1066) the duty paid on the sale of a slave is described; whereas the payment here is said to be for the tax of a certain year. A similar formula occurs in G. O. 473—ὑπὲρ ἐνκύκλιου ζ L; and on an ostracon from Denderah in my possession there is a record of a payment ἐγκύκλιου ια L. The latter appears to belong to the same group as a number of demotic ostraca found with it, which all relate to members of the same family as the one Greek example, but describe the tax paid as 'one-twentieth' simply. These demotic ostraca show that the tax for a given year was regularly paid early in the succeeding year; that the amounts paid by the same man were different in different years; but that the amounts paid by different members of the family were the same in any one year. It seems probable that in this case the twentieth or ἐγκύκλιον was assessed at the close of the year on the year's profits of some trade carried on by the family; and the same explanation may be suggested for the ἐγκύκλιον of no. 40, which was similarly paid after the close of the year for which it was assessed; but in this case some other expansion of κλ than κληρονομιῶν seems desirable.

### (*h*) Ἐπικεφάλαιον.

The nature of the tax known as ἐπικεφάλαιον is discussed below (p. 153), where I have argued that it is to be taken as equivalent to χειρωνάξιον and not to *λαογραφία*. It seems natural to consider the abbreviation *ἐπι*[κ] in the following ostracon and in G. O. 681, 686, and 696 as standing for *ἐπικεφαλαίου*, in view of the long lists of persons paying *ἐπικεφάλαια* given in no. 136 and other instances quoted in the notes on that text.

**73.** (G. 427). ·059 × ·096. Second to third century A.D.

*Παῦνι ι̅β̅ τοῦ κγ∫ ὀνό(ματος) Βήσιος*
*Χαβονχώνσιος ὑπ(ὲρ) ἐπικ(εφαλαίου) καὶ χωμ(ατικοῦ)*
*∫ ὀκτὼ / ∫η. Πανί(σκος) σ(εσημείωμαι).*
p ḥmt n (?) nbe (?) n Bs s Ḫf-Ḫns n ḥ-sp 23 (?)
ʾbt-2 šm ss-12

'Pauni 12 in the twenty-third year in respect of Besis son of Chabonchonsis for trade-tax (?) and dyke-tax eight dr. = 8 dr. Signed, Paniskos.

The bronze of (?) (the) dyke-tax (?) of Bes son of Khef-khons, year 23 (?), Pauni 12.'

(*i*) *Ἠπητικόν*.

The receipts for the tax on cobblers show much the same characteristics as those for the tax on weavers (section (*e*) above). The tax is usually stated to be for a particular month, though this does not hold good of no. 74 and G. O. 464, and the amounts paid by different individuals vary; so that it seems probable that the assessment was on the extent of the business of the individual.

As in the case of the *γερδιακόν*, the earlier receipts are given by *τελῶναι*, the later by *ἐπιτηρηταί*.

**74.** (G. 405). ·140 × ·125 (broken above on right and left). 44 A.D.

*]ε̣ικῶνις Πεχύτο(υ) [*
*τέ]λ̣ος ἡπητῶν διὰ Ἀμμωνο(ῦτος ?) [*
*] ∫ζ∫. ∟δ Τιβερίου Κλαυδ[ίου*
*Καίσαρος Σεβαστοῦ Γερμανικοῦ*
*Αὐτοκράτορος Φαρμοῦθ(ι) ι̅δ̅. Ὁμ[οίως*
*Φαρμοῦθ(ι) κ̅θ̅ ∫δ.*
whm (?) n ʾbt-3 šm ss-2 sttr 1.t qt $\frac{1}{2}$ a qt 1.t (*οβολ*) 3
a sttr 1.t qt $\frac{1}{2}$ ʿn

'. . eikonis son of Pechutes [has paid] as tax on cobblers through Ammonous (?) [ ] 7 dr. 3 obols. Year 4 of Tiberius Claudius Caesar Augustus Germanicus Imperator, Pharmouthi 14. Likewise on Pharmouthi 29, 4 dr.

Likewise, Epeiph 2, 1 stater ½ kite = 1 kite 3 obols = 1 stater ½ kite again.'

7. The demotic entry refers to a further transaction in continuation of the Greek.

**75.** (G. 249). ·081 × ·102. 190 A.D.

*Τιθοῆς καὶ μ(έτοχοι) ἐπιτ(ηρηταὶ) τέλ(ους) ἠπητ(ῶν)*
*Φατρῆτι Φατρήο(υς) χαί(ρειν). Ἐσχήκ(α)μ(εν)*
*παρὰ σοῦ τὸ καθῆκ(ον) τέλ(ος) ὑπ(ὲρ) μηνὸς*
*Παῦνι τοῦ λ∫. ∟λ Αὐρηλίου*
*Κομμόδου Ἀντω(νίνου) Καίσαρος τοῦ κυρίου*
*Παῦνι κϛ̅.*

'Tithoes and his colleagues, supervisors of the tax on cobblers, to Phatres son of Phatres, greeting. We have received from you the appointed tax for the month Pauni of the thirtieth year. Year 30 of Aurelius Commodus Antoninus Caesar our lord, Pauni 26.'

1. Τιθοῆς: this collector is possibly identical with Τιθοῆς Πετεμίνιος who gave the receipts G. O. 1069, 1070, 1071 for the tax on cobblers in the twenty-second, twenty-third, and twenty-fifth years of Commodus.

**76.** (G. 423). ·081 × ·076. Second to third century A.D.

*Πασῆμις Φατρήους*
*ἐπιτηρητ(ὴς) τέλ(ους) ἠπητ(ῶν) καὶ μ(έτοχοι)*
*Ἀντωνίῳ χαίρειν. Ἔσχον*
*παρὰ σοῦ τὸ τέλ(ος) τοῦ Παχὼ(ν)*
*∫ι ὀβ(ολοὺς) ε. ∟ϛ⸗*
*Παῦνι β̄.*

'Pasemis son of Phatres, supervisor of the tax on cobblers, and his colleagues to Antonius, greeting. I have received from you the tax for Pachon, 10 dr. 5 obols. Year 6, Pauni 2.'

(*k*) *Κυνηγίδων πλοίων.*

Wilcken published five ostraca relating to payments for this tax, the name of which is usually written *κυνη*, but in one case *κυνηγιδ*; and he appears to have found the correct explanation in expanding this contraction as κυνηγίδων and translating this as 'hunting-boats' (*Ostr.* i, p. 229). The addition in no. 78 of π after κυνη supports Wilcken's rendering. There is, however, a point arising in connexion with the formula shown in these receipts which he had to leave unexplained. In four out of the five examples the name of the payer is preceded or followed by the symbol ϙ, which occurs similarly in no. 78; but fortunately in no. 77 the word is written out as δεκανº, which supplies a suitable expansion of the symbol. It would appear therefore that δεκανοί were responsible for this tax; and this gives a point of contact with the entry in B. G. U. I. 1 of a payment of 60 drachmae δεκανικοῦ ὁμοίως τῶν αὐτῶν πλοίων, which suggests the existence at Soknopaiou Nesos in the Fayûm of a similar responsibility of δεκανοί for certain boat-taxes.

**77.** (G. 406). ·071 × ·128. 75 A. D.

*Κυνη(γίδων) ζL Οὐεσπασιανοῦ τοῦ κυρίου*
*Τῦβι ιθ Ἀγο(ρῶν) Νό(του). Φαῆρι(ς) Ἁρβήχ(ιος)*
*δεκανὸ(ς) καὶ μέ(τοχοι) ῥυπ(αρὰς) ηϝ.*
*Πεχύ(της).*

'For hunting-boats in the seventh year of Vespasianus our lord, Tubi 19, in Agorai South. Phaeris son of Harbechis, decurion, and his colleagues (have paid) 8 bad (dr.) 4 obols. (Signed), Pechutes.'

3. καὶ μέ(τοχοι): cf. G. O. 1564, where the payment is similarly made by a man described as ϙ (see above) and μέ(τοχοι).

**78.** (G. 270). ·123 × ·120. 100 A. D.

*Κυνη(γίδων) π(λοίων) γL. Τεῶς Φατρῆο(υς)*
*(δεκανὸς) κυνη(γίδων) ῥυπ(αρὰς) δρ(αχμὰς) ὀκτὼ / ϛη.*
*Lγ Τραιανοῦ τοῦ κυρίου*
*Μεχ(εὶρ) ιε. Ἡρακ(λείδης) σ(εσημείωμαι).*

'For hunting-boats in the third year. Teos son of Phatres, decurion of hunting-boats, (has paid) eight bad drachmae = 8 dr. Year 3 of Trajanus our lord, Mecheir 15. Signed, Herakleides.'

2. (δεκανός): written ϙ (see above).

(*l*) *Κωμητικά.*

As pointed out by Grenfell and Hunt on P. Tebt. 365, the term *κωμητικά* is used of village-dues in a purely general sense; it includes various classes of payments in kind, and, as here, in cash. The tax in this case, though collected by the *πράκτορες ἀργυρικῶν* in money, is on land.

**79.** (G. 91). ·070 × ·062. Third century A.D.

*Α(ὐρήλιος) Καρούνιος Πλύνιο(ς)*
*καὶ μέτοχ(οι) πράκ(τορες) ἀργ(υρικῶν)*
*κωμητικῶν Μεμνο(νείων).*
*Ἔσχ(ο)μ(εν) ὑπ(ὲρ) γε(νήματος) δϛ= ὀνόμα-*
*τος Τελώρου Σαμσούσι(ος)*
ϛ ζ 𐅵. Lεϛ= *Τῦβι* κ̄.

'Aurelius Karounios son of Plunis and his colleagues, collectors of money-taxes, for the village-dues in the Memnonia. We have received for the produce of the fourth year in respect of Teloros son of Samsousis 7 dr. 3 obols. Year 5, Tubi 20.'

(*m*) *Λαογραφία.*

Wilcken has shown (*Ostr.* i, pp. 230 ff.) that the rate of the poll-tax apparently differed considerably, not only in various parts of Egypt, but even in separate districts of Thebes; and he drew up the following table as giving the results of his investigations with regard to Thebes. The districts and rates were, according to this:—

| | |
|---|---|
| Charax . . . | 10 dr., after 113–14 rather more. |
| Ophieion . . . | 10 dr., later 10 dr. 4 ob. |
| Agorai North . . | 10 dr. |
| Kerameia . . . | 10 dr. 4 ob. |
| Memnonia . . . | 16 dr. |
| South and South-west. | 24 dr. |

But this table appears to require modification in some respects. In the first place it is based on the highest sums which occur on any single ostracon for any district, except in the case of Kerameia, the only two examples from which show payments of 5 dr. 2 ob.: Wilcken assumes that these must be instalments, and, in order to bring the rate for Kerameia into line with that for Ophieion at the same period, that they must be one-half the tax for the year. But they might equally well be one-third of 16 dr., or indeed any proportion of any sum. Similarly the receipts from other districts for 10 dr. might be half or some other proportion of a larger sum. That the receipt for a year's poll-tax was not necessarily entered in full on a single ostracon, even if a series of instalments were paid, is shown by two receipts in this collection (no. 36 and G. 217, not published) given by the same collector Erieus to the same taxpayer Petechonsis son of Phthomonthes son of Hatres. These contain the following record of instalments of taxes for the sixteenth year of Trajan:—

| | | | | | |
|---|---|---|---|---|---|
| G. 217. | Pharmouthi | 6, year 16 | 4 dr. | for λαογραφία. |
| | " | 21 " | 4 dr. | " " |
| | " | 23 " | 4 dr. | " " |
| No. 36. | " | 28 " | 4 dr. | " " |
| | Pachon | 19 " | 4 dr. | " " |
| | Mesore | 6 " | 2 dr. | " " |
| | " | 15 " | 2 dr. | " " |
| | " | " " | 2 dr. | for ποταμοφυλακία. |
| | Phaophi | 21, year 17 | 3 dr. 4½ ob. | for χωματικόν. |
| | Hathur | 18 " | 6 dr. | " " |

This gives a higher total—24 dr.—for the Memnonia than Wilcken's; and still larger sums occur on other ostraca from the same district. G. 417 shows payments amounting to 32 dr. as one man's poll-tax in the seventeenth year of Trajan, and G. 272 similar payments amounting to 28 dr. in the fourth year of Hadrian.

At the same time there is no reason to assume that the divergence between the rates of 10 dr. and 24 dr. or even 32 dr. for neighbouring districts is too wide. It is fairly certain that the usual poll-tax at Syene was 16 dr.; and the same rate is shown to have been the regular one at Tentyra under Tiberius by a series of 49 demotic ostraca given to members of one family (an account of which I hope to publish shortly). At Oxyrhynchus there were apparently two rates of 12 and 16 dr.; while in the Fayûm even more variation occurs. The commonest rate in the district was 20 dr.; but at Tebtunis alone payments of 8 dr., 16 dr., 22 dr. 4 ob., 24 dr., and 40 dr. also occur (cf. Grenfell and Hunt, *Tebtunis Papyri*, ii, p. 99). It can only be concluded that the amount payable by any individual was determined by some circumstances not at present known to us.

**80**. (G. 248). ·058 × ·076 (right top corner broken). 19 B.C.

Ψενθαῆσις Πασήμ[ιος
τέ(τακται) λαογ(ραφίας) ιαL ͵ϛη. Lια Καίσα(ρος)
Μεχ(εὶρ) δ̅. Κέφα(λος) τρ(α)π(εζίτης).

'Psenthaesis son of Pasemis has paid for poll-tax for the eleventh year 8 dr. Year 11 of Caesar, Mecheir 4. (Signed), Kephalos, banker.'

3. Κέφα(λος): this banker occurs on ten of Wilcken's ostraca, of dates ranging between the thirteenth and twenty-third years of Augustus.

**81**. (G. 287). ·076 × ·109. 107 A.D.

Ἀπολ(λώνιος) καὶ μ(έτοχοι) πράκ(τορες) ἀργ(υρικῶν) μητ(ροπόλεως)
Παχομ(νεῖ ?) Ψενχνο(ύμεως) Πετεχεσ̣θ(ῶτος).
Ἔσχ(ομεν) ὑπ(ὲρ) χ̣ω̣(ματικοῦ) Χά(ρακος) δέκ(α) / ι, ὑπ(ὲρ) λαο(γραφίας)
ὀκτὼ / η. Lδεκ(άτου) Τραιανοῦ
Φαμ(ενὼθ) λ κ̅α̅. Ἀρυώτη(ς) σ(εσημείωμαι).
Ἄλ(λας) Παῦνι λ κ̅γ̅ ὑπ(ὲρ) λαο(γραφίας) Σ̣ε̣β . . . . τέσσαρ(ας)
/ ϛδ. Ἀρυώτη(ς) σεση(μείωμαι).

'Apollonios and his colleagues, collectors of money-taxes of the metropolis, to Pachomneus son of Psenchnoumis son of Petechesthos. We have received for dyke-tax in Charax ten (drachmae) = 10, for poll-tax eight = 8. Tenth year of Trajanus, Phamenoth 30–21. Signed, Haruotes.

Also on Pauni 30–23 for poll-tax in Seb....(?) four (drachmae) = 4 dr. Signed, Haruotes.'

1. Ἀπολ(λώνιος): cf. G. O. 497, 498, 503, of the eleventh and thirteenth years of Trajan, where the same collector appears.

**82.** (G. 78). ·073 × ·082. 114 A.D.

*Πετοσῖρις γενόμ(ενος) πράκ(τωρ) ἀργ(υρικῶν)*
*Μεμ(νονείων) Κολάνθης Πασήμι(ος).*
*Ὑπ(ὲρ) λαο(γραφίας) ιδ$ αἱ διαγραφεί-*
*σης ὀνό(ματι) ἡμῶν ὑπὲρ σοῦ*
*$δ. L ιζ Τραιανοῦ Καίσαρος*
*τοῦ κυρίου Παχὼ(ν) ιγ.*

2. l. Κολάνθῃ. 3. l. διαγραφεῖσαι?

'Petosiris, formerly collector of money-taxes in the Memnonia, to Kolanthes son of Pasemis. In regard to the poll-tax of the fourteenth year, the 4 dr. entered in our name are for you. Year 17 of Trajanus Caesar our lord, Pachon 13.'

1. Πετοσῖρις: this collector is shown by G. O. 1613 and no. 35 above to have been in office in the Memnonia district in the twelfth and thirteenth years of Trajan. The purport of this ostracon is not very clear, but it appears to relate to a correction in his accounts after he laid down his office.

**83.** (G. 238). ·105 × ·109. 132 A.D.

*Φθομώ(νθης) πράκ(τωρ) ἀργ(υρικῶν) Ἑρμώνθεως*
*Ψενταση(μει) Ψεμώ(νθεως) καὶ Πετεχώ(νσει)*
*υἱ(ῷ). Ἔσχο(ν) ὑπ(ὲρ) λαο(γραφίας) ις$ ῥυ(παρὰς) ὀκτὼ*
*$η. L ις Ἁδριανοῦ*
*Καίσαρος τοῦ κυρίου Ἐπεὶφ ιθ.*

'Phthomonthes, collector of money-taxes of Hermonthis, to Psentasemis son of Psemonthes and Petechonsis his son. I have received for poll-tax of the sixteenth year eight bad (drachmae) = 8 dr. Year 16 of Hadrianus Caesar our lord, Epeiph 19.'

**84.** (G. 407). ·092 × ·098. 134 A.D.

*Πικῶς καὶ μ(έτοχοι) πράκ(τορες) ἀργ(υρικῶν)*
*Ψεναρπβήχ(ει) Ἁρπβήχ(ιος) διὰ Ὥρο(υ).*
*Ἔσχ(ομεν) ὑπ(ὲρ) λαο(γραφίας) ιθ$ ῥυπ(αρὰς) δραχ(μὰς) πέντε*
*F / ῥυπ(αρὰς) $εF. L ιθ Ἁδριανοῦ*
*Καίσαρος τοῦ κυρίου Φαμε(νὼθ)*
*λ*

'Pikos and his colleagues, collectors of money-taxes, to Psenharpbechis son of Harpbechis, through Horos. We have received for poll-tax of the nineteenth year five bad drachmae 4 obols = 5 bad dr. 4 obols. Year 19 of Hadrianus Caesar our lord, Phamenoth 30.'

1. The beginning of the first line is nearly washed out.

**85.** (G. 416). ·091 × ·113. 157 A.D.

*Ἀμμώνιο(ς) καὶ Παχνο(ῦμις) γενο(μένοι) πράκ(τορες) ἀργ(υρικῶν) Ἄ̣ν̣ω̣ (το)π(α̣ρχίας)*
*Ἀσκλᾶτι ν̣(εωτέρῳ̣) Ἐρ⟨ι⟩έως Φαή(ριος). Ἔσχ(ομεν) ὑπ(ὲρ) λαο(γραφίας)*
*καὶ ἄλ(λων) κϛ δραχ(μὰς) τέσσαρας / ϛδ. Lκα*
*Ἀντωνίνου Καίσαρος τοῦ κυρίου Ἀθὺρ κ̅δ̅. Ἀμμ(ώνιος) σ(εσημείωμαι).*

'Ammonios and Pachnoumis, formerly collectors of money-taxes of the upper toparchy, to Asklas the younger, son of Erieus, son of Phaeris. We have received for poll-tax and other taxes of the twentieth year four drachmae = 4 dr. Year 21 of Antoninus Caesar our lord, Hathur 24. Signed, Ammonios.'

**86.** (G. 66). ·085 × ·084 (face chipped). Probably 213 A.D.

*Αὐρήλιος Τύρανος Ἐπωνύχ(ου)*
*καὶ μέ(τοχοι) πράκ(τορες) ἀργ(υρικῶν) κώ(μης) Ταυρ̣( )*
*διὰ Αὐρήλιος Ψεμώ(νθου). Ἔσχ(ομεν)*
*ὑπ(ὲρ) λαογρα(φίας) καὶ ἄλ(λων) καϛ*
*ὀνόμ(ατος) Π[ανι]ομῶς Παῶ(τος)*
*ϛιβ. [Lκ]αϛ*
*Φαρ[μοῦθ]ι ι̅α̅.*

3. l. Αὐρηλίου. 5. l. Πανιομῶτος.

'Aurelios Turanos son of Eponuchos and his colleagues, collectors of money-taxes of the village Taur...., through Aurelios Psemonthes. We have received for poll-tax and other taxes of the twenty-first year in respect of Paniomos son of Paos 12 dr. Year 21, Pharmouthi 11.'

[See also nos. 33, 35, 36, 37, 38, 39, 45, 49, 53, and 97 for other receipts for *λαογραφία*.]

(*n*) Ξενικά.

The *τέλος ἐπιξένων* is mentioned in a Cairo ostracon published by Wilcken (*Archiv* i, p. 153), which is dated in the reign of Nero, and, like this one, shows a payment of 2 drachmae a month. It is probably to be explained by P. Tebt. 391, which relates to the collection of poll-tax: from this it appears that two of the collectors were responsible for *τὸ ἐπίξενον*—the inhabitants of Tebtunis who were away from home. If the payment in this ostracon was for poll-tax, it points to a rate of 24 drachmae a year (cf. last section, p. 118). As the collection here is made by *ἐπιτηρηταί*, it seems to have been taken out of the hands of the usual collectors of poll-tax, and transferred to the *ἐπιτηρηταὶ ξενικῶν πρακτορίας*, who were responsible for recovering debts from people living outside their own district (cf. Grenfell and Hunt on P. Oxy. 712).

**87**. (G. 236). ·070 × ·094. 133 A.D.

*Ἀπολλινάριος Ἀκάμαντος*
*καὶ μέτοχ(οι) ἐπιτηρητ(αὶ) τέλ(ους) ἐπι-*
*ξένω(ν) διὰ Φθομώ(νθου) γρα(μματέως) Πετέ-*
*χων Τεμ(  ). Ἔσχ(ομεν) παρὰ σο(ῦ) ὑπ(ὲρ)*
*Με⟨χ⟩χεὶρ τοῦ ιζ𐅵 𐅵β. Lιζ*
*Ἀδριανοῦ Καίσαρος τοῦ κυρίου*
*Φαμ(ενὼθ) ζ̄.*

3. l. Πετέχωντι.

'Apollinarios son of Akamas and his colleagues, supervisors of the tax on strangers, through Phthomonthes their clerk, to Petechon son of Tem... We have received from you for Mecheir of the seventeenth year 2 dr. Year 17 of Hadrianus Caesar our lord, Phamenoth 7.'

5. Με(χ)χείρ: the first χ is only partly written on a rough spot in the surface of the ostracon.

(*o*) *Οἴνου τιμή.*

As suggested by Wilcken (*Ostr.* i, p. 271), the payments entered on ostraca *ὑπὲρ τιμῆς οἴνου* were probably money equivalents of a tax payable in kind. The latest of the three examples given here (no. 90) furnishes a clue to the rate—144 drachmae to the aroura; but the rate may very probably have varied for different estates, as the *οἴνου τέλος* (cf. Wilcken, p. 270) apparently did.

**88.** (G. 280). ·079 × ·093. 90 A.D.

Διαγ(εγράφηκε) Τιθοῆ(ς) Πετοσόρκο(ντος)
διὰ Ὥρο(υ) ὑπ(ὲρ) τιμ(ῆς) οἴ(νου) ι∫ Ἄνω (το)π(αρχίας)
ƒ. Lι Δομιτ(ιαν)οῦ τοῦ κυρίου Ἀθὺρ ια̅.

'Tithoes son of Petosorkon has paid through Horos for the valuation of wine for the tenth year in the Upper toparchy 4 obols. Year 10 of Domitianus our lord, Hathur 11.'

**89.** (G. 70). ·076 × ·084. 181–2 A.D.

Μιῦσις καὶ μ(έτοχοι) ἐπιτ(ηρηταὶ) τιμ(ῆς) οἴνου
καὶ φοι(νίκων) Πεκρίχ(ει) Πεκρίχ(ιος)
Ἡρακλᾶτο(ς). Ἔσχο(μεν) παρὰ σο(ῦ)
ὑπ(ὲρ) τιμ(ῆς) οἴ(νου) γενή(ματος) κβ∫
∫ ἕνδεκα = / ∫ια =,
ἃς καὶ διαγρά(ψομεν) ἐπὶ τὴν δημ(οσίαν) τράπ(εζαν).

'Miusis and his colleagues, supervisors of the valuation of wine and palms, to Pekrichis son of Pekrichis son of Heraklas. We have received from you for the valuation of wine of the produce of the twenty-second year eleven dr. 2 obols = 11 dr. 2 obols, which we will pay into the official bank.'

1. Μιῦσις: this collector occurs in G. O. 1264, dated in 183 A.D., which gives a date for the present example.
6. ἃς καὶ κτλ. For a similar note cf. G. O. 662.

**90.** (G. 253). ·102 × ·114. Early third century A.D.

Α(ὐρήλιος) . . . άθης Ἰναρώους καὶ Πλῆνις
Ψενενφῶ(τος) οἱ β̅ ἀπαιτ(ηταὶ) τιμῆς
οἴ(νου) καὶ φοι(νίκων) γ∫ ὀνόμ(ατος) Α(ὐρηλίου) Πεχύτης
Πρεμτώτου ἀρ(ούρης) ς̅ ∫κδ.
Lγ∫ Μεσορὴ η̅.
Καὶ ὑπ(ὲρ) δ∫ ∫η.

3. l. Πεχύτου.

'Aurelios ... athes son of Inaros and Plenis son of Psenenphos, collectors of the valuation of wine and palms of the third year, in respect of Aurelios Pechutes son of Premtotes, on $\frac{1}{8}$ aroura 24 dr. Year 3, Mesore 8. Also for the fourth year 8 dr.'

(*p*) *Πεντηκοστή*.

The octroi-charges on goods entering or leaving various districts in Egypt have been illustrated by many references on papyri and ostraca. The charges seem to have varied locally: at Thebes the rate, both for *εἰσαγωγή* (G. O. 1569) and for *ἐξαγωγή* (G. O. 801, 806), was two per cent. The ostracon given here does not specify whether the produce on which the charge was levied was going in or out.

**91.** (G. 296). ·072 × ·075. First century A.D.

Γερμανὸς καὶ μ(έτοχοι) τελ(ῶναι)
ν̄ Πετενχ(ώνσει) χα(ίρειν). Ἔχωι
τέλο(ς) ϟ ὄνου ἑνός.
L. [Φαμεν]ὼθ κ̄β̄.

'Germanos and his colleagues, farmers of the two per cent. tax, to Petenchonsis, greeting. I have received the tax on one ass loaded with corn. Year [?], Phamenoth 22.'

3. ϟ: it would be expected that the number of artabae of corn would be specified, as in G. O. 801 and 806; but instead the customs-officer has contented himself by simply stating the quantity as an ass-load.

(*q*) *Πλι(νθευομένη)*.

The contraction πλῑ, which specifies the tax to which the following ostracon refers, may most probably be taken as connected with bricks; and the tax is very likely identical with the *μερισμὸς πλινθευομένης* of P. Oxy. 502 and 574 and the *ὑπὲρ πλινθ* of G. O. 512, 572, 592, 1421. In these ostraca, as here, the collection is made by *ἀπαιτηταί*, though the tax is described as a *μερισμός*, not a *τέλος*: but the two words are sometimes used indifferently. The nature of the tax is still obscure: possibly, as suggested by Grenfell and Hunt on P. Oxy. 502. 43, it was a payment in lieu of providing bricks for the government.

**92.** (G. 279). ·091 × ·104. 141 A.D.

ʽΩρος καὶ μ(έτοχοι) ἀπαιτ(ηταὶ) πλι(νθευομένης) τέλ(ους)
κβ ς θεοῦ Ἁδριανοῦ
Πικῶς Θοτεύτης.
Ἔσχ(ομεν) παρὰ σοῦ δρ(α)χ(μὰς)
πέντε / ῥυπ(αραὶ) ς πέντε.
∟δ Ἀντων(ίν)ου Καίσαρ(ος) τοῦ κυρίου
Ἐ(πεὶ)φ κε̅.

3. l. Πικῶτι Θοτεύτου.

'Horos and his colleagues, collectors of the brick-tax of the twenty-second year of the deified Hadrianus, to Pikos son of Thoteutes. We have received from you five drachmae = five bad dr. Year 4 of Antoninus Caesar our lord, Epeiph 25.'

(γ) *Ποταμοφυλακία.*

The tax for policing the river is one which offers no difficulties, except as regards the variations in the rate at which it was paid. Possibly, as suggested by Wilcken (*Ostr.* i, p. 285), it was assessed annually for each locality and paid as a poll-tax by every one. In no. 36 above the amount was apparently 2 drachmae for A.D. 112–13 in the Memnonia; in no. 93 three men pay 33 obols—i.e. probably 1 drachma 5 obols each—a year later in Charax; but in G. O. 507 there is a payment in Charax of 4 obols only in the former year. There may, therefore, have been other considerations which entered into the determination of the assessment of each individual.

**93.** (G. 425). ·158 × ·067. 113 A.D.

Ἰμούθης καὶ μέτοχ(οι)
Φατρῆς Παμώνθη(ς) Φατρή(ους)
μη(τρὸς) Θερμ(ούθιος) καὶ Παμώνθη(ς) ἀδελ(φὸς)
καὶ Παμμῖνις ἄλ(λος) ἀδελ(φός).
Ἔσχ(ομεν) ὑπ(ὲρ) ποταμο(φυλακίας) Χά(ρακος) ιζ ς

ὀβολ(οὺς) τριάκοντα τρῖς
/ ὀβολ(οὺς) λγ. L ιζ Τραιανοῦ
τοῦ κυρίου Θὼθ λ̄. Α(    ) σ(εσ)ημ(είωμαι).
Ἄλ(λο) Φαῶφι ᾱ ὁμο(ίως) Παμῖ(νις)
Παμώνθη(ς) Φατρή(ους) μη(τρὸς) Θ̣ε̣ρ̣μ̣(ούθιος)
σκοπ(έλων) καὶ ἄλ(λων) Χά(ρακος) ιζς ῥυπ(αρὰς) ς
τρεῖς κέρμ(ατος) ε / ςγ κέρμ(ατος) ε.
Α(    ) σ(εσ)ημ(είωμαι).

2. l. Φατρῆτι Παμώνθου. 3. l. Παμώνθῃ ἀδελ(φῷ).
4. l. Παμμίνει ἄλ(λῳ) ἀδελ(φῷ). 10. l. Παμώνθου.

'Imouthes and his colleagues to Phatres son of Pamonthes, son of Phatres, and Thermouthis, and to his brothers Pamonthes and Pamminis. We have received for the river-police in Charax for the seventeenth year thirty-three obols = 33 obols. Year 17 of Trajanus our lord, Thoth 30. Signed, A . . . . .

Also on Phaophi 1 likewise Paminis son of Pamonthes, son of Phatres, and Thermouthis (paid) for guard-tax and other taxes in Charax for the seventeenth year three bad dr. 5 (obols) copper = 3 dr. 5 (obols) copper Signed, A . . . . .'

1. Ἰμούθης: cf. G. O. 507, 511, 512, where the same collector appears; in the first for the previous, in the two latter for the succeeding, year.

**[See also no. 36 for another receipt for** *ποταμοφυλακία.*]

(s) Σκοπέλων.

Like the last tax, the payment for maintenance of guard-posts shows some variations in rate. As a rule, the amounts for which receipts were given in Charax in the opening years of the second century were about 4 drachmae (cf. Wilcken, *Ostr.* i, p. 293, and no. 93 above). But in no. 34 above, which belongs to the same period, the sum paid in the Memnonia was only 1½ drachmae, unless the later payments, amounting to 16 dr., refer to the same tax. Presumably the rate was fixed by the needs of the locality.

**94.** (G. 285). ·125 × ·108. 119 A.D.

Χεσφμόις πράκ(τωρ) ἀργ(υρικῶν) μη(τροπόλεως)
Πετεχνοῦβις Ψεναμο(ύνιος). Ἔσχ(ον) ὑπ(ὲρ)
σκοπ(έλων) καὶ ἄλ(λων) δ∽ ῥυπ(αρὰς) δραχ(μὰς) τρῖς τετρώ(βολον) καὶ (προσδιαγραφόμενα)
/ ∽γ𐅵. L δ Ἀδριανοῦ Καίσαρος
τοῦ κυρίου Φαῶφι κη̅. Πανίσκο(ς) σ(εσ)η(μείωμαι).

2. l. Πετεχνούβει.

'Chesphmois, collector of money-taxes of the metropolis, to Petechnoubis son of Psenamounis. I have received for guard-tax and other taxes for the fourth year three bad drachmae four obols, with the extra charges = 3 dr. 4 obols. Year 4 of Hadrianus Caesar our lord, Phaophi 28. Signed, Paniskos.'

1. Χεσφμόις: the same collector occurs in G. O. 1241 and 1570, both of the following year; these receipts are also subscribed by Paniskos.

[See also nos. 34 and 93 for other receipts for σκοπέλων.]

(*t*) Στεφανικόν.

The practice of raising contributions for *aurum coronarium* in Egypt under the Roman emperors has been well illustrated by recent discoveries. The only noteworthy point in the following ostraca is the occurrence of πράκτορες στεφανικοῦ at Thebes; hitherto these officials have only been named in papyri from the Fayûm, the Theban receipts being normally given by the banks.

**95.** (G. 206). ·052 × ·115. Second century A.D.

Φαρ(μοῦθι) κη̅ τοῦ κβ∽ ὀνό(ματος) Ταλῶτο(ς) πρ(εσβυτέρας)
Σετο( ) ὑπ(ὲρ) στεφα(νικοῦ) χρή(ματος) Ἀγο(ρῶν) 𐅃 / 𐅃. Σεση(μείωμαι).
t ꜣpwkh n p rn n Ta-lw ta Z-ḥr (?) ḥr n bne-w
n ḥ-sp 22 ʾbt-4 pr ss-29 (ὀβολ.) 3 n šbte-w (?)

'Pharmouthi 28 of the twenty-second year in respect of Talos the elder, daughter of Seto .... for crown-tax in Agorai 3 obols = 3 obols. Signed.

The receipt in the name of Talou daughter of Zeho (?) for the palm-trees, year 22, Pharmouthi 29, 3 obols, the merchants (?).'

2. ὑπ(ὲρ) στεφα(νικοῦ) χρή(ματος): presumably the relation between this entry and the 'palm-trees' of the demotic text is that the latter were the property on which the tax was assessed.

4. (ὀβολ.): the reading of the demotic sign for obol is uncertain, though its meaning is certain; so I have used the Greek equivalent in brackets. [H. T.]

šbte-w (?): reading uncertain; perhaps an abbreviation of a locality frequently mentioned in the demotic ostraca, 'the houses of the merchants.' [H. T.] (Cf. note 3 on D. 5, p. 23.)

**96.** (G. 403). ·085 × ·100. Possibly 222 A.D.

*Α(ὐρήλιος) Πλήνιος υἱὸς* [[.]] *Σενκαλασί(ριος)*
*καὶ μέτ(ο)χ(οι) πράκ(τορες) στεφ(ανικοῦ) χρήμ(ατος) ἔσχ(ομεν)*
*ὑπ(ὲρ) ὀνόμ(ατος) Α(ὐρηλίου) Πεχύτης Πρεμ-*
*τώτου ἀρ(ούρης)* ϛ̄ ϛδ
L ε″ *Τῦβ(ι)* ιβ̄.

'Aurelios Plenis son of Senkalasiris and his colleagues, collectors of the crown-tax, have received in respect of Aurelios Pechutes son of Premtotes on $\frac{1}{6}$ aroura 4 dr. Year 5, Tubi 12.'

1. l. Πλῆνις: the letter following *υἱός* seems to have been intentionally erased.

3. l. Πεχύτου: this Aur. Pechutes son of Premtotes is doubtless the same person who occurs in no. 90 above, possibly rather more than a year earlier, in which also the tax is paid on $\frac{1}{6}$ aroura.

5. L ε″: the year may be of Elagabalus; the hand is an early third century one, and presumably the date is after 212, in view of the Aurelii; also receipts for *στεφανικόν* occur rather frequently in Egypt in the reign of Elagabalus.

### (*u*) *Χωματικόν*.

The *χωματικόν*, as has been shown by Wilcken (*Ostr.* i, pp. 333 ff.), was normally paid at the annual rate of 6 dr. 4 obols in most of the districts of Thebes and in the Fayûm during the first century and a half of Roman rule in Egypt; and the same rate holds good at Oxyrhynchus (see Grenfell and Hunt's note in *P. Oxy.* ii, p. 281) and Tentyra. It is most probable, as suggested by Kenyon (*B. M. Cat.* ii, p. 103), that it represented an *adaeratio* of the five days' work on embankments which was required in Egypt.

The rate, however, is not absolutely uniform in all instances. Wilcken pointed out (p. 335) that a Fayûm papyrus of the year 178–9 shows a payment of 7 drachmae 4 obols 2 chalki, which may be due to a rise in the assessment—or, possibly, to a rise in the standard rate of wages; and this agrees very closely with the sum entered in no. 100 below. Even at an earlier date there are abnormal amounts on Theban ostraca; thus in no. 98 we have a payment of 7 drachmae for the fifteenth year of Trajan, in some unspecified district; and in no. 99 one of 8 drachmae 2 obols 2 chalki for the nineteenth year of Trajan in the Memnonia. With the latter may be compared G. O. 1613, which contains an entry of two sums amounting to 8 drachmae 4 chalki for the twelfth year of Trajan, and no. 36 above, with similar entries amounting to 9 drachmae 4 obols 4 chalki for the seventeenth year of Trajan, both alike from the Memnonia. It would seem, therefore, that in the latter part of the reign of Trajan there was an increase in the assessment in the Memnonia; and that this extended to other districts of Thebes appears from no. 81, which probably shows a payment of 10 drachmae for the tenth year of Trajan in Charax.

**97**. (G. 418). ·104 × ·113. 46 A.D.

*Διαγεγρ(άφηκε) Πασίω(ν) Φθομώ(νθου) Πικῶ(τος) μη(τρὸς) . . .*
*ὑπ(ὲρ) λαο(γραφίας) Μεμνο(νείων) ϛL ∫δ. Lϛ Τιβερίου*
*Κλαυδίου Καίσαρος Σεβαστοῦ*
*Γερμανικοῦ Αὐτοκράτ[ορος]*
*Παχὼ(ν) γ̄. Ὁμο(ίως) Παῦνι ζ̄ ∫δ. Ὁμο(ίως)*
*Ἐπεὶφ κᾱ ∫δ. Ὁμο(ίως) κη̄ ∫δ. Ὁμο(ίως)*
*Μεσορὴ η̄ ὑπ(ὲρ) χω(ματικοῦ) ∫γ⊢c*

'Pasion son of Phthomonthes, son of Pikos, and ...... has paid for poll-tax in the Memnonia for the sixth year 4 dr. Year 6 of Tiberius Claudius Caesar Augustus Germanicus Imperator, Pachon 3. Likewise on Pauni 7, 4 dr. Likewise on Epeiph 21, 4 dr. Likewise on (Epeiph) 28, 4 dr. Likewise on Mesore 8 for dyke-tax 3 dr. 4½ obols.'

**98**. (G. 288). ·082 × ·083. III A.D.

*Πεμσ(αῶς) γρ(αμματεὺς) θη(σαυροῦ) Πετεχῶ(ντι)*
*Πετεμφθῶ(τος) μη(τρὸς) Κρονιαίνη(ς).*
*Ἔσχ(ον) ὑπ(ὲρ) χωμ(ατικοῦ) ιδ∫ ῥυπ(αρὰς) δρ(αχμὰς) ἑπτὰ / ∫ζ.*
*Lιε Τραιανοῦ Καίσ(αρος) Φαῶφι*
λ ιγ̄. Γ

'Pemsaos, clerk of the granary, to Petechon son of Petemphthos and Kroniaina. I have received for dyke-tax for the fourteenth year seven bad drachmae = 7 dr. Year 15 of Trajanus Caesar, Phaophi 30–13. (Signed) G........'

1. γρ(αμματευς) θη(σαυροῦ): it is a novelty to find an official of the θησαυρός collecting the dyke-tax, though the ἐπιτηρηταί or τελῶναι θησαυροῦ ἱερῶν frequently occur as collectors of the bath-tax, which was paid in money.

**99.** (G. 257). ·098 × ·095. 116 A.D.

*Ἐριέως Παμώ(νθου) πρά(κτωρ) ἀργ(υρικῶν) Μεμ(νονείων) ⟦γ⟧*
*⟦. .⟧ Καμῆτις Παμώνθου Ψενπο̣ . . .*
*ὑπ(ὲρ) χω(ματικοῦ) Μεμ(νονείων) ιθϛ ϛη = $\chi^{\beta}$. ∟ιθ*
*Τραια(νοῦ) Ἀρίστου Καίσαρος τοῦ κυρίου*
*Μεσ(ορὴ) ἐπαγο(μένων) β̄.*

1. l. Ἐριεὺς. 2. l. Καμήτει.

'Erieus son of Pamonthes, collector of money-taxes of the Memnonia, to Kametis son of Pamonthes son of Psenpo .... (I have received) for dyke-tax in the Memnonia for the nineteenth year 8 dr. 2 obols 2 chalki. Year 19 of Trajanus Optimus Caesar our lord, Mesore second extra day.'

1. Ἐριέως: cf. note on 36. 1.
3. ϛη: the η is apparently written over θ; possibly the actual payment was 9 drachmae, which was reduced as in the cases discussed above (p. 90).

**100.** (G. 222). ·085 × ·053 (only the right-hand side preserved). Plate XII. 177 A.D.

*. . . . . τ]οῦ ιηϛ Αὐρηλίων Ἀντων(ίνου)*
*καὶ Κομ]μόδου Καισάρων*
*τῶν κυρί]ων ὀνόμ(ατος) Φθουμώνθου*
*. . . . . ὑπ(ὲρ)] χωμ(ατικοῦ) ιζϛ Ἀγο(ρῶν) ϛ ἑπτὰ Ϝ $\chi^{\beta}$.*
*ϛζϜ$\chi^{\beta}$ . .] σ(εσ)η(μείωμαι).*
p(?) ḥmt p(?) nbe n [. . . . .

'[ ] of the eighteenth year of Aurelii Antoninus and Commodus Caesars our lords, in respect of Phthoumonthes [ ] for dyke-tax for the seventeenth year in Agorai seven dr. 5 obols 2 chalki [= 7 dr. 5 ob. 2 ch.]. Signed, [ ].

[ ] the (?) bronze (of) the (?) dyke-tax of [ ].'

[See nos. 33, 34, 35, 36, 38, 43, 48, 50, 51, 73, 81, for other receipts for χωματικόν.]

(*w*) Ὠνίων.

The exact nature of the tax on marketable goods is still an open question; the sums paid for it are normally small, the highest recorded by Wilcken being 4 drachmae. Wilcken's suggestion (*Ostr.* i, p. 343) that it represents a payment for a stand in the market seems to suit the facts sufficiently well. It may be related to a 'dromos' tax named on a series of demotic ostraca from Denderah, which refer to the years 37 Augustus to 21 Tiberius, and show apparently an annual payment of 2 to 2¼ drachmae, which is about the average of the amount in the Theban ostraca.

**101.** (G. 424). ·103 × ·098. 142 A.D.

Ὧρος καὶ μ(έτοχοι) ἀπαιτ(ηταὶ) μερισμ(οῦ) τέλ(ους) ὠνίω(ν) Ἀγ(ορῶν) Ν(ότου)
Σεντιθο(ήτι) νε(ωτέρᾳ) Ἰναρῶ(τος) διὰ Ἰναρῶ(τος)
Ὥρου. Ἔσχομ(εν) ὑπ(ὲρ) μερισμ(οῦ) εL ὀβ(ολοὺς) δ
/ ὀβ(ολοὺς) δ. Lϛ Ἀντωνίνου Καίσαρος
τοῦ κυρίου Φαῶφι κ̄.
Πικῶς σεση(μείωμαι).

'Horos and his colleagues, collectors of the rate for the tax on marketable goods in Agorai South, to Sentithoes the younger, daughter of Inaros, through Inaros son of Horos. We have received for the rate of the fifth year 4 obols = 4 obols. Year 6 of Antoninus Caesar our lord, Phaophi 20. Signed, Pikos.'

1. Ὧρος: probably this head collector is the same individual who appears in G. O. 608, a receipt for the same tax dated in the previous year.

2. διὰ Ἰναρῶ(τος): the name is written over another word, which cannot be deciphered.

## II. Receipts for Taxes paid in Kind.

(*a*) Ἀννώνη.

The receipts for ἀννώνη are almost certainly, as pointed out by Wilcken (*Ostr.* i, p. 155), to be referred to the *annona militaris*—the contributions levied in kind for the troops stationed in Egypt. Very often this was converted into a payment in money, and the majority of the instances published by Wilcken are receipts for such money-payments. There are, however, a few, like the one given below, which specify payments in kind.

**102.** (G. 276). ·059 × ·084. Second to third century A.D.

Μεσο(ρὴ) η̄ τοῦ θϛ ὀνόμ(ατος)
Σενπικῶ(τος) Χάροπος
ὑπὲρ λόγ(ου) ἀν(νώνης) Lι κριθῆς
ἀρτάβης μίας / ∸ ᾱ.
Lθϛ. Φιδά(μμων) σ(εσ)η(μείωμαι).

4. l. ἀρτάβην μίαν.

'Mesore 8 of the ninth year, in respect of Senpikos daughter of Charops on account of the annona of the tenth year, one artaba of barley = 1 art. Year 9. Signed, Phidammon.'

3. Lι: the tax was apparently paid in advance, in the last month of the year before that in which it became due—a very unusual proceeding.

(*b*) Ἀχυρικά.

Receipts for the delivery of chaff are common on ostraca; but in spite of their frequency it remains doubtful on what system the collection was made. Practically all that is certain is contained in Wilcken's summary (*Ostr.* i, pp. 162 ff.); the chaff was, in almost all cases, for the use of the troops, and served as fuel; sometimes the destination is more definitely stated as the furnaces of the baths; in a very few instances it seems to have been required for brick-making. The levy was presumably made on landholders or cultivators, but there is no evidence as to the rate of assessment.

**103.** (G. 401). ·088 × ·122. 77–8 A.D.

Κ]άσσιος στρατιώτης Ψεννήσι Ψενο-
σείρεος χαί(ρειν). Ἀπέχω παρὰ σοῦ γόμ(ον) ἀχύρου.
Lι Οὐεσπασιανοῦ τοῦ κυρίου.

'Cassius, soldier, to Psennesis son of Psenosiris, greeting. I have received from you a load of chaff. Year 10 of Vespasianus our lord.'

1. Κάσσιος: another receipt given by the same Cassius in the same year, also for one load of chaff, is G. 52 (not published). The man is perhaps identical with the Κᾶσις of G. O. 776, a similar receipt of the previous year. The receipts for chaff of the first century seem to have been normally given by soldiers, while those of the second century, where the collectors are named, are from ἀχυροπράκτορες or ἀχυράριοι or ἀπαιτηταὶ ἀχύρου, except for one or two from centurions; many of the second century receipts, however, do not specify the office or rank of the collector, and these may still have been soldiers; in some cases the names are Roman.

**104.** (G. 256). ·070 × ·101. 88–9 A.D.

*Ἄρριος Ἄτερ στρατιώτης*
*Ὥρῳ Οὐσερουήρεως χαίρειν.*
*Εχω παρὰ σοῦ γόμον ἀχύρου*
*ἕνα τοῦ ζL Δομιτιανοῦ*
*τοῦ κυρίου. Ἐγράφη ηL μη(νὸς)*
*Δομιτιανοῦ κ̄ᾱ.*

'Arrius Ater, soldier, to Horos son of Osoroueris, greeting. I have received from you one load of chaff for the seventh year of Domitianus our lord. Written in the eighth year, month Domitianus 21.'

2. Ὥρῳ Οὐσερουήρεως: presumably the same man who appears in no. 46 above.

**105.** (G. 100). ·078 × ·095. 148 A.D.

*Παῆρις . . . . . . . . . . .*
*Κολλάνθῃ Πετεμενού-*
*φι(ος) χα(ίρειν). Ἐλάβαμεν παρὰ σοῦ*
*ἀχύρου δημοσίου γόμου*
*ἑνὸς ἡμίσους. Lια*
*Ἀντενείνου Καίσαρος*
*τοῦ κυρίου Παῦνι*
*ζ̄.*

4, 5. l. γόμον ἕνα ἥμισυ.

'Paeris [and his colleagues, collectors of chaff in the metropolis?] to Kollanthes son of Petemenouphis, greeting. We have received from you one and a half loads of chaff for public use. Year 11 of Antoninus Caesar our lord, Pauni 7.'

1. Παῆρις: the line, the end of which is obscured by discoloration, may perhaps be completed καὶ μ(έτοχοι) ἀχυρ(άριοι) μητροπ(όλεως).
3. ἐλάβαμεν: Wilcken pointed out (*Ostr.* i, p. 109) that all the instances of the use of λαβεῖν in receipts on ostraca known to him were written by Romans; this case appears to be an exception, as the name of the writer is clearly Egyptian.

**106.** (G. 268). ·065 × ·084. Plate XII. 160 A.D.

*Παμώ(νθης) Φθομώ(νθου) καὶ Παύνχη(ς) πρ(εσβύτερος) Ἀθᾶς*
*ἀχυράρι(οι) Μεμ(νονείων) ὀν(όματος) Κοιντῶν β̄*
*θυγ(ατέρων) Κοίντου διὰ πε̣( ) υ( ) Αὐλήριος*
*Ψενώρου. Ἔσχ(ομεν) ὑπ(ὲρ) γενή(ματος) κβ𐅵*
*ἀχύρου γόμου[ς] ε.*
*∟κγ Ἀντωνίνου Καίσαρος*
*τοῦ κυρίου Παῦ(νι) ᾱ.*

3. l. Αὐρηλίου.

'Pamonthes son of Phthomonthes and Paunches the elder, son of Athas, collectors of chaff in the Memnonia, in respect of the two Quintae, daughters of Quintus, through . . Aurelios Psenoros. We have received on account of the produce of the twenty-second year 5 loads of chaff. Year 23 of Antoninus Caesar our lord, Pauni 1.'

3. πε̣( ) υ( ): I am unable to suggest a meaning for this contraction; π and υ seem clear, and the former is followed by a letter above the line which is probably meant for ε, while the υ has a stroke over it.

**107.** (G. 209). ·125 × ·141. 160 A.D.

*Παμώ(νθης) Φθομώ(νθου) καὶ Παύνχη(ς) πρ(εσβύτερος) Ἀθᾶς*
*ἀχυράρι(οι) Μεμ(νονείων) ὀνόμ(ατος) Ψεμμώ(νθου) ἀπε̣λ̣(ευθέρου) Ἀμενώθου.*
*Ἔσχο(μεν) ὑπ(ὲρ) γενήμ(ατος) κγ𐅵 γόμου(ς) ἀχύρου ιε.*
*∟κγ Ἀντωνίνου Καίσαρος τοῦ κυρίου Ἐ(πεὶφ) ῑη̄.*

'Pamonthes son of Phthomonthes and Paunches the elder, son of Athas, collectors of chaff in the Memnonia, in respect of Psemmonthes freedman (?) of Amenothes. We have received on account of the produce of the twenty-third year 15 loads of chaff. Year 23 of Antoninus Caesar our lord, Epeiph 18.'

2. ἀπε̣λ(ευθέρου): the reading is very doubtful; the first two letters are clear, but the following contraction is obscure.

**108.** (G. 65). ·065 × ·065 (broken on right). 166 A.D.

Ἄπριος Γέμελλος (ἑκατοντάρ)χ(ης) [. . . . . . . . . . . .
χα(ίρειν). Ἔλαβον παρὰ σοῦ [εἰς ὑπόκαυσιν
βαλανείο(υ) ἀχύρο(υ) δη[μοσίου γενήμ(ατος)
ϛL γό(μου) ἥμυσου. [Lϛ Ἀντωνίνου
καὶ Οὐήρου τῶν [κυρίων Σεβαστῶν
Ἐπεὶφ ιγ̄.
Σε[σημείωμαι.

4. l. ἥμισυ.

'Aprius Gemellus, centurion, [to . . . .], greeting. I have received from you [for the heating] of the baths half a load of chaff for public use [from the produce] of the sixth year. [Year 6 of Antoninus] and Verus our [lords Augusti], Epeiph 13. Signed.'

The restorations are on the analogy of G. O. 927, a similar receipt of a year later.

**109.** (G. 254). ·078 × ·092. 176 A.D.

Παρεκομ(ίσθη) εἰς τὴν σπ(εῖραν) ὀνόμ(ατος) Πετεμ(ίνιος)
Πεμσ̣ε̣ῦ̣τ(ος) ἀχύρου γόμ(ου) τρίτ(ον) / γόμ(ου) γʹ
ὑπ(ὲρ) γενήμ(ατος) ιϛ Αὐρηλίου Ἀντωνίνου
Καίσαρος τοῦ κυρίου Μεσ(ορὴ) γ̄. Ἀπολλ(ώνιος) σ(εσ)η(μείωμαι).

'Delivered to the cohort in respect of Peteminis son of Pemseus one-third of a load of chaff = ⅓ load, on account of the produce of the sixteenth year of Aurelius Antoninus Caesar our lord, Mesore 3. Signed, Apollonios.'

**110.** (G. 408). ·065 × ·101. 182 A.D.

*Παρεκομ(ίσθη) εἰς Ὠφιῆο(ν) ὑπ(ὲρ) γενήμ(ατος)*
*κβϛ ὀνόμ(ατος) Πεχύ(του) Τιθο(ήους) ἀχ(ύρου) γόμ(ου) ∠δ′*
*ἕκτο(ν) τετραк(αιεικοστὸν) / γ(όμου) ∠δ′ϛκδ. Lκγ Αὐρηλίου*
*Κ(ομ)μόδ(ου) Ἀντ(ωνίνου) Καίσαρ(ος) τ(οῦ) κυρίου Ἀθὺρ ιγ.*
*Πανίσ(κος) σεσημ(είωμαι).*

'Delivered to Ophieion on account of the produce of the twenty-second year in respect of Pechutes son of Tithoes twenty-three twenty-fourths of a load of chaff = $\frac{23}{24}$ load. Year 23 of Aurelius Commodus Antoninus Caesar our lord, Hathur 13. Signed, Paniskos.'

**111.** (G. 219). ·084 × ·142. 215 A.D.

*Μάρκος Αὐλήριος Ὧρος ὁ καὶ Πκοῖλ(ις) καὶ Μάρκ(ος) Αὐλ(ήριος)*
*Πλῆνις Πλῆνις οἱ β̄ ἀχυροπ(ράκτορες) Μεμνον(είων) ἐσχήκ(αμεν)*
*ὑπ(ὲρ) ὀνόμ(ατος) Πασήμιο(ς) Πατσέβ(θιος) γόμ(ου) κδ καὶ ὀνόμ(ατος) Πασήμιος*
*Ἀτρήους Πατσέβ(θιος) γόμ(ου) ϛκδ καὶ ὀνόμ(ατος) Πασήμιος*
*Πατσέβ(θιος) γόμ(ου) κδ / γόμω τέταρτον τετρακαιεικοσ-τόν. Lκγ Ἐπεὶφ ιϛ.*
*Μάρκος Αὐλ(ήριος) Ὧρος ὁ καὶ Πκοῖλ(ις) σ(εσ)η(μείωμαι).*
*Μάρκ(ος) Αὐλ(ήριος) Πλ(ῆνις) Πλ(ήνιος) διὰ τοῦ πατρὸς σ(εσ)η(μείωμαι).*

2. l. Πλῆνις Πλήνιος. 5. l. γόμου.

'Marcus Aurelius Horos, also called Pkoilis, and Marcus Aurelius Plenis son of Plenis, collectors of chaff in the Memnonia, have received in respect of Pasemis son of Patsebthis $\frac{1}{24}$ load, and in respect of Pasemis son of Hatres son of Patsebthis $\frac{5}{24}$ load, and in respect of Pasemis son of Patsebthis $\frac{1}{24}$ load = seven twenty-fourths of a load. Year 23, Epeiph 16.
Signed, Marcus Aurelius Horos, also called Pkoilis.
Signed, Marcus Aurelius Plenis son of Plenis, through his father.'

**112.** (G. 419). ·087 × ·109. Probably 212 A.D.

*Παρεκομίσ(θη) εἰς τὴν χώρ(την) γ(εν)ήμ(ατος)*
*ιθ∫ ὀνόμ(ατος) Πεκύσιος Τρεμπαπουήσιος*
*ἀχύρου γόμου ἕκτον κδ / γό(μου) ϛκδ.*
∟κ∫ *Παῦ(νι) ιθ. Πịḳ(ῶς ?) γ(ραμματεύς).*
*Ὧρος σεση(μείωμαι).*

'Delivered to the cohort from the produce of the nineteenth year in respect of Pekusis son of Trempapouesis five twenty-fourths of a load of chaff = $\frac{5}{24}$ load. Year 20, Pauni 19. (Signed), Pikos (?), scribe. Signed, Horos.'

4. ∟κ∫: this date may be taken as of Caracalla, on the assumption that the Pekusis of this ostracon is the same man who appears in no. 123.

(*c*) *Κριθηλογικόν.*

A tax for the expenses of collection of barley has not hitherto been noted from Egyptian records; but there are close parallels in the payment *ὑπὲρ οἰνολογίας* of G.O. 711 of Ptolemaic times, in the *σιτολογικόν* of P. Oxy. 740[2] 22, and probably in the entries for *σ^λ*, which contraction Wilcken (*Ostr.* i, p. 294) thinks may represent *σιτολογία*, on four ostraca of the reigns of Augustus and Tiberius. The existence of the term *κριθολογία* is shown by Wilcken (*Ostr.* i, p. 270, note 1) from an entry in the Codex Theodosianus.

**113.** (G. 282). ·072 × ·081. Late second or early third century A.D.

*Ἐ(πεὶ)φ κ̣θ̣ τοῦ α∫ ὀνό(ματος) Πετεχεσπ(οχράτου)*
*Ψεναπάθου ὑπ(ὲρ) κριθηλογί(ας) Νή(σων)*
*κρι(θῆς) ∸ τρίτον δωδέκατο(ν) / ∸ γ̄ ιβ.*
*Ἀμμώ(νιος) σ(εσημείωμαι).*

'Epeiph 29 of the first year in respect of Petechespochrates son of Psenapathes for the collection of barley in the Islands, five-twelfths of an artaba of barley = $\frac{5}{12}$ art. Signed, Ammonios.'

2. Νή(σων): the district known as *Νῆσοι* occurs in many ostraca dealing with payments in kind (cf. Wilcken, *Ostr.* i, p. 714). A *θησαυρὸς Νήσων* is mentioned in a list of entries of corn in an unpublished text (G. 191) of this collection.

(*d*) *Πρόσθεμα.*

The exact nature of the payments for *πρόσθεμα* which occur on ostraca is not clear; but evidently, as pointed out by Wilcken (*Ostr.* i, p. 288), it must have been an extraordinary demand above the regular payments for a given year. It is noticeable that in the instance given here, as in three out of Wilcken's four examples, the payment is made after the close of the year for which it is assessed; in one case (G. O. 973) it is made two years after.

**114.** (G. 409). ·115 × ·112. 192 A.D.

Σερῆνος γενόμ(ενος) πρά(κτωρ) σιτικ(ῶν) Χάρα(κος)
ἔσχο(ν) εἰς πρόσθ(εμα) γενήμ(ατος) λβ∫ ὀνόμ(ατος)
Σεναπάθης Πλή(νιος) Ἁρ̣σ̣ι̣η̣σ̣ο̣ήου(ς) νε(ωτέρου)
⳨αϛ̅/ καὶ ὀνόμ(ατος) Ἐσουή(ριος) Παχώ(μιος)
⳨ϛ̅ καὶ ὀνόμ(ατος) Παχώ(μιος) π(ρεσβυτέρου) ⳨ϛ̅
καὶ ὀνόμ(ατος) Ἐσουή(ριος) Ἁτρήο(υς) ⳨κ̅δ̅ / ÷ κ̅δ̅
/ ἐπ(ὶ τὸ αὐτὸ) ⳨βκ̅δ̅. Lλγ∫
Θὼθ κ̅. Σερῆ(νος) σεσημ(είωμαι).

3. l. Σεναπάθου.

'Serenus, formerly collector of corn-taxes in Charax, has received for the extra charge from the produce of the thirty-second year in respect of Senapathes daughter of Plenis son of Harsiesoes the younger $1\frac{2}{3}$ art. corn, and in respect of Esoueris son of Pachomis $\frac{1}{6}$ art. corn, and in respect of Pachomis the elder $\frac{1}{6}$ art. corn, and in respect of Esoueris son of Hatres $\frac{1}{24}$ art. corn $= \frac{1}{24}$ art.: total, $2\frac{1}{24}$ art. corn. Year 33, Thoth 20. Signed, Serenus.'

(*e*) *Σιτικά.*

A very large proportion of the receipts on ostraca found at Thebes consist of *μετρήματα θησαυροῦ* of corn and other produce, without any mention of the name of the tax. There can be little doubt that these represent the *σιτικὰ τελέσματα* mentioned in papyri, and referred to the levy made on the crops from which the corn required to feed the populace of Rome was drawn (cf. Wilcken, *Ostr.* i, p. 201). There is not much variation in the formulae, and a small selection out of the numerous examples in this collection will suffice.

**115.** (G. 54). ·073 × ·147. 16 B.C.

*Ἔτους ιδ Καίσαρος Μεσορὴ λ̄ μεμέτρη(κε) Καλλία(ς)*
*Ἀμενώθου ἰς τὸν Πισιρ̣ . . . θησαυρὸν Λιβύης τοῦ κολ̣( )*
*μισθώσεως 𐅵μ*
*ἀπὸ χέρσου 𐅵κε*
*/ ξε. Τι( ) γρα(μματεύς).*

'Year 14 of Caesar, Mesore 30: Kallias son of Amenothes has paid into the ..... granary of Libya .....

from rented land 40 art. corn
from unwatered land 25 art. corn .
= 65 (art.). (Signed) Ti( ), scribe.'

2. Πισιρ̣ . . .: presumably a proper name; the surface of the ostracon is discoloured by spots, one of which covers the termination of this word.

**116.** (G. 262). ·073 × ·142. 61 A.D.

*Μεμέτρηκε Ὧρος Πασῆμις*
*Λάβαις εἰς θησαυροῦ ἱερατικοῦ*
*Κάτο τοπαρχ(ίας) γενή(ματος) τοῦ ζL ὑπ(ὲρ) Μεμ(νονείων)*
*πυροῦ σωροῦ ἀρτάβας ἥμισυ δοδέ-*
*κατον / 𐅵∠ιβ. Lη Νέρωνος*
*τοῦ κυρίου Φαῶφι λ̄.*

1. l. Πασήμιος.

'Horos son of Pasemis son of Labais has paid into the granary of the temples of the Lower toparchy from the produce of the seventh year on account of the Memnonia seven-twelfths of an artaba of sifted corn = $\frac{7}{12}$ art. corn. Year 8 of Nero our lord, Phaophi 30.'

2. θησαυροῦ (l. θησαυρὸν) ἱερατικοῦ: cf. for the title the θησαυρὸς ἱερῶν commonly found on Theban ostraca.

**117.** (G. 411). ·132 × ·108. 99 A.D.

*Μέ(τρημα) θη(σαυροῦ) ἱερῶ(ν) Κωμ(ῶν) γενή(ματος)*
*β ς Τραιανοῦ τοῦ κυρίου Ἐπεὶφ*
*κ̄ζ̄ ὀνόμ(ατος) Ὧρος Πετεχεσ(ποχράτου) Πικῶ(τος)*
*διὰ Ἀσκλᾶτο(ς) Ὥρου ⳨ δύο*
*/ ⳨ β. Νεμ( ) σεση(μείωμαι).*

3. l. Ὥρου.

'Payment into the granary of the temples in the Villages from the produce of the second year of Trajanus our lord, Epeiph 27, in respect of Horos son of Petechespochrates son of Pikos, through Asklas son of Horos, two artabae of corn = 2 art. corn. Signed, Nem( ).'

1. θη(σαυροῦ) ἱερῶ(ν) Κωμ(ῶν): ἱερῶν is not to be taken as an epithet of Κωμῶν; there were θησαυροὶ ἱερῶν for various districts, as Ἑρμώνθεως (G. O. 779) and Ἄνω τοπαρχίας (G. O. 783), and the district known as Κῶμαι occurs frequently.

**118.** (G. 57). ·140 × ·148 (chipped at bottom). 107 A.D.

*Μέτρη(μα) θησ(αυροῦ) Κάτω (το)π(αρχίας) γενή(ματος) ι ς Τραιανοῦ*
*τοῦ κυρίου Ἐπεὶφ ῑγ̄ ὀνό(ματος) Νήσο(υ) Ἀκρυο( )*
*Πόστυμος Θέωνο(ς) καὶ Ἀσκλᾶς Ὥρου καὶ μέ(τοχοι)*
*διὰ γεω(ργῶν) Πεκύσιος Ὀσορουή(ριος) καὶ με(τόχων) ⳨ εἴκοσι*
*ἐννέα ἥμισυ τρίτον τετρακ(αιεικοστὸν) / ⳨ κθ∠γ̄κδ̄.*
*Ἀπολλόδ(ωρος) σεση(μείωμαι).*
*Ἄλλο γενήμ(ατος) διὰ τῶν α(ὐτῶν) ⳨ τέταρτον / [⳨ δ̄.*
*Ἁρπχ[ῆμις σεση(μείωμαι).*

'Payment into the granary of the Lower toparchy from the produce of the tenth year of Trajanus our lord, Epeiph 13, in respect of the Island of Akruo( ) (from) Postumus son of Theon and Asklas son of Horos and their colleagues, through the husbandmen Pekusis son of Osoroueris and his colleagues, twenty-nine and twenty-one twenty-fourths artabae of corn = $29\frac{21}{24}$ art. corn. Signed, Apollodoros.

A further payment through the same, one quarter of an artaba of corn = [$\frac{1}{4}$ art. corn]. [Signed], Harpchemis.'

1. Κάτω (το)π(αρχίας): this is doubtless the meaning of the contraction κατῶ (cf. Wilcken, *Ostr.* i, p. 308). The name θησαυρὸς Κάτω τοπαρχίας is written out in full in an unpublished list (G. 191).

2. ὀνό(ματος) Νήσο(υ) Ἀκρυο(    ): there appears to be a variant from the usual formula here, possibly due to a slip of the writer; the normal form would be ὑπὲρ Νήσου Ἀκρυο(    ) ὀνόματος Ποστύμου κτλ. The Νῆσος Ἀκρυο(    )—possibly to be read Ἀβρυο(    )—does not occur elsewhere, but several νῆσοι with various names are mentioned on Theban ostraca.

**119.** (G. 261). ·120 × ·139. 114 A.D.

*Μεμέτρη(κε) Ψεναμοῦνις Πατφουή(ους)*
*Ψενθ(υντασήμιος) εἰς θησ(αυρὸν) Μεμνο(νείων) γενήματος ιϛ∠*
*ὑπὲρ α∠ Τραιανοῦ τοῦ κυρίου ε̣ἰ̣ς̣ τ̣ὰς̣ ἀ̣κολ(    )*
*Λίμνης ἀπὸ̣ τ(ῶν) Μεμνο(νείων) πυροῦ σωρο(ῦ) τέταρτον*
*τετρακ(αιεικοστὸν) / ₰δκ̅δ̅, καὶ ὀνό(ματος) Πετέχω(ντος) ἀδελφὸς*
*ὁμοίως πυροῦ σωρο(ῦ) τέταρτον τετρακ(αιεικοστὸν)*
*/ ₰δκ̅δ̅. ∟ιζ Τραιανοῦ Καίσαρος τοῦ*
*κυρίου, Μεχεὶρ ϛ̅.*

5. l. ἀδελφοῦ.

'Psenamounis son of Patphoues son of Psenthuntasemis has paid into the granary of the Memnonia from the produce of the sixteenth year on account of the same (?) year of Trajanus our lord for the ..... of the Lake from the Memnonia seven twenty-fourths (of an artaba) of sifted corn = $\frac{7}{24}$ art. corn, and in respect of Petechon his brother likewise seven twenty-fourths (of an artaba) of sifted corn = $\frac{7}{24}$ art. corn. Year 17 of Trajanus Caesar our lord, Mecheir 6.'

2. Ψενθ(υντασήμιος): this expansion is given on the assumption that the payer is the same who appears in no. 37 of the same year.

3. ὑπὲρ α∠: if this is to be taken in the natural sense as for the first year of Trajan, the payment was extraordinarily late; the corn-tax was usually collected promptly, and Wilcken (*Ostr.* i, p. 215) only notes two cases of the debt to the state being allowed to run on over a year. It would give an easier explanation if α∠ could be taken to mean (τοῦ) α(ὐτοῦ) ἔτους, i. e. the payment was made from the produce of the sixteenth year in respect of that year, although in the seventeenth year.

ε̣ἰ̣ς̣ τ̣ὰς̣ ἀκολ(    ): the reading is very doubtful, as the writer of the ostracon is apt to degenerate into a mere scribble, and the meaning remains uncertain.

4. Λίμνης: probably the basin now known as the Birket Habu, lying a little way south of the Colossi, which would be included in the district of the Memnonia.

**120.** (G. 203). ·051 × ·065. 126 A.D.

*Μέτρη(μα) θησ(αυροῦ) μητροπ(όλεως) γενή(ματος)*
*ιϛ Ἀδριανοῦ τοῦ κυρίου Μεσορὴ κ̄β̄*
*ὀνό(ματος) Μαιεύριο(ς) Ἁρφμόιτος*
*ὑπ(ὲρ) Ἀγο(ρῶν) πυρο(ῦ) τέταρτ(ον) / ⳨δ̄.*
*Ἐφ( ) σ(εσ)η(μείωμαι).*

'Payment into the granary of the metropolis from the produce of the tenth year of Hadrianus our lord, Mesore 22, in respect of Maieuris son of Harphmois for the Agorai, one quarter (of an artaba) of corn = ¼ art. corn. Signed, Eph( ).'

3. Μαιεύριος Ἁρφμόιτος: this is the latest appearance in our collection of this man, who first occurs in the tenth year of Vespasian (no. 44 above).

**121.** (G. 97). ·096 × ·145. 163 A.D.

*Μέ(τρημα) θησ(αυροῦ) μη(τροπόλεως) γενήμ(ατος) βϛ Ἀντωνίνου καὶ Οὐήρου*
*τῶν κυρίων Σεβαστῶν Τῦβι θ̄ τοῦ γϛ ὑπ(ὲρ) Νη(σῶν) ὀνό(ματος)*
*Ταλῶτο(ς) Ἰναρῶτο(ς) λαχ(άνου) ∻ τέταρτο(ν) / λαχ(άνου) ∻ δ̄.*
*Ἄλλο ὁμοίως λαχ(άνου) ∻ ἥμισυ τρίτο(ν) κ̄δ̄ / λαχ(άνου) ∻ ∠γ̄κ̄δ̄.*
*/ ἐπ(ὶ τὸ αὐτὸ) λαχ(άνου) ∻ αη̄. Ἀμώ(νιος) σ(εσ)η(μείωμαι).*

'Payment into the granary of the metropolis from the produce of the second year of Antoninus and Verus our lords Augusti, Tubi 9 of the third year, for the Islands in respect of Talos daughter of Inaros one quarter of an artaba of vegetables = ¼ art. vegetables. A further payment likewise of twenty-one twenty-fourths of an artaba of vegetables = $\frac{21}{24}$ art. vegetables: total, 1⅛ art. vegetables. Signed, Ammonios.'

**122.** (G. 77). ·078 × ·073. 197 A.D.

*Μέ(τρημα) θησ(αυροῦ) μη(τροπόλεως) γενή(ματος) εϛ Λουκίου*
*Σεπτιμίου Σεουήρου Εὐ-*
*σεβοῦς Περτίνακος Καί-*
*σαρος τοῦ κυρίου Παῦνι κ̄δ̄*

ὑπ(ὲρ) Χά(ρακος) ὀνόμ(ατος) Φθουμί(νιος) Τιθοήους
πυροῦ τέταρτον τε-
τρακαιικοστὸν / 𐅶δ̅κ̅δ̅.
Φ( ) σεσημ(ειώμαι) 𐅶δ̅κ̅δ̅.

'Payment into the granary of the metropolis from the produce of the fifth year of Lucius Septimius Severus Pius Pertinax Caesar our lord, Pauni 24, for Charax in respect of Phthouminis son of Tithoes, seven twenty-fourths (of an artaba) of corn = $\frac{7}{24}$ art. corn. Signed, Ph( ), $\frac{7}{24}$ art. corn.'

5. Φθουμί(νιος) Τιθοήους: the same payer occurs in G. O. 983 two years later.

**123.** (G. 271). ·105 × ·098. 211 A.D.

Μέ(τρημα) θησ(αυροῦ) μη(τροπόλεως) γ(εν)ή(ματος) ιθ\ Ἀντωνίνου καὶ
Γέτα Εὐσ(εβῶν) Σεβ(αστῶν)
Παῦ(νι) κ̅η̅ ὑπ(ὲρ) Νό(του) ὑπ(ὲρ) γ(εν)ή(ματος) ιη\ ὀνόμ(ατος) Πεκύσιο(ς) Τρεμ-
παπουή(σιος) κρ(ιθῆς) ∸ ἕκτο(ν) κ̅δ̅ / κρ(ιθῆς) ∸ ϛ̅κ̅δ̅. Εὔκη( )
σ(εσ)η(μείωμαι).
Ἄλ(λο) Θὼθ ι̅ϛ̅ ὑπ(ὲρ) γ(εν)ή(ματος) ιη\ ὀνόμ(ατος) Πεκύ(σιος) κρ(ιθῆς) ∸ ὄγδοον.
/ κρ(ιθῆς) ∸ η̅. Εὔκη( ) σ(εσ)η(μείωμαι).

'Payment into the granary of the metropolis from the produce of the nineteenth year of Antoninus and Geta Pii Augusti, Pauni 28, for the South district on account of the produce of the eighteenth year in respect of Pekusis son of Trempapouesis, five twenty-fourths of an artaba of barley = $\frac{5}{24}$ art. barley. Signed, Euke( ).

A further payment, Thoth 16, on account of the produce of the eighteenth year in respect of Pekusis, one-eighth of an artaba of barley = $\frac{1}{8}$ art. barley. Signed, Euke( ).'

2. ὑπ(ὲρ) γ(εν)ή(ματος) ιη\: a similar instance of the settlement of a debt due from a previous year with the produce of the next is to be found in G. O. 995.

Πεκύσιο(ς) Τρεμπαπουή(σιος): probably identical with the payer of no. 112.

**124.** (G. 239). ·092 × ·091.    233 A.D.

Μέ(τρημα) θησ(αυροῦ) μη(τροπόλεως) γ(εν)ή(ματος) ιβ϶ Μάρκου Αὐρηλίου
Σεουήρου Ἀλεξάνδρου Καίσαρος
τοῦ κυρίου Ἀδρ(ιανοῦ) ιᾱ τοῦ ιγ϶ ὑπ(ὲρ) γ(εν)ή(ματος)
ιβ϶ ὑπ(ὲρ) . . . ὀνόμ(ατος) Ἀπολοδώ(ρου) Ποριεύθο(υ)
5 κριθῆς ⸗ δίμοιρο(ν)/ κρ(ιθῆς) ⸗ ϑ̣] . . Α(ὐρήλιος) Δι( ) σ(εσ)η(μείωμαι).

'Payment into the granary of the metropolis from the produce of the twelfth year of Marcus Aurelius Severus Alexander Caesar our lord, Hadrianus 11 of the thirteenth year, on account of the produce of the twelfth year for ..... in respect of Apollodoros son of Porieuthes, two-thirds of an artaba of barley = ⅔ art. barley. Signed, Aurelios Di( ).'

3. τοῦ ιγ϶ : apparently corrected from τοῦ ια϶.
4. ὑπ(ὲρ) . . . : the name of the district is obscured by discoloration of the surface.

**125.** (G. 414). ·134 × ·095 (top left-hand corner broken).

Plate XII. 253 A.D.

[Μέ(τρημα)] θησ(αυροῦ) μη(τροπόλεως) γενή(ματος) β϶ τῶν κυρίων ἡμῶν
Γάλλου καὶ Οὐολουσιανοῦ Σεβαστῶν Ἐπεὶφ η̄
ὑπ(ὲρ) Ἀγο(ρῶν) α ὀνόμ(ατος) Ἰσιδώ(ρου) νε(ωτέρου) Ἀπολλοδώ(ρου)
πρ(εσβυτέρου) διὰ Φθομ(ώνθου)
ἀπὸ γενή(ματος) τοῦ α(ὐτοῦ) β϶ πυ(ροῦ) ⸗ δύο ἥμισυ
5 τρίτον / ᴅβ∠γ̄. Αὐ(ρήλιος) Διόσκ(ορος) Α . . . σ(εσ)η(μείωμαι)
καὶ ἔσχον τὸν ὀβολ(όν).

'Payment into the granary of the metropolis from the produce of the second year of our lords Gallus and Volusianus Augusti, Epeiph 8, for the first district of the Agorai in respect of Isidoros the younger, son of Apollodoros the elder, through Phthomonthes, from the produce of the said second year, two and five-sixths artabae of corn = 2⅚ art. corn. Signed, Aurelios Dioskoros ....., who has received the fee.'

3. Ἀγο(ρῶν) α : there seems to be a variation between the earlier and later subdivisions of the quarter of Thebes known as Ἀγοραί, the change occurring about the time of Hadrian. Up till this reign the usual forms are Ἀγο βο and Ἀγο νο, which are doubtless correctly taken by Wilcken as Ἀγοραὶ βορρᾶ and Ἀγοραὶ νότου; the latest instance of either form seems to be in A.D. 142 (no. 101). But in G. O. 1471 (A.D. 250) and 1474 (A.D. 261) there is mentioned Ἀγο(ραὶ) γ, which would belong to the same series as the Ἀγοραὶ α of this text; and possibly

the 'Αγο(ραὶ) β of G. O. 643, 834, 1008, 1583, and 1594 should be taken as falling into the same numeration; they are all of the reign of Hadrian or later, and the contraction is 'Αγο or 'Αγορ$^{ω}$ β, not β$^{o}$; in three of the five instances the β is apparently marked $\bar{β}$ as a numeral. A transitional form may be found in 'Αγο(ραὶ) δ νό(του) of no. 42, dated A.D. 133. It may be suggested that about A.D. 130 the quarter, formerly subdivided into the districts βορρᾶ and νότου, was rearranged in four numbered districts. The new arrangement would not, however, appear to have been universally accepted at once; the earliest instance of 'Αγοραὶ $\bar{β}$ is in A.D. 131 (G. O. 834), but 'Αγοραὶ βορρᾶ occurs in A.D. 138 (G. O. 857) and 'Αγοραὶ νότου in A.D. 142 (no. 101).

6. καὶ ἔσχον τὸν ὀβολ(όν): cf. G. O. 1008.

## III. Receipts for Personal Service.

The final section of the Roman tax-receipts is concerned with those given in respect of the liturgy on dykes and embankments to which the inhabitants of Egypt were liable. As has been seen above (p. 129), the personal service could probably be commuted by a money-payment; but it is not uncommon to find receipts for the actual work done. The general problem arising from these receipts so far as they appear on ostraca is the basis on which they were given. If the liability of the individual was simply to work for five days, the natural form of the quittance would be a statement that the man had worked for five days; and such a form is actually found on papyri (e.g. P. Tebt. 371, 641–74). On ostraca, however, the usual course of the receipt is that the man has dug a number of naubia, which suggests piecework rather than day-work. But the numbers of naubia stated in different receipts vary widely; the highest amount is in G. O. 1399, where three brothers are stated to have dug 15 naubia; and this agrees with a small series of receipts from Denderah, where the ἀναβολὴ χωμάτων is regularly given as 5 naubia for each man; on the other hand, in G. O. 1567, a man and his two sons are credited with only half a naubion, which seems a very small amount of work for five days, and in no. 128 two men have a receipt for two-thirds of a naubion. As Wilcken has pointed out (*Ostr.* i, p. 337), the phraseology of the receipts leaves little doubt that they are for compulsory, not for paid, work; but it is rather mysterious why the officials should have taken the trouble to measure up the number of naubia dug, and to enter it in the receipts, if the obligation was only for service by time; they would hardly be anxious to preserve a record of the comparative diligence of different workers. The simplest explanation would be to suppose that, in common acceptance, *ναύβιον* was regarded as meaning a day's compulsory work, and a statement that a man had dug five naubia was equivalent to saying that he had worked on the dykes for five days.

**126.** (G. 13). ·076 × ·058. Early part of first century A.D.

Lγ Χοιὰχ χω-
ματικοῦ Ψον-
όντηρ πάν-
τε διαποεῖτα-
ι.

(Traces of a line, apparently of demotic, below.)

3–4. l. πάντα.

'Year 3, Choiak. Psononter has done the whole of his dyke-work.'

The ostracon is inscribed in rude capitals, obviously by an illiterate person; it reduces the formula of quittance practically to its simplest elements.

**127.** (G. 260). ·097 × ·146. 117–18 A.D.

Ἰσίδωρο(ς) Φθο(μώνθου ?) χω(ματεπιμελητὴς) Ἑρμ(ώνθεως) διὰ Μέμνο(νος) γρα(μματέως)
Ψε̣μ̣ώ(νθη) Ἁρπαήσιο(ς) Ἰμο̣ύ̣(θου ?) χα̣(ίρειν). Ἤργ(ασαι) ἐπὶ
περιχώ(ματος) Κλου τοῦ Φμου τῶι β𐅵
Ἁδριανοῦ Καίσαρος τοῦ κυρίου ναύβ(ια) δύο
/ ναύβ(ια) β, καὶ ὀνόμ(ατος) Παμο̣ύ̣(νιος) ἀδελ(φοῦ) ὁμ(οίως)
ναύβ(ια) ἓν ἥμισυ / ναύβ(ια) α𐅵.

'Isidoros son of Phthomonthes, dyke-supervisor of Hermonthis, through Memnon his clerk, to Psemonthes son of Harpaesis son of Imouthes (?), greeting. You have dug two naubia on the dyke of Klouphis (?) of Phmou (?) in the second year of Hadrianus Caesar our lord, = 2 naubia, and in respect of Pamounis your brother likewise one and a half naubia, = 1½ naubia.'

2. Ἰμο̣ύ̣(θου): as this ostracon follows the same general formula as G. O. 1043–7, the word standing here should be the name of the district; but the letters cannot be made into νό(του) καὶ λ(ιβός), the district of those five ostraca.

3. Κλου τοῦ Φμου: possibly this should be read as a single word, the local name of the embankment; the first four letters suggest the περίχωμα Κλούφιος of G. O. 1043–7, which are, like this ostracon, from Hermonthis, and perhaps the title here is a fuller form of the same—Κλού(φιος) τοῦ Φμου(  ).

**128.** (G. 290). ·068 × ·081 (broken at bottom). Plaṭe XII. 139 A.D.

*Ψεννήσιο(ς) Ἰσιδώρου χω(ματεπιμελητὴς) δι(ὰ) Ψεν-*
*σενφθομ(ώνθου) βοηθοῦ*
*Ἰναρώους Καβίριο(ς) καὶ Κολ̣λ̣ε̣ύ̣θ̣η(ς)*
*υἱό(ς) οἱ β̄ χα(ίρειν). Ἀναβ(εβλήκατε) εἰς περίχω(μα)*
*Ψαμ(    ) ναυβ(ίου) ⅔*
*∟γ Ἀντωνίνου τοῦ κυρίου*
*Φαμ(ενὼθ) [.]*

1. l. Ψεννῆσις.    3, 4. l. Ἰναρῶτι Καβίριος καὶ Κολλεύθῃ υἱῷ τοῖς β̄.

'Psennesis son of Isidoros, dyke-supervisor, through Psensenphthomonthes his assistant, to Inaros son of Kabiris and Kolleuthes his son, greeting. You have thrown up on the dyke of Psam(    ) $\frac{2}{3}$ naubion. Year 3 of Antoninus our lord, Phamenoth [    ].'

**129.** (G. 433). ·128 × ·081 (top right-hand corner lost). 140 A.D.

*Φθομώ(νθης) Ὥρου χω(ματεπιμελητὴς) [*
*Ἁρπαήσιος Πασήμιο(ς) Πκ̣ο̣[ίλιος (?) χαίρειν.*
*Ἀνέβ(αλες) εἰς περίχω(μα) Ψαμ(    ) καὶ ἄ̣λ̣(λο) χῶ(μα) Ψ̣[*
*ναύβ(ια) βδ̄η̣̄. ∟δ Ἀντωνίνου*
*Καίσαρος τοῦ κυρίου Φαμ(ενὼθ) ῑᾱ.*

2. l. Ἁρπαήσει.

'Phthomonthes son of Horos, dyke-supervisor [    ], to Harpaesis son of Pasemis son of Pko[ilis?] [greeting]. You have thrown up on the dyke of Psam(    ) and the mound of Ps[    ] $2\frac{3}{8}$ naubia. Year 4 of Antoninus Caesar our lord, Phamenoth 11.'

The following text appears to belong to the class of receipts for work on dykes; but it is distinguished from the ordinary type of these receipts by the fact that it specifies a payment for the work, and so can hardly be regarded as dealing with the five days' compulsory service. Further, the quittance is not given by *χωματεπιμεληταί*, but by officials—if they were officials—whose title does not occur elsewhere. Perhaps, as it seems to have been permitted for men liable to this compulsory service to compound for it by a money-payment (see p. 129), and considerable numbers must have availed themselves of this permission, to judge by the frequency of receipts for money-payments on account of *χωματικόν*, the revenue derived from the compositions might be devoted to hiring men for the dyke-work as required to supplement the forced labour, and this ostracon may be taken as a statement of a payment for this purpose; though it would have appeared more natural for the men who did the work to give a receipt for their payment.

If the standard amount of work was one naubion a day, the value of five days' work at the rate shown in this ostracon would be ten drachmae five obols, which is higher than any recorded payment for *χωματικόν* as a composition in money. Possibly, however, the forced labour was not reckoned at so high a value as paid labour; it would almost certainly be worth less in fact.

**130.** (G. 434). ·1 × ·096 (broken at right below). Second cent. A.D.

*Ψενμώ(νθης) Πλή(νιος) νε(ωτέρου) καὶ Φθομ(ώνθης) Ὥρου*
*πεντηκ( ) Μεμνονίων δ̣ι̣ὰ̣ γρ̣(αμματέως) Ἐ̣π̣ῶ̣τ(ος)*
*Σαχούμνεους χαί(ρειν). Ἀναβέβλ(ηται)*
*ὑπὸ σοῦ ναύβ(ια) ηδ/ ὧν καὶ*
*τὸν μισθῶν ἔσχες*
*ἑκάστου ἑνὸς ναυβ(ίου) ὀβο(λοὺς) ιγ*
*καθαροῦ ἐφ' ᾧ τὰς ἀ[πο-]*
*χὰς τὰς πω̣[*
*ἀκυρῶ̣[σαι*
L ιε̣[

3. l. *Σαχούμνει.* 5. l. *μισθὸν.*

'Psenmonthes son of Plenis the younger and Phthomonthes son of Horos, . . . . . . . of the Memnonia, through Epos (?) their clerk, to Sachoumnes, greeting. $8\frac{2}{3}$ naubia have been thrown up by you, for which you have received pay at the rate of 13 obols for each naubion clear, on condition that th former (?) receipts are annulled. Year 15 [ ].'

2. πεντηκ(   ): the officials here can hardly be the πεντηκοστῶναι (cf. Wilcken, *Ostr.* i, p. 277), who were collectors of customs. It seems more probable that some local title analogous to δεκανός or δεκάπρωτος is to be sought in the contraction.

7–9. ἐφ' ᾧ τὰς ἀ[πο]χὰς τὰς πω[   ] ἀκυρῶ[σαι]. Dr. Hunt remarks that the ordinary phrase to be expected would be ἐφ' ᾧ τὰς ἀποχὰς τὰς προτέρας ἀκυρῶσαι, but he cannot make the remaining letters at the end of l. 8 fit προτέρας, and suggests that πω[   ] may be a name.

## IV. Miscellaneous.

### (*a*) *Receipts.*

The first of these receipts is clearly a private one.

**131.** (G. 15). ·090 × ·095 (broken below and on right).

First to second century A.D.

Θαμυδάρης καὶ Δημή-
τριος Ἡρακλείῳ καὶ
Ἀπολλωνίῳ χαίρειν.
Ὁμολογοῦμεν ἀπέχ[ει-]
ν παρ' ὑμῶν τὰς διὰ τ[ῆς]
μισθώσεως πυροῦ [ἀρ-]
τάβας πέντε /
[καὶ ο]ὐθὲν ὑμῖν ἐνκα-
[λοῦμε]ν. Ἔγραψεν
[. . . . . . . .]φης
[. . . . . . . . Μεσ]ορὴ η̄.

'Thamudares and Demetrios to Herakleios and Apollonios, greeting. We acknowledge the receipt from you of the five artabae of corn due for rent, and make no claim against you. Written by . . . ., Mesore 8.'

The next list appears to give the number of men, probably soldiers, for whom certain nomes contributed supplies in kind—oil, vinegar, pulse, and other articles, the names of which are lost. So far as can be judged from the fragment, which accounts for over half the total of 140 men, there can only have been a small proportion of the nomes of the whole country concerned, and the nomes mentioned are all in Lower or Middle Egypt. It is noticeable that the totals of *ξέσται* specified at the end are divisible not by 140 but by 167 in each case, which looks as if some of the 140 men got double or treble allowances or more.

**132.** (G. 22). ·096 × ·075 (broken above and on right).

Third century A.D.

*Ἡρα]κλεο[πολίτου*
*. .]. /Φλαβωνίτου/ ἀνδ(ρῶν) κ[*
*ἀνδρ(ῶν) θ/ Νιλούπολιν ἀνδρ(ῶν) [*
*ἀνδρ(ῶν) δύο/ Ἀφροδίτω ἀνδ[ρ(ῶν)*
*Καβασίτου ἀνδρῶν ἕξ/ Λεο[ντοπολίτου*
*ἀνδρ(ῶν) κ/ Διοσπολίτου κάτω [ ἀνδρῶν*
*κδ/ γί(νεται) ἀνδρ(ῶν) ρμ/. ἐλέο[υ*
*ξ̄ ρξζ/ ὄξους ξ̄ ωλε[*
*τος ξ̄ τλδ φακ[οῦ*
*. . . . ρι . . . [*

2. *Φλαβωνίτου*: this may be meant for *Φραγωνίτου*, as the nomes are not arranged in a strict geographical order; Phragonis seems to have risen in importance at the expense of the neighbouring Buto in late Roman times.

## (*b*) *Orders.*

The three following ostraca may be grouped together, as they are all private notes conveying orders.

The first is of some interest in connexion with the *μετρήματα ἐς θησαυρόν* (pp. 139–46), as showing the relations of the landholders and the *γεωργοί*. In this case it would appear that the *γεωργός* is not a tenant, but a person in the position of a bailiff; and the numerous instances of *μετρήματα* made *διὰ γεωργοῦ* which occur on ostraca probably relate to similar transactions, where the corn was not delivered by the landholder in person, but by deputy through one of his servants.

**133.** (G. 12). ·079 × ·118 (broken at bottom). Second century A.D.

Σενπλῆ(νις) γυνὴ Πλ(ήνιος) Ἀνδρονίκῳ
κολ' τσαυ γεωργῷ μου χαίρειν.
Μέτρησον εἰς τὸν δημόσιον θησαυρὸν πυροῦ ἀρτάβας τριάκοντα
καὶ κριθῆς ἀρτάβας εἴκοσι μό-
νας ἔστ' ἂν σε ἰδ[[. .]]ησω καὶ με-
τρήσω τὴν γῆν μου· ἐπεὶ γὰρ
ἐμέτρησα ἐνταῦθα καὶ νιλοκαμιν
τηρ̣η̣[

'Senplenis wife of Plenis to Andronikos ..... my husbandman, greeting. Pay into the public granary thirty artabae of corn and twenty artabae of barley only till I see you and measure my land ; for when I measured it and having perceived there was a failure of the Nile (?) .......'

6. ἰδ[[. .]]ησω: apparently ἴδω was first written and then altered.
8. νιλοκαμιν: possibly this should be read νιλοκαμεῖν τηρή[σασα], with a reference to a low inundation ; or Dr. Hunt suggests that Νιλόκαμιν may be a proper name.

**134.** (G. 18). ·075 × ·101. First to second century A.D.

Σαραπί[ω]ν Φθομών(θει) χαίρ(ειν).
Τὰ πρὸς Κράτητα εὐθέως
ἀπάλλαξον κατὰ τὰς συνθ[ή]-
κας, οὐδὲν γὰρ ζητεῖ-
ται πρὸς αὐτόν.

'Sarapion to Phthomonthes, greeting. Discharge the debt to Krates at once in accordance with the agreement, for there is no question against him.'

**135.** (G. 21). ·071 × ·105 (surface chipped). First century A.D.

Ποίησον τὸν ἀναδι-
τὸ ὄστρακον
δόντα σοι φυτὰ κάρου
τοῦ ἐνιαυτοῦ τούτου
δι[. . . .]υ̣[.] π̣ρ̣αγματικὰς
τῆ̣ς [. . . . .] μ̣ετ̣ [. . . . .]

4. πραγματικὰς: the final ς is on the edge of the ostracon.

'Supply the man who delivers this ostracon to you with caraway plants of this year . . . . . . . . .'

### (*c*) *Lists.*

A considerable proportion of the Greek ostraca in our collection consists of lists and accounts. In many cases the lists are merely of names, with no indication of their purpose; or the names have against them entries of sums in money or kind, but again without any definition of the reason of the entries. There is, however, one group, represented by a large number of fragments, from which six fairly complete documents have been made up; these are referred to as G. 151 (consisting of G. 151 and an unnumbered fragment), G. 158 (G. 158, G. 330, and G. 197), G. 159 (G. 200, G. 322, G. 159, and G. 196), G. 161 (G. 166 and G. 161), G. 172, and no. 136 (G. 310, G. 187, and an unnumbered fragment). All these ostraca, besides several other fragments which do not fit together, are in the same hand, and appear to be summaries of the accounts of Paeris son of Psensenplenis. The names in the lists for the most part recur, though not always in the same order; nearly all are found in three or four of the six lists; and against the names are entered numbers of *μη/*, which can be nothing but *μηνιαῖα*, in view of some of the headings, and must apparently be taken in the sense of monthly payments. The number of *μηνιαῖα* entered is regularly less than twelve; but, from a comparison of G. 151, G. 158, and G. 159, it appears that these three relate to one year and are complementary: thus Paeris of Thebes is credited with 11 *μηνιαῖα* on G. 151 and 1 on G. 158; Mauos son of Hatres with 10 and 2; Sisois son of Suros with 11 on G. 151 and 1 on G. 159; the sum being always 12. The clearest evidence that a total of 12 *μηνιαῖα* was required is to be found in no. 138, belonging to another series, where the number of *μηνιαῖα* credited is followed by a note of the balance of the 12 remaining. The nature of these *μηνιαῖα* may be gathered from the headings of the lists: G. 151 is headed [*Παῆ*]*ρις Ψενσενπλή(νιος)* | [*π*]*ρᾶξις ἐπὶ κεφαλῆς ἀργυρίου*: G. 159, *λόγ(ος) λινο(υργῶν) καταμην(ιαίων)* | *διὰ Παήρις Ψενσενπλ(ήνιος)*: G. 161, [? *λόγος ἐξ*]*ουσίας ἐπικεφαλείων*: and no. 136, *λόγ(ος) ἐξουσίας ἐπικεφαλείων Παῆρις* | *Μεσωρὰ λα*. The *μηνιαῖα* were therefore for *ἐπικεφάλαιον*, and this *ἐπικεφάλαιον* cannot be taken in the sense of poll-tax, *λαογραφία*, which was not collected as a monthly tax at Thebes, so far as the ostraca show, but is presumably one of the taxes on trades, like the *γερδιακόν* and *ἡπητικόν* already discussed; and the λιν° of G. 159, which is presumably for λινουργῶν or λινοπώλων, shows the trade concerned in one instance. The ostraca from Syene supply numerous instances of a *χειρωνάξιον μηνιαῖον* paid by linen-workers or sellers at Elephantine (cf. Wilcken, *Ostr.* i, pp. 322 ff.); and it may be assumed with reason that the tax here was also a *χειρωνάξιον*, and that Wilcken (*Ostr.* i, p. 249, note 1) was wrong in rejecting Marquardt's interpretation of the pseudo-Aristotelian phrase *ἐπικεφάλαιόν τε καὶ χειρωνάξιον προσαγορευομένη*, as showing that the two terms applied to the same tax. The monthly payments do not appear to have been collected with great regularity; on G. 151, indeed, the normal entry is either 10 or 11 *μηνιαῖα*, but G. 161 shows entries varying from 3 to 10, and G. 172 and no. 136 are similar. The sums entered against individuals also vary: thus *Χολλῶς Σύρου* is credited with 11 *μηνιαῖα* on G. 151, 1 on G. 159, 10 on G. 172, and 3 on no. 136; *Καλασῖρις Ἀλείκει* with 11 on G. 151, 1 on G. 159, 6 on G. 161, 9 on G. 172, and 8 on no. 136; and so forth. In two cases, not belonging to the accounts of Paeris, some of the entries are not in *μηνιαῖα*, but in denarii; the more complete of these is given below (no. 137), and the figures given suggest that 19 denarii, which would be the equivalent of 76 drachmae, were the unit of the *μηνιαῖον*. This is unusually high for *χειρωνάξιον*, even though the ostracon is a late one; the rates for various trades at Arsinoe about 300 A.D., as shown by B. G. U. 9, ranged from 8 to 60 drachmae a month (cf. Wilcken, *Ostr.* i, p. 325). The ostracon is complete, but bears no note of the trade which was the subject of the *μηνιαῖα*.

**136.** (G. 310 + G. 187 + unnumbered). ·134 × ·179.

Second century A.D.

*Λόγ(ος) ἐξουσίας ἐπικεφαλείων Παῆρις*
*Μεσωρὰ $\overline{λα}$.*
*Ἀντῆλε μη(νιαῖα) γ.*
*Ἀτρῆς παραχύτου μ(ηνιαῖα) ζ.*
*Σελεῦε Παῆρις μη(νιαῖα) ια.*
*Ἀλείκει μη(νιαῖα) η.*

*Καλασῖρις υἱὸς μη(νιαῖα) η.*
*Σοισόιτος Σύρους μη(νιαῖα) ε.*
*Καλασῖρις Πεκ(ύσιος) μ(ηνιαῖα) γ.*
*Ψενσενφθο(μώνθης) μη(νιαῖα) ε.*
*Πλ(ῆνις) Πεκ(ύσιος) Καμή(τιος) μη(νιαῖα) ζ.*
*Χολλῶς Σύρ(ου) μη(νιαῖα) γ.*
*Πλῆ(νις) παραχύτου μη(νιαῖα) η.*
*Φθομῖν Πεκ(ύσιος) μη(νιαῖα) γ.*
*Παῆρις Παῆρις π(ρεσβυτέρου) μη(νιαῖα) β.*
*Παῆρις ἀπὸ Θηβῶν μη(νιαῖα) δ.*
*Σύρους Πατέσβ(θιος) μη(νιαῖα) η.*

1. l. Παήριος: so also in ll. 5 and 15. 17. l. Σῦρος Πατσέβθιος.

3. Ἀντῆλε: this name is spelt Ἀντιλε in G. 159, which looks as if it was a Greek form; from G. 172, however, it appears that the bearer of the name was a son of Πλῆνις, though this would not exclude the possibility of his having a Greek name.

4. παραχύτου: probably not a proper name here and in line 13, but simply giving the trade of the father; so in G. 151 and elsewhere Πκοῖλις ἡπητοῦ occurs.

8. l. Σίσοις Σύρου: this name seems to have given Paeris much difficulty; in G. 159 he spells it Σισύιτος.

**137.** (G. 156). ·164 × ·105. Second to third century A.D.

*Παμῖνις Παχώμιος μη(νιαῖα) γ̄.*
*Ψῦρος Παποντῶ(τος) μη(νιαῖα) δ̄.*
*Πλῆ(νις) Στράβ(ωνος) πρ(εσβυτέρου) μη(νιαῖα) β̄.*
*Παῆρις Παή(ριος) νεωτ(έρου) μη(νιαῖον) ᾱ.*
*Ἀμενώθ(ης) Κυμαικὸς μη(νιαῖα) ε̄.*
*Σενπεχύτης ⳨ ν.*
*Πρεμμοῦν ⳨ ρ̅ι̅δ̅*
*Γυνὴ Παττσέβθιος Φθομ(ώνθου)* (above: Πεκύ(σιος))
*⳨ ι̅θ̅.*

6. ⳨ ν: if the unit was 19 denarii, as suggested above, this should be ν̅ζ̅: but there is no sign of a ζ.

**138.** (G. 176). ·115 × ·143. Second century A.D.

*Δεκ(    ) λ̅α̅ ἕως λ̅ε̅*
*διὰ Ἀρσιήσιος Καλήους*
*Πετεμενώφιος Πετεμενώφιος μη(νιαῖα) θ, λοιπ(ὰ) γ.*
*Πετεχώ(νσιος) Πετεχώνσιος ὁμ(οίως) γ, λοιπ(ὰ) θ.*
*Παέρμιος Παέρμιος ὁμ(οίως) ζ, λοιπ(ὰ) ε.*
*Σανσν(ῶτος) Τρύφωνος ὁμ(οίως) ι, λοιπ(ὰ) β.*
*Παμού(νιος) νεω(τέρου) Ὥρου ὁμ(οίως) ζ, λοιπ(ὰ) ε.*

The following ostracon is a fragment only, but is interesting on account of the heading, which shows it to have contained a list of the night-police for a particular month.

**139.** (G. 195). ·071 × ·086 (broken below). Second century A.D.

*Νυκτοφύλ(ακες) Θὼθ τοῦ ιε*ϛ
*(δεκανὸς) Ἀμενώθ(ης) Καμήτιο(ς) Ἀβῶτ(ος)*
*Φθομώνθ(ης) Χεστφνάχθ(ιος) [*
*Ὀννῶφ[ρις] Ὥρο(υ) Ὀν[νώφριος]*
*[    ]φρι(ς) Παμώ(νθου) [    ]*
*[    ]ης Π[    ]*

2. Δεκανός: written Ϯ; cf. p. 117.

One list occurs in two copies (G. 153 and G. 188), written in different hands; it contains a numbered statement of κλῆροι ἐργατῶν for a certain year. Unfortunately both copies are broken, and the end of the first line, which may have contained a statement of the purpose of the κλῆροι, is lost in both. In view of the duplication of the list, it may be suggested that, when the lots were drawn for rota of duties, each man concerned was supplied with a copy of the list. The text given is that of the more complete copy.

**140.** (G. 153). ·110 × ·087 (broken on right and below).
Second century A.D.

Κλῆρ(οι) ἐργατῶν ιες κ̣α̣ι̣ γ[
ᾱ Πλῆ(νις) Παβῆκ(ιος) Γαΐου
β̄ Ἀλείκει Πατσέβθις
γ̄ Παμῖν Γαΐου
δ̄ Πλῆ(νις) ν(εώτερος) Πλή(νιος) κε[
ε̄ Πλῆ(νις) Ψενσενπαή[ριος
ϛ̄ Πλῆ(νις) Πλή(νιος) ν(εωτέρου) κ[
ζ̄ Καλασῖρις Ἀλεί[κει
η̄ Πουώριος Νε[
θ̄ Παῆρις Ἀμμ[ωνίου ?
[ῑ . . . . . .]μ[

2. Γαΐου: in G. 188 written here and in l. 4 Γαεΐου.
3. Ἀλείκει Πατσέβθις: l. Πατσέβθιος: this name and that of Καλασῖρις Ἀλείκει (l. 8) occur in the Paeris lists (no. 136 above).
9. Πουώριος: l. Πουῶρις: in G. 188 it is written Πουορις.

Another fragment presents a problem, the solution of which is obscure. Entries are made of quantities of corn, barley, and pulse, and one-third is taken of each entry; and at the end a valuation in money appears to have been made.

**141.** (G. 168). ·093 × ·094 (broken on all sides). Second century A.D.

]α . . φ̣σι . . . [
]ητρο(ς) ἀπὸ Ἰσιδίου ὄρους ϟα τὸ γ̄ [ϟγ̄
]ος Δολοῦτος ϟε τὸ γ̄ ϟαδ/
]ν̣ου παστοφό(ρου) ϟβ τὸ γ̄ ϟδ/
] Ὥρου ϟβ κρι(θῆς) ÷ γδ̄ τὸ γ̄ ϟδ/ κ(ριθῆς) ÷ αιβ̄
]ῶσις γυνὴ Πχόρσ(ιος) ϟγ τὸ γ̄ ϟα
]ς ϟγ τὸ γ̄ ϟα
]ωρος φακ(οῦ) ÷ ας τὸ γ̄ φακ(οῦ) [÷ ς
κρι(θῆς)] ÷ γ τὸ γ̄ κριθ(ῆς) ÷ α
] ÷ ∠δ′
]μ̣ης φακ(οῦ) χμγ[
] ÷ ἀργ(υρίου) παλ(αιοῦ) ςτ[
X

6. ϡγ: γ is corrected, apparently from α.

11. χμγ: this number is written over another, possibly χπγ.

12. ἀργ(υρίου) παλ(αιοῦ): this may refer to the Ptolemaic tetradrachms, which were still in circulation in Egypt till late in the third century; or, if the ostracon was written after the debasement of the currency in the reign of Commodus, the reckoning may be in the older Roman tetradrachms, which appear, from the evidence of hoards, to have been more appreciated than the debased issues.

The following account, which is almost complete, concerns a society of worshippers of Amenothes, probably connected with the temple of Hatasu at Deir-el-bahri, the upper court of which was given over in Ptolemaic and Roman times to the cult of this god of healing; the graffiti scribbled on the walls suggest that it became a sanatorium. The ostracon gives a list of names with entries of one *ρο*[δ] or *κε*[ρ] against each; the contractions are presumably for *ῥόδιον* and *κεράμιον*, and the account is one of the contributions of jars of wine made by members of the society, no doubt for the common benefit at their meetings.

**142.** (G. 334). ·178 × ·162 (top right-hand corner broken).
Second century A.D.

*Λόγος συνόδου Ἀμενώθου θεοῦ [μεγίστου*
*Μεσορὴ ε̄ Ψεντιτουῆ(s) γ̣ ῥόδ(ιον) [α.*
*ς̄ Φθομώνθ(ης) ο· Ἀπολλωνί(ου) ῥόδ(ιον) α.*
*ια̅ Σισόις Ἀπολλωνί(ου) ῥόδ(ιον) α.*
*Ἐπαγο(μένων) ᾱ Ἀμώνιο(s) Ψεντιτουή(ους) ῥόδ(ιον) α.*
*δ̄ Παμώνθ(ης) Φθομώνθ(ου) ῥόδ(ιον) α.*
*ζL Θὼθ ᾱ Πεκῦσι(s) Καμήτι(ος) ῥόδ(ιον) α.*
*β̄ Ψεντιτουῆ(s) γ̣ ῥόδ(ιον) α.*
*ζ̄ Ψεντιτουῆ(s) γ̣ ῥόδ(ιον) α.*
*Σισόις Ἀπολλωνί(ου) ῥόδ(ιον) α.*
*ῥόδ(ια) β*
*η̄ Ψεντιτουῆ(s) γ̣ ῥόδ(ιον) α.*
*Φθομώνθ(ης) ο· Ἀπολλωνί(ου) ῥόδ(ιον) α.*
*Πεκῦσι(s) Καμήτι(ος) ῥόδ(ιον) α.*
*Παμώνθ(ης) Φθομώνθ(ου) κερ(άμιον) α.*
*θ Ἀμώνιο(s) Ψεντιτουή(ους) ῥόδ(ιον) α.*

ῑᾱ Σισόις Ἀπολ(λωνίου) ῥόδ(ιον) α.
Παμώνθ(ης) Φθομ(ώνθου) κερ(άμιον) α.
Σενκα(μῆτις ?) κερ(άμιον) α.
(col. 2) ῑδ̄ Πεκῦσι(ς) ῥόδ(ιον) α.
Ψενκαλ(αμῆς ?) κερ(άμιον) α.
Σισόις Ἀπολ(λωνίου) ῥόδ(ιον) α.
Σενκα(μῆτις ?) κερ(άμιον) α.
ις Ψεντιτουῆ(ς) ῥόδ(ιον) α.

2. γ: this letter regularly follows the name of Psentitoues, except in the last entry; it may be suggested that it represents γραμματεύς, and he was secretary of the society; at any rate he is the most frequent contributor in this list.

ῥόδιον: the Rhodian measure of wine is already known from an ostracon (Wilcken, *Ostr.* i, p. 765); it probably originated from the Rhodian amphorae, the stamped handles of which are common at Alexandria, though I know no instance of their having been found at Thebes; they are rare outside the Delta. Another measure of wine which occurs in Egyptian documents is the κνίδιον (Wilcken, *l.c.*). This may have been connected with amphorae similarly, as Knidian amphora-handles also have been found fairly frequently at Alexandria.

3. ο·: the symbol following the name of Phthomonthes here and in l. 12 is obscure; it appears to be 𝛿/, possibly for διάδοχος.

Another list possibly concerned with wine gives particulars of διπλοκεράμια distributed to various persons, in the same manner as G. O. 1485. The offices of the recipients suggest that the occasion of the distribution was a festival.

**143**. (G. 305). ·098 × ·075. Third century A.D.

Φαρ(μοῦθι) κ̣ζ
Σαραπίων βοηθ(ῷ) διπ(λοκεράμιον) α.
Ἀντισθένης ὁμοί(ως) διπ(λοκεράμιον) α.
γραμματῖ ἐπιτρόπ(ου) διπ(λοκεράμια) β̄.
ἀγραμήσαντι διπ(λοκεράμια) β.
κορνουκλαρίου διπ(λοκεράμιον) ᾱ.
ῥήτωρι Ἐπισθ(ένῃ ?) διπ(λοκεράμιον) ᾱ.
πρινκίπῳ διπ(λοκεράμιον α.
ἑρμηνῖ διπ(λοκεράμιον) α.

βοηθ(ῷ) βασιλ̣ι̣κ̣(οῦ) διπ(λοκεράμια) ε.
στρατηγῷ διπ(λοκεράμια) γ.
γ(ίγνεται) διπ(λοκεράμια) ι̅θ̅ γ° π°
λ(οιπὸν) βουτ( ) διπ(λοκεράμιον) α.

2. l. Σαραπίωνι. 3. l. Ἀντισθένῃ. 6. l. κορνουκλαρίῳ. 8. l. πρίνκιπι.

1. κζ: the date appears to have been altered from κϛ.

5. ἀγραμήσαντι: Dr. Hunt suggests that this may be meant for ἀγορανομήσαντι.

The following account of 'heliotrope' wood presents some novelties.

**144.** (G. 192). ·104 × ·084. First century A.D.

Λόγ(ος) ξύλου ἡλιοτροπίου
π̣ρ̣υ̣σ̣μοῦ πρώτου
δέσμαι τρίξυλ(οι) ξ̄
ἄλ(λο) ὁμ(οίως) ἑπτάξυλοι ρ̄ — καὶ ἠθετή(θησαν) κ̄ ἄχρι πρυσμοῦ
ἄλ(λο) ὁμ(οίως) δεκάξυλ(οι) ξ̄
ἄλ(λο) ὁμ(οίως) πολύξυλ(οι) κ̄
– ἐπὶ τὸ α(ὐτὸ) δέσμ(αι) σμ
$χ^{ω}$ των κ̣ ῑ β̄
ξύλ(α) ἀχπ.

1. ἡλιοτροπίου.

2. π̣ρ̣υ̣σ̣μοῦ: presumably for πρισμοῦ.

8. This line is badly rubbed; possibly it should be completed χω(ρὶς), and is intended to convey that the 20 πολύξυλοι, which may be those referred to in the side-note as put aside for sawing, were not to be reckoned in: but in this case the arithmetic is wrong, and it does not appear for what the ῑ and β̄ are meant.

Two lists of names may be given in conclusion: the first, written in good capitals, contains a curious metronymic; the second is interesting for the occupations noted.

**145.** (G. 6). ·092 × ·154. First century A.D.

Ταυσῖρις μητρὸς Τφοι-
ρείας καὶ Καλατηφόις
μητρὸς Θεᾶς μεγίστης
ἀπὸ τοῦ Περὶ Θήβας.

**146**. (G. 154). ·089 × ·098. Second century A.D.

*Ἱέραξ Πελιλέως*
*Ἱέραξ Φμόιτος*
*Πλελοῦς Πετέχωντος.*
*Κλωτεῖς τέκτων.*
*Καλῆς ἀδελφός.*
*Φμόις λεγ(όμενος) Φόρσις ναυτικ(ός).*
*Παχοῦμις Σανσνῶτ(ος) ὀνηλ(άτης).*
*καὶ Παχοῦμις υἱός.*
⟦*Φμόις Σενψάϊτος ὀνηλ(άτης).*⟧

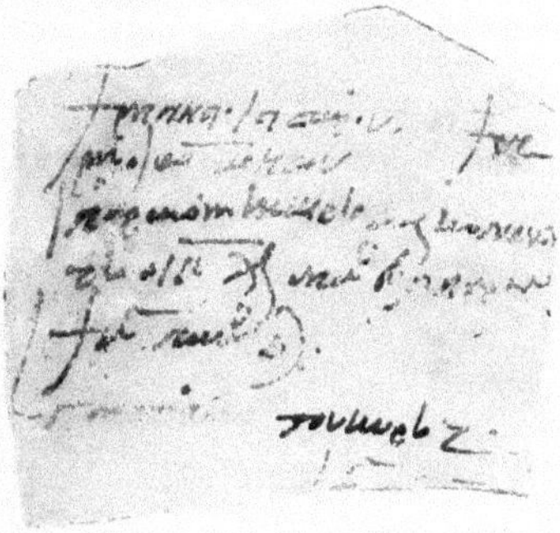

128

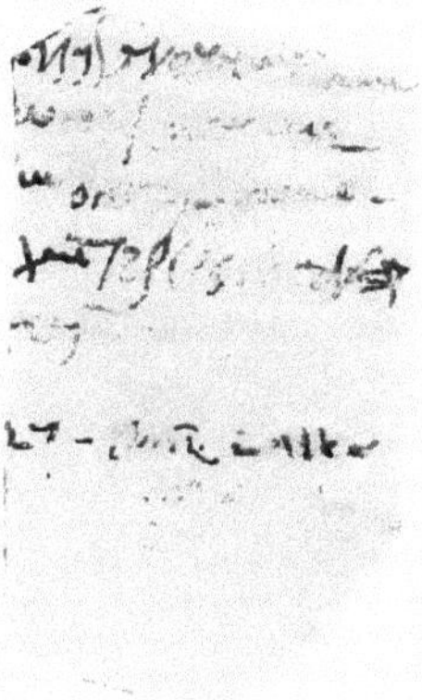

100

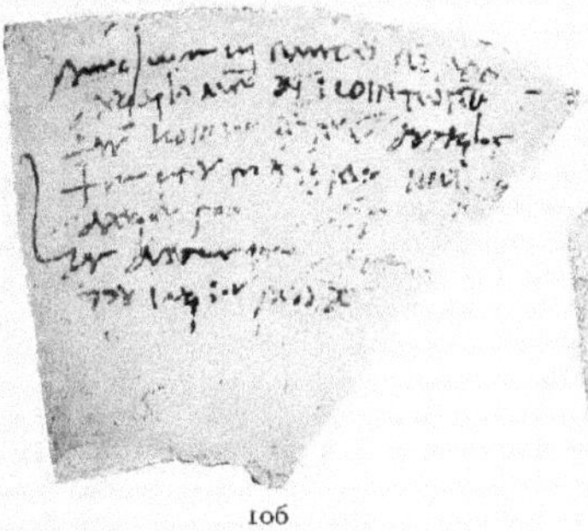

106

125

# INDEXES

## I. Emperors.

## II. Taxing-officers.

[Note:—The date of each reference is given in angular brackets: in the Ptolemaic list B.C. is to be understood; in the Roman, except where otherwise specified, A.D.]

### A. *Ptolemaic.*

#### (i) *Money-taxes.*

**Τραπεζῖται** (by districts).



#### (ii) *Taxes in kind.*

**Σιτολόγοι.**



*Signers of receipts* (by districts).



### B. *Roman.*

#### (i) *Money-taxes.*

**Πράκτορες ἀργυρικῶν** (by districts).

## III. Personal Names.

*Demotic texts.*



## IV. Geographical.

## V. Words.

# IV

# COPTIC TEXTS

| NOS. | | |
|---|---|---|
| 1–11. | LEGAL DOCUMENTS. | |
| 12–26. | TAX RECEIPTS. | |
| 27–42. | LETTERS. | |
| 43. | ACCOUNTS. | |
| 44. | LIST OF NAMES. | |
| 45. | SCHOOL EXERCISE. | 2 SAMUEL i. 1. |
| 46. | „ „ | ACTS ii. 9. |
| 47, 48. | „ „ | |

# INTRODUCTION

The Coptic Ostraca in this collection number about 90. They all come from Thebes and its neighbourhood, and they are very similar to others which have been published from the same locality. None of them offer material of any special interest and many are very fragmentary; hence it seemed to me that a selection of the better preserved examples would suffice. They may probably all be dated in the seventh and eighth centuries after Christ.

H. T.

## 1. Repayment of Loan.

⳨ ⲁⲛⲟ
ⲕ ⲉⲩⲇⲟ
ⲝⲓⲁ ϩⲓ
. . . . . ⲉⲓⲥϩ
*sic* ϩⲁⲓ ⲛ̄ⲙⲁⲛⲓϩⲁ
ϫⲁⲕⲁ ϫⲉⲉⲡⲉⲓ
ⲇⲏ ⲁⲓⲁⲡⲟⲇⲁⲥⲉ ⲛ̄
ⲛⲕⲁⲇⲟⲥ ⲛⲁⲕ ϣⲁⲡⲉ
ⲕⲗⲁⲩⲉ ϫⲉⲓⲭⲣⲉⲓⲱⲥⲧⲁ
ⲛⲁⲕ ⲧⲉⲛⲟⲩ ⲉⲛⲉⲗⲁⲩⲉ ⲛ̄ⲣ
ⲱⲙⲉ ⲉⲓ ⲉⲃⲟⲗ ⲉⲣⲟⲕ ⲉⲛⲉϩ
ⲟⲩⲇⲉ ⲁⲛⲟⲕ ⲟⲩⲇⲉ ϣⲏⲣ[ⲉ]
ⲉϥⲉⲓⲣⲉ ⲙ̄ⲡⲁⲡⲣⲟⲥⲟⲡⲟⲛ
ⲟⲩⲇⲉ ⲗⲁⲁⲩⲉ ⲛ̄ⲣⲱⲙⲉ ⲉ
ϥⲉⲛ ⲉⲣⲟⲓ ⲡⲉⲧⲛⲁⲉⲓ ⲉ
ⲃⲟⲗ ⲉⲣⲟⲕ ⲉϥⲛⲁϯⲟⲩ
ϩⲟⲗⲕ/ ⲛ̄ⲛⲟⲩⲃ ⲁⲛ
ⲟⲛ ⲉⲩⲇⲟⲝⲓⲁ ϯⲥⲧⲟ
ⲭⲉ ⲉϯⲃⲉⲗϫⲉ
ⲙⲛ̄ϩⲱⲣ ⲛ .
ⲉ . . ⲉϩⲁ . .
. .

*Verso* 1 . . . . . ⲟⲧⲕ
ll. 2–5 illegible.
6 [ⲙ]ⲁⲣⲧⲩⲣⲟⲥ

'I, Eudoxia, with (?) . . . . . write to Ma . . . . . to the effect that I have assigned (ἀποτάσσειν) to thee the casks (κάδος) towards your amount[1], for I am in debt to thee; now no man shall have a claim on thee for ever, neither I nor a child representing (*πρόσωπον*) me, nor any man belonging (l. ⲉϥⲛⲡ) to me. If one shall make a claim on thee, he[2] shall pay a gold solidus. I, Eudoxia, assent to this contract, together with (?) Hor . . . .'

[1] Lit. your something. ⲗⲁⲁⲩ is used elsewhere in begging petitions where the petitioner asks for 'something' meaning money; but I do not know of any other instance comparable to its use here. The form of acknowledgement is a common one.

[2] We should expect 'I,' but the reading is clear, and the same phrase is found in Turaieff, *Ostr.* no. 4 (*Bull. Ac. Sci. St.-Pétersb.* 1899, x, no. 5).

## 2. Bond for Repayment of Loan.

*sic*
[ⲁ]ⲛⲟⲕⲩⲣⲓⲁⲕⲟⲥ ⲡϣⲏⲣⲉ ⲙⲫⲓⲗⲟ
ⲑⲉⲟⲥ ⲉⲓⲥϩⲁⲓ̈ ⲛⲁⲓ̈ⲱⲛⲁⲥ ⲡϣⲏⲣⲉ ⲙⲡⲁⲅⲗ
ⲱⲣⲓⲟⲥ ϫⲉⲉⲡⲓⲇⲏ ⲁⲓ̈ⲡⲁⲣⲁⲕⲁⲗⲉⲓ ⲙ̄ⲙⲟⲕ
ⲁⲕⲣϩⲓⲧⲁϩⲏ ⲁⲕϫⲓ ⲟⲩⲡϣⲧⲣⲓⲙ/ ⲛ̄ⲛⲟⲩ
ⲃ̄ ⲛ̣ⲁ̣ ⲉⲧⲁⲭⲣⲓⲁ ⲧⲉⲛⲟⲩ ϯⲟ ⲛ̄ϩⲉⲧⲉⲙⲟⲥ ⲛ̄ⲧⲁ
ⲁⲡⲟⲗⲟⲅⲓⲍⲉ ⲛⲁⲕ ⲛⲧⲡϣⲧⲣⲓⲙⲏⲥⲉ ⲛⲉⲓ
ⲱⲧ ϩⲙⲡⲁⲱⲛⲉ ⲥⲉⲥⲟⲟⲩ ⲛ̄ⲣⲧⲟⲃ̄ⲛⲉ ⲛ
ⲧⲁⲧⲁⲗⲟⲟⲩ ⲉⲡⲉⲕⲏⲓ̈ ϩⲛⲧⲁϩⲏⲙⲉ
ⲉⲡⲉⲕⲱⲣϫ ⲁⲓ̈ⲥϩⲁⲓ̈ ⲛⲧⲓ̈ⲁⲥⲫⲁⲗⲓⲁ
ⲉⲥⲟⲣϫ ϩⲙⲙⲁ ⲛⲓⲙ ⲁⲛⲟⲕ ⲕ
ⲩⲣⲓⲁⲕⲟⲥ ϯⲥⲧⲉⲭⲉ ⲉⲧⲓⲁⲥⲫⲁ
ⲉⲅⲣ/ ⲥ̣ⲟ̣ⲩ ⲓⲉ ⲭⲓⲁϩⲕ ⲧⲉ̣ⲩⲧⲉⲣⲁⲥ
ⲡⲯⲙⲱ ⲡⲇⲓⲁⲕ/ ϯⲟ ⲙⲛⲧ
ⲣⲉ· ⲁⲛⲟⲕ ⲡⲁϩⲁⲙ ϯⲟ
ⲙⲛⲧⲣⲉ· ⲙⲏⲛⲁⲥ ⲡ
ⲉⲗⲁⲭ ⲙ̄ⲡⲣⲉⲥ ⲁⲓ
ⲥⲙⲛⲧ̄ⲥ̄ ϯⲟ ⲙ
ⲙⲛⲧⲣⲉ
+

'I, Cyriacus son of Philotheus, write to Jonas[1] son of Paglorios that, as I begged (παρακαλεῖν) of thee, thou didst come before me[2], thou didst bring me (l. ⲛⲁⲓ?) a half tremision of gold for my need. Now I am ready (ἕτοιμος) to repay (ἀπολογίζειν) thee the half tremision in barley in Payni[3]; they are six artabas and I will deliver them at your house at my (expense for) freight. For thy confirmation I have written this bond (ἀσφάλεια) which is valid everywhere.

'I, Cyriacus, assent to this bond (l. ⲁⲥⲫⲁⲗⲓⲁ). Written (ἐγράφη) on the 15th day of Khoiak, second (δευτέρας) (indiction-year).

'I, Psemo, the deacon, bear witness.

'I, Paham, bear witness.

'I, Menas, the humble (ἐλάχιστος) priest (πρεσβύτερος), have drawn it up (and) I bear witness. +'

[1] Written Aionas, but Jonas is meant. Cf. nos. 13, 14, 15.
[2] i.e. didst anticipate my request, or hastened to meet it. Cf. Crum, *Ostr.* no. 160 ⲁⲕⲣϩⲉⲧⲁϩⲉ in a similar context; also John xx. 4 (Boh.) ⲁϥϭⲟϫⲓ ⲁϥⲉⲣⲉⲧϩⲏ (var. l. ⲁϥⲉⲣϩⲓⲧϩⲏ) ⲙ̄ⲡⲉⲧⲣⲟⲥ = προέδραμεν τάχειον, praevenit Petrum.
[3] After the harvest and six months from the date of the contract.

## 3. Bond for Repayment of Loan.

. . . ⲉⲙⲫⲏⲩ̣ . . . . .
ⲡϣ]ⲏⲣ$^{ⲉ}$ ⲛⲓⲱϩⲁⲛⲛⲏⲥ ϩⲛϫⲏ
]ⲛⲏⲕ ⲛ̄ⲟⲩϩⲱⲗⲟⲕ/ . . . . .
ϯⲟ ⲛϩⲉⲧⲉ]ⲙⲟⲥ ⲛ̄ⲧⲁⲧⲁϥ ⲛⲏⲕ ⲛ . .
]ⲙⲁ ⲛ̄ϫⲏⲡⲉ ϩⲉⲛⲁϩⲓⲧ
]ⲙ̄ⲙⲁϩⲉ ⲛⲏⲕ ⲙ̄ⲙⲏⲥⲉ .
]ⲛⲁⲛⲧⲉⲗⲟⲅⲓⲁ
]ϯⲥⲧⲟⲓⲭⲟⲓ ⲉⲡⲉⲁⲥ
]ⲡ̣ⲟ̣ⲩ̣ϩ̣ⲁⲣ ⲙⲁⲣⲧⲉⲣⲱ
. . . ⲭ . . ⲙⲁⲣⲧⲩⲣⲱ
. . . . ⲙⲁⲣⲧⲩⲣⲱ

'[I, X. the son] of Pheu(?) [write to Y. the] son of John in Jê[me, I owe] thee a solidus [of gold and I am rea]dy to pay it thee on . . . . . .

[at thy] threshing-floor in Ahit (?) [and I will give so much] flax to thee for interest [without any] dispute. [I, . . . . . .] assent to this bond[1].'

Three witnesses also sign; the name of the first is probably Pouhar; those of the others are lost.

[1] This form of document is so familiar that ⲁⲥ . . . . here can hardly be other than the equivalent of ἀσφάλεια. The Coptic article is undoubtedly masculine however, which is either a scribe's blunder or some such form as ⲁⲥⲫⲁⲗⲓⲥⲙⲁ must have been used.

### 4. Loan of Corn.

+ ⲁⲛⲁⲛ ⲛ̄ⲕⲗⲏⲣⲟⲛⲟ[ⲙⲟⲥ]
ⲛ̄ⲓ̈ⲣⲁⲝ ⲉⲛⲥϩⲁⲓ̈ ⲛ̄ⲁϩⲁⲙ
ϫⲉⲉⲥ ⲟϩⲟⲛ ⲥⲟⲩⲟ ⲁⲕⲧⲓϥ [ⲛⲁⲛ]
ⲧⲉⲛⲟ ⲛ̄ϩⲉⲧⲟⲓⲙⲟⲥ ⲛ̄ⲕ . . . .
ⲛⲏⲕ ϩⲛ̄ⲡⲉⲛⲙⲉⲟ̣ . . . .
ⲧⲉⲥ ⲛⲁⲧⲗⲁ[ⲁⲩ ⲛ̄ . .
ⲫⲱⲗ̣ . . .

'We, the heirs of Hierax, write to Aham that behold (l. ⲉⲓⲥ) there is (l. ⲟⲩⲟⲛ) wheat that thou hast given [to us]. We are ready to [repay it] to thee in our . . . . without any dispute . . . .'

### 5. Agreement.

+ ⲁⲛⲟⲕ ⲡⲉⲧⲣⲟⲥ ⲛ̄ϩⲏⲗⲓ[ⲁⲥ ⲉⲓⲥϩⲁⲓ
ⲛ̄ⲧⲥⲩⲣⲟⲥ ⲑⲓⲙⲉ ⲓ̈ⲱ[
ⲡⲏⲗⲕ ⲉⲃⲟⲗ ⲛⲉ [
ⲇⲉ
ⲉⲣⲟⲡ̅ⲥ̅ ⲉϩⲟⲩⲛ̄ [
ⲛ̄ϩⲁ̣ⲙ ⲉⲧⲉⲧⲛ̄[
ϣ̣ⲁⲛⲣⲱⲙⲉ [
ⲧ︦ⲟⲩϩⲟⲗⲟⲕ/ [ⲛ̄ⲛⲟⲩⲃ̣ ⲛⲉ
ⲛϥ̅ϩⲱⲛ ⲉⲧ[ⲉⲓⲃⲉⲗϫⲉ . . .
ⲧⲥⲏⲃ̣ⲧⲑⲓⲟ
. . . ⲱ̣ⲙⲛ̄

'I, Peter (the son) of Eli[as, write] to Tsyros, the wife of Io . . . . [I] agree with thee . . . . but if thou[1] reckon it among . . . . . . . . . If any man [make a claim on thee, I will] pay a solidus [of gold to thee] and he shall submit to this [agreement] . . . .'

[1] Apparently the ⲣ (2nd sing. fem.) has been written over ⲕ (2nd sing. masc.).

## 6. Fragment of an Agreement for the Lease of Land.

+ . . . . . . .
ϫⲉ̣ⲡ̣ⲉ̣ⲥⲙ . . .
ⲡϫⲟ ⲉϩⲣⲁⲓ . . .
ⲛⲟⲩⲧⲓⲡⲉϥⲡⲁⲕⲧ̣ⲟ[ⲛ
ϫⲛⲗⲁⲁⲩ ⲛⲧ̣ⲁ̣ . . .
ⲕⲁⲥⲓⲟⲛ ϩⲛ̣ . . .
ⲉⲥⲱⲣϫ ⲁⲩ . . .
ⲛϩⲏⲧϥ ⲉⲟⲩⲣ . . .
ⲡ̣ⲓ̣ⲕⲟⲥⲙ . . .
ⲧⲟⲗⲟ̣ . . . .

'. . . . . . . . the seed . . . . and thou shalt pay its rent . . . . without any [dispute] . . . . kasion[1] in . . . . . [this agreement] being valid [in every place] in which it is. Written . . . . . Kosma (?) . . . . [P]tolo[my ?] . . . .'

[1] Perhaps part of a place-name.

## 7. Fragment of a Contract.

. . .
]ⲛ̄ⲛⲟ̣[. . . .
]ⲙ̄ⲫⲉⲧⲉⲙ̣[
]ϣⲉ ⲛϫⲛⲟϥ[
]ϣⲟⲩ ⲉϩⲣⲁï ⲛ̄ⲟⲩⲡ[

]ⲙⲟⲟⲩ ⲉϩⲣⲁⲓ̈: ⲁⲛⲟⲕ ϩ[
]ⲛⲁⲕ ϩⲙ̄ⲛⲁϩⲏⲙⲉ ⲛⲟⲩⲓ̣ϩ[
. . . ⲁⲙ]ⲫⲩⲃⲟⲗⲓⲁ ⲙⲛ̄ⲡ̄ⲥⲱⲥ ⲧⲁ[ . .
. . . ]ⲁⲕ: ⲉⲡϩⲏⲙ̄ϫ̄ ⲉⲡⲗⲱⲙ̄ⲥ̄
]ⲁ̣ⲧ̣ⲉⲣ̣ⲙⲟ̣ⲩ

The words in l. 8 'if vinegar, if impurity' suffice to show that this is a contract relating to the sale of wine (cf. Krall, *Kopt. Texte*, no. xxix, Crum, *Cat. Rylands Pap.* no. 206). The amount seems from l. 3 to have been '100 baskets'—for baskets of wine see Crum, *Ostr.* no. 160. The text is too fragmentary for reconstruction.

## 8. ATTESTATION OF AN AGREEMENT.

]ⲉ ⲛⲁⲙⲫⲓⲃ[ⲟⲗⲓⲁ . . .]ⲱⲣϫ[
]ⲧ̣ⲓ̣ⲥⲧⲟⲓ^χ ⲉⲣⲟⲥ ⲉⲥ̄ⲣ ⲙ́ ⲫ̣/ω ⲓⲅ ⲓⲛⲇ/ ⲋ + ⲁⲛⲟⲛ
ⲕⲩⲣⲓ]ⲁⲕⲟⲥ ⲡ̣ⲁ̣ⲫⲉⲩ ⲙⲛⲓⲁⲕⲱⲃ ⲥⲟⲗⲱⲙⲱⲛ ⲧⲛ
ⲟ ⲙ]ⲙⲛⲧⲣⲉ + ⲁⲑⲁⲛⲁⲥⲓⲟ ⲓⲱⲁⲛⲛⲏⲥ ϩⲙⲡⲁⲧⲟⲩ
ⲃⲁⲥⲧⲛ ⲁⲩⲉⲓⲧⲉⲓ ⲙⲟⲓ ⲁⲓⲥⲙⲛⲧⲉⲁⲥⲫⲁⲗⲉⲓⲁ ⲁⲓ
ⲥϩⲁⲓ ϩⲁⲛⲙⲛⲧⲣⲉⲉⲩ ϫⲉ̣ⲛ̣ⲥ̣ⲉⲛⲟⲓ ⲁⲛ ⲡⲣⲟⲥ
ⲧⲉⲩⲉⲧⲏ̣ⲥⲓⲥ +

'without question . . . . confirmed . . . . [I, X.] assent thereto. Written in the month of Phamenoth (?) 13, indiction 6. + We, [Cyri]acus (son of) Papheu (?) and Jacob (son of) Solomon, are witnesses + I, Athanasius (son of) John in Patoubasten[1], at their request have drawn up this bond, (and) I have written for the witnesses[2] who were unable to do so, at their request.'

[1] A place near Thebes containing a monastery. Cf. Crum, *Ostr.* no. 301, *Berl. Kopt. Urk.* no. 78.

[2] I do not know another instance of this plural form in Sahidic. ⲙⲉⲑⲣⲉⲩ occurs in Bohairic (cf. Peyron, *Lex. s. v.*).

## 9. Attestation of an Agreement.

]ⲉ̣ⲥϩ̣ⲣ̣ⲟⲩ
]ⲧⲣⲓⲧⲏ : ⲁϫⲛ̅
]ⲗⲟⲅⲓⲁ : ⲁⲛⲟⲕ ⲇⲁ
]ⲉ̣ⲧⲓⲃⲗϫⲉ ⲁⲩⲱ ⲥ̅ⲣ̅
]ⲉ̣ⲩⲛⲁϫⲓⲧ̅ⲥ̅ ⲉⲣⲟϥ
]ⲉⲱⲛ ⲙⲁⲣⲧⲩⲣⲱ
]ⲁ ⲙⲁⲣⲧⲩⲣⲱ

'. . . . . third [indiction ?]; without [any] dispute. I, Dav[id, assent] to this contract and it is [valid[1], wherever] it shall be taken. [I, Sim]eon bear witness, [I, Men]a (?) bear witness.'

[1] l. ⲥ̅ⲣ̅ϫⲟⲉⲓⲥ ϩⲙⲙⲁ ⲛⲓⲙ ⲉⲧⲉⲩⲛⲁϫⲓⲧ̅ⲥ̅ ⲉⲣⲟϥ.

## 10. Guarantee (?).

]ⲛⲁⲑⲁⲛ̣ⲁ̣[
]ⲧⲏ ⲅⲉⲱⲣⲅⲓⲟⲥ[
]ⲏ̣ⲣⲉ ⲙⲙⲱⲧⲛ[
]ⲥⲛⲁⲩ ⲛⲥ[
ⲛ̣ϩⲟⲗⲟⲕ/ ⲉϯϣ̅ⲡ̅ⲧⲱ[
ⲙⲙⲟⲟⲩ ϣⲁⲧⲉⲛ̣[
]ⲕⲣ̣ⲏⲥ̣ⲓ̣[

l. 5 seems to show that this is a guarantee of some sort; but the fragment is too slight for translation.

## 11. Injunction.

+
. . ⲡⲟⲟⲩ ⲛ̅
ϩ[ⲟⲟ]ⲩ ⲉⲧⲉⲥⲟⲩ
ⲙⲏⲧⲡⲉ ⲛ̅ⲉⲙⲭⲉⲓⲣ

A a

ⲉⲓⲥ ⲡⲗⲟⲅⲟⲥ ⲙ̄ⲡⲛⲟⲩⲧⲉ
ⲛ̄ⲧⲟⲟⲧⲉ ⲛ̄ⲧⲱ ⲕⲩⲣⲁ ⲛ̄ⲧⲉ
ϩⲙⲟⲟⲥ ⲛ̄ϩⲟⲩⲛ ⲙ̄ⲡⲏ̈ⲓ
ⲙ̄ⲙⲏⲛⲁ ⲡⲟⲩϣⲏⲣⲉ ϫⲉⲛ̄
ⲛⲉⲩϩⲉ ⲉⲣⲱ ϩⲛ̄ⲕⲉⲗⲁⲁⲩ
ⲛ̄ϩⲱⲃ ⲛ̄ⲡⲁⲣⲁⲡⲧⲱⲙⲁ ⲁⲗⲗⲁ
ⲛ̄ⲧⲉϩⲙⲟⲟⲥ ⲛ̄ϩⲟⲩⲛ ⲛ̄ⲡⲏ̈ⲓ
ⲛ̄ⲡⲟⲩϣⲏⲣⲉ ϩⲛ̄ⲟⲩⲕⲁⲧⲁⲥⲧⲁⲥⲓⲥ
[ⲡ]ⲣⲟⲥⲑⲉ ⲛⲧⲁⲥϩⲁⲓ̈ ϩⲟⲙⲟⲗⲟⲅⲓ
. . ⲱ ⲉⲧⲉⲛⲉⲉⲅⲅⲩⲏⲧⲏⲥⲛⲉ ϫⲉ
. . . . . . ϩⲛ̄ⲕⲉϩⲱⲃ ⲛ̄
. . . . . . . ⲕ̣ⲉ

'On this day which is the tenth of Mechir, lo, here is the word of God to thee [1], Cyra, that thou live in the house of Mena, thy son, so that thou be not found in any other offence, but that thou live in the house of thy son permanently (?) [2], according as I have written a declaration . . . being the guarantors . . . . . [3]'

[1] This formula occurs usually, as here, in an order to do a specified thing. Cf. Crum, *Cat. Rylands Pap.*, p. 79 n. and references there.
[2] Cf. *Cat. Gk. Pap. Brit. Mus.* iv, no. 1597.
[3] This refers to the class of document known as ὁμολογία ἐγγυητική whereby persons of standing made themselves liable to produce other persons at a given place and time for government purposes (taxation, enforced labour, &c.) under penalties. There are numerous examples in the *Brit. Mus. Cat. u. s.*, in Krall, *Kopt. Texte*, in Crum, *Cat. Rylands Pap.*, and elsewhere.

## **12.** Tax Receipt.

+ ⲁⲛⲟⲕ ⲙⲱⲩⲥⲏⲥ
ⲙⲛ̄ⲡⲁⲙⲟⲩⲧⲉ ⲉⲛⲥϩⲁⲓ̈ ⲙⲡⲁⲡⲛⲟⲩⲧⲉ
ⲡⲙⲟⲛⲁⲭⲟⲥ ⲁⲩⲱ ⲡ̄ⲡⲥⲟⲛ ϫⲉⲉⲡⲉⲓⲇⲉ
ⲁⲛϫⲛⲟⲩⲕ ⲉⲡⲇⲓⲙⲟⲥⲓ̈ⲟⲛ ⲛⲧⲉⲓⲣⲟⲙ̄ⲡⲉ
ⲧⲉⲓ̈ ⲉⲧⲉⲩⲟⲥⲉⲡⲉ ⲁⲩⲱ ⲁⲛϯⲉⲓ̈ϥ ⲧⲉ

ⲛⲟⲩ ϫⲓⲛⲡⲟⲟⲩ ⲛϩⲟⲟⲩ ⲉⲃⲟⲗ ϣⲁⲟⲩⲟⲉⲓ̈ϣ
ⲛⲓⲙ ⲉⲛ̄ⲉϩ ⲉⲛⲛⲏⲩ ⲉⲃⲟⲗ ⲉⲣⲟⲕ ⲛⲕⲉⲥⲟⲡ̄
ϩⲁⲧⲉⲓ̈ⲇ̣ⲓ̈ⲙⲟⲥⲓⲟⲛ ⲧⲛⲱ ⲛϩⲉⲧⲉⲙⲟⲥ ⲛ
ⲧⲛϯⲇⲓⲟⲩ ⲛϩⲟⲗⲟⲕ" ⲛⲧⲛϩⲱⲛ ⲁⲧⲉⲓ̈ⲃ̄ⲗⲁϫⲉ
ⲁⲛⲟⲛ ⲙⲱⲩⲥⲏⲥ ⲙⲛⲡⲁⲙⲟⲩⲧⲉ ⲧⲛⲥⲧⲉⲭⲉⲓ
ⲁⲧⲉⲓⲃ̄ⲗⲁϫⲉ ⲁⲛⲟⲕ ⲁⲃ̄ⲣⲁϩⲁⲙ ⲁⲩⲡⲁⲣⲁⲕⲁⲗⲉⲓ
ⲙⲟⲓ̈ ⲁⲓⲥⲁϩⲧⲉⲓⲃ̄ⲗⲁϫⲉ ⲧⲁϭⲓϫ ⲛⲥⲟⲩϫⲟⲩⲱⲧⲁ
ⲡⲉⲧⲣⲉ
ⲥⲉ ⲛϩⲧⲑⲱⲣ ⲛⲁϩⲣⲁⲓ̈ ⲛⲉⲗⲉⲥⲉⲩⲟⲥ ⲡⲗⲁϣⲁⲛⲉ
ⲙⲁⲣⲧⲩⲣⲱ ⳨ ⲅⲉⲣⲙⲁⲛⲟⲥ ⲛⲧⲩⲣⲱⲣ
ⲓ̈ⲱϩⲁⲛⲛⲏⲥ

on lower edge ⲇⲁⲛⲓⲏⲗ ⲡⲱⲓⲏ ⲙⲁⲣⲧⲩⲣⲱ

'I, Moses, together with Pamoute, we write to Papnoute the monk (μοναχός) and our brother, that we have applied to thee for the tax (δημόσιον)[1] of this year, which is a (year of?) loss and thou hast paid it now from to-day henceforth for ever. We will not come against thee again for this tax. We are ready to pay five solidi[2] and we adhere to this contract[3]. We, Moses and Pamoute, assent to this contract. I, Abraham, at their request (παρακαλεῖν) have written this contract (with) my own hand on the twenty-sixth day of Athyr in the presence of Eleseuos (son of) Peter[4], the *lashane*.

I bear witness ⳨ Germanus (son) of Tyror[5]

John

I bear witness, Daniel (son of) Poie[6].'

[1] This is a general term for all the public ordinary taxes, and included poll-tax, a land-tax, and δαπάνη (probably expenses of collection, &c.), all paid in money, and the corn-tax paid in kind. See H. I. Bell's *Introduction* to *Greek Papyri in the Brit. Mus.* vol. iv, p. xxv, 169.

[2] i.e. as a fine in case of the contract being broken.

[3] Lit. this potsherd (ostracon).

[4] Inserted above the line; the last two letters are not quite certain.

[5] Cf. proper name ⲧⲓⲣⲱⲣⲏ in *Berl. Kopt. Urk.* no. 119. It may however be a place-name—Germanus of Tyror; such a place is not known.

[6] For this form of tax receipt cf. *Berl. Kopt. Urk.* no. 80.

## 13. Tax Receipt.

\+ ⲉⲓⲥ ⲟⲩϩⲟⲗⲟⲕ/
ⲛⲁⲣⲓⲑⲙⲓⲁ ⲁϥⲉⲓ ⲉ
ⲧⲟⲟⲧ ϩⲓⲧⲟⲟⲧⲕ ⲛⲧⲟⲕ ⲓⲱ
ⲛⲁⲥ ⲡⲕ̣ⲉⲗⲗⲱⲣⲓⲟⲥ ϩⲁⲡⲉⲕⲇⲓⲁⲅⲣⲁⲫⲟⲛ
ϩⲓⲧⲡⲣⲱ^ⲧ ⲕⲁⲧⲁ^ⲃ ⲛ̣ϯ̣ⲣⲟⲙⲡⲉ
ⲡⲉⲛⲧⲉⲕⲁⲓⲇⲕⲧ/ *γι̣ αρ α̣ φω ι ινδ*
*πρω^τ* + ⲗⲟⲛⲅⲓⲛⲟ̣ ⲡⲁⲡⲉ
ϯⲥⲧⲟⲓⲭ/ ⲯⲁⲧⲉ ⲡⲓⲥⲣⲁ
ⲏⲗ ⲁϥⲁⲓⲧⲉⲓ ⲙⲙⲟⲓ
ⲁⲓⲥⲙⲛⲡⲉⲓⲉⲛⲧⲁⲅ/

'Behold a solidus by reckoning (*ἀρίθμια*)[1] has come to me from thee, Jonas (son of) Pkellorios[2], for thy poll-tax (*διάγραφον*)[3] for the first payment (*καταβολή*)[4] of this fifteenth year = 1 solidus, Phaophi[5] 10, first indiction[6]. + Longinus[7], the headman, I assent. I, Psate[8] (son of) Pisrael, at his request (*αἰτεῖν*) have drawn up this receipt (*ἐντάγιον*)[9].'

[1] The coinage at this time was debased, and, contrary to what one would expect, the government taxes seem to have been assessed at the debased value (*νομίσματα ἀρίθμια*), coins reckoned, i.e. by weight, not at the standard value (*νομ. ἐχόμενα*). The word ⲁⲣⲓⲑⲙⲓⲁ is often used alone for ϩⲟⲗⲟⲕⲟⲧⲧⲓⲛⲟⲥ ⲛ̄ⲁⲣ. = solidus. See on the whole subject the discussion by H. I. Bell in *Greek Pap. in the Brit. Mus.* iv, p. 84 seq.

[2] Cf. nos. 2, 14, 15. For the father's name cf. *P. Ox.* vi, no. 992 *πεκολάριος* (fifth cent.).

[3] Cf. H. I. Bell, *u. s.*, pp. 168–9.

[4] Ibid., p. 87. There were at this time, it seems, two payments in the year for poll-tax. There is no certain instance in the Coptic tax receipts of a third *καταβολή*; but the payment might be made by instalments. The amount of the tax is uncertain, probably about two solidi (see discussion, ibid., pp. 171–2).

[5] The abbreviation is written with the ω at the bottom of the tail of the φ. The expansion of the Greek summation is *γίνεται ἀρίθμιον α' φαῶφι ι' ἰνδικτιόνος πρώτης*.

[6] The tax was assessed in the last year of one indiction and paid—as is usually the case—in the following year. Occasionally assessment and payment are made in the same year; rarely two years intervene between them.

[7] Longinus, cf. no. 14. For the headman of a village see Crum, *Ostr.*, p. 23 (no. 308); there might be several headmen in a village at the same time.

[8] Known elsewhere as a scribe of papyri and ostraca.

[9] The ἐντάγιον was strictly the order for payment of taxes (H. I. Bell, *u.s.* xxvii), but as these documents state that the sum in question has been paid and at a date usually a year after the year of the tax, it is evident that they are really receipts.

This and the following tax receipts belong to a well-known group to which attention was first called by Dr. Crum in his *Coptic Ostraca* (1902), p. 36. They are mostly written on pieces of pottery covered with a white or yellowish slip and glazed. The handwriting is easily recognizable, but often difficult to decipher with certainty. Besides the specimens published by Crum, others are to be found in the *Koptische Urkunden* of the Berlin Museum, Bd. I, nos. 84–93; Cairo Mus. Cat. (Crum, *Copt. Monuments*), nos. 8266–91 and 8293, 8295, 8296; Hall, *Texts*, pp. 118, 122, 124–8, 147; Guidi, *Coptica* (1906), p. 16. Their date has been proved by Crum to be about the middle of the eighth century.

## 14. Tax Receipt.

+ ⲉⲓⲥ ⲟⲩϩⲟⲗⲟⲕ$^{ⲧ}$/

ⲛⲁⲣⲓⲑⲙⲓⲁ ⲁϥⲉⲓ ⲉⲧⲟⲟⲧ

ϩⲓⲧⲟⲟⲧⲕ ⲛⲧⲟⲕ ⲓⲱⲛⲁⲥ

ⲡⲁⲅⲉⲗⲗⲱⲣⲓⲟⲥ ϩⲁⲡⲉⲕⲇⲓⲁ

ⲅⲣⲁⲫⲟⲛ ϩⲓⲧⲉⲩⲧⲉⲣⲁ ⲕⲁⲧⲁⲃ$^{ⲗ}$

ⲛϯⲣⲟⲙⲡⲉ ⲡⲣⲱ γι ρ α

μ́ μ$^{χ}$ ις̣ ινδ/ β +

ⲗ̣ⲟⲛⲅⲓⲛⲟⲥ ⲡⲁⲡⲉ ϯⲥⲧⲟⲓ$^{χ}$/

[ⲯⲁⲧ]ⲏ ⲡⲓⲥⲣⲁⲏⲗ ⲁϥⲁⲓⲧⲉⲓ

[ⲁⲓⲥⲙⲛ]ⲡ̣ⲉⲓⲉⲛⲧⲁⲅ/

'Behold a solidus by reckoning has come to me from thee, Jonas (son of) Pagellorios, for thy poll-tax for the second payment of this first year = 1 solidus[1] in the month of Mechir 16, indiction 2. + I, Longinus the headman, assent. I, Psate (son of) Pisrael, at his request have drawn up this receipt.'

[1] ρ stands for ἀρ(ίθμια). Cf. no. 13, n. 1, and Crum, *Ostr.* no. 419, n. 2.

## 15. Tax Receipt.

+ ⲉⲓⲥ ⲟⲩⲧⲣⲓⲙ/ ⲛⲡⲓ
ⲑⲙⲓⲁ ⲁϥⲉⲓ ⲉⲧⲟⲟⲧ ϩⲓ
ⲧⲟⲟⲧⲕ ⲛⲧⲟⲕ ⲓⲱⲛⲁⲥ
ⲡⲁⲅⲉⲗⲗⲱⲣⲓⲟⲥ ϩⲁⲡⲉⲕ
ⲇⲓⲁⲅⲣⲁⲫⲟⲛ ϩⲓⲧⲡⲣⲱ$^{ⲧ}$
ⲕⲁⲧⲁⲃⲟⲗⲏ ⲛϯⲣⲟⲙⲡⲉ
ⲡⲣⲱ$^{ⲧ}$ *γι ρ γ̄ φρμ*$^{\theta}$
*ιθ ινδ/ πρω*$^{\tau}$ ⲇⲁⲛⲓⲏⲗ
ⲡⲁⲡⲏ ϯⲥⲧⲟⲓⲭ/
ⲯⲁⲧⲉ . . . . .
. ⲁⲓⲥ[ⲙⲛ]

'Behold a tremision by reckoning has come to me from thee, Jonas (son of) Pagellorios, for thy poll-tax for the first payment of this first year $=\frac{1}{3}$ solidus, Pharmuthi 19, first indiction. I, Daniel the headman, assent. I, Psate, . . . . have drawn it up.'

## 16. Tax Receipt.

+ ⲉⲓⲥ ⲟⲩϩⲟⲗⲟⲕ/
ⲛⲁⲣⲓⲑⲙⲓⲁ ⲁϥⲉⲓ ⲉ
ⲧⲟⲟⲧ ϩⲓⲧⲟⲟⲧⲕ ⲛⲧⲟⲕ
ⲅⲉⲱⲣⲅⲓⲟⲥ ⲟⲛⲟⲫⲣⲓⲱ̣ⲥ
ⲃⲓⲕⲧⲱⲣ ϩⲁⲡⲉⲕⲇⲓⲁⲅⲣⲁⲫⲟⲛ
ϩⲓⲧⲡⲣⲱ$^{ⲧ}$ ⲕⲁⲧⲁⲃⲟⲗⲏ ⲛ̣ϯⲣⲟⲙ
ⲡⲉ ⲡⲣⲱⲧⲏⲥ *ρ α αθυρ ιθ*
*ινδ/ β* ⲇⲁⲛⲓⲏⲗ ⲡⲁⲡⲏ ϯ
ⲥⲧⲟⲓ$^{ⲭ}$/ ⲯⲁⲧⲉ ⲡⲓⲥⲣⲁⲏⲗ
ⲁϥⲁⲓⲧⲉ̣ⲓ̣ ⲙ̣ⲙⲟⲓ ⲁⲓⲥⲙⲛ
ⲡⲉⲓⲉⲛⲧⲁⲅⲓ/

'Behold a solidus by reckoning has come to me from thee, George (son of) Onuphrios Victor[1], for thy poll-tax for the first payment of this first year = 1 sol., Athyr 19, indiction 2. I, Daniel the headman, assent. I, Psate (son of) Pisrael, at his request I have drawn up this receipt.'

[1] There is little doubt that these double names, in spite of the fact that the second is usually written in the nominative form, represent filiation. This is shown by instances where the filiation is fully written out. Cf. 'Jonas son of Paglorius' in no. 2 with the 'Jonas Paglorius' of nos. 13–15, or again, the second name is put in the genitive, 'Psate ⲡⲓⲥⲣⲁⲏⲗⲓⲟⲩ' of no. 18 compared with the usual 'Psate Pisrael.' In Coptic this is at this time expressed by ⲡ̄, e.g. ⲓⲱϩⲁⲛⲛⲏⲥ ⲡ̄ⲗⲁⲍⲁⲣⲟⲥ of *Berl. Kopt. Urk.* nos. 86, 87 is the same person as the John Lazarus of our no. 20. When, as in this case, we have three names, presumably George is the son of Onuphrios who was the son of Victor, and the latter must have been always known by his patronymic to distinguish him from some other contemporary Onuphrios.

## 17. Tax Receipt.

+ ⲉⲓⲥ ⲟⲩϩⲟⲗⲟⲕ/ ⲛ̄ⲁⲣⲓⲑ
ⲙⲁ ⲁϥⲉⲓ ⲉⲧⲟⲟⲧ ϩⲓⲧⲟⲟ
ⲧⲕ ⲛⲧⲟⲕ ⲑⲉⲟⲇⲱⲣⲟⲥ
ⲓⲱⲛⲁⲥ ϩⲓⲡⲉⲕⲇⲓⲁⲅⲣⲁⲫⲟⲛ (*sic*)
ϩⲓⲧⲡⲣⲱ^ⲧ ⲕⲁⲧⲁⲃⲟⲗⲏ ⲛ†ⲣⲟⲙⲡⲉ
ⲧⲣⲉⲓⲧⲏ *γι ρ α* ⲁⲡⲉⲓⲁ ⲡⲁⲡⲏ †
ⲥⲧⲟ^χ ⲯⲁⲧⲉ ⲡⲓⲥⲣⲁⲏⲗ ⲁϥⲁⲓⲧⲉⲓ
ⲙⲙⲟⲓ ⲁⲓⲥⲙⲛⲡⲉⲓⲉⲛⲧⲁⲅ/

'Behold a solidus by reckoning has come to me from thee, Theodore (son of) Jonas, for thy poll-tax for the first payment of this third year = 1 sol. I, Apeia[1] the headman, assent. I, Psate (son of) Pisrael, at his request have drawn up this receipt.'

[1] Cf. Abeia, Crum, *Ostr.* nos. 414, 415.

## 18. Tax Receipt.

. . . . . .
ⲟⲩⲕ [ⲛⲧⲟⲕ ⲃⲁ]
ⲥⲓⲗⲉ . . [. . . ϩⲁⲡⲉ]
ⲕⲁⲓⲁⲅⲣⲁⲫⲟⲛ ϩⲓⲧ̣[ⲡ]ⲣ̣[ⲱ^ⲧ]
ⲛⲕⲁⲧⲁⲃⲟⲩⲗⲏ ⲛⲧⲉⲓⲣⲟ
ⲙⲡⲉ ⲧⲉⲧⲁⲣⲧⲏ̣ *γι ρ α μ́ τοβι κη*
*ινδ/ δ* ⲙⲁⲑⲓⲁⲥ ⲡⲁⲡⲏ ϯⲥⲧⲟⲓⲭ/
ⲯⲁⲧⲏ ⲡⲓⲥⲣⲁⲏⲗⲓⲟⲩ ⲁϥⲁⲓⲧⲉⲓ
ⲙⲙⲟⲓ ⲁⲓⲥⲙⲛⲡⲉⲓⲉⲛ
ⲧⲁⲅⲓⲟⲛ +

'[Behold a solidus has come to me] from thee [Ba]sil (son of) . . . . . [for thy] poll-tax for the first (?)[1] payment of this fourth year = 1 sol. in the month of Tybi 28, indiction 4. I, Mathias the headman, assent. I, Psate son of Pisrael[2], at his request have drawn up this receipt.'

[1] There is little doubt of the reading.
[2] The reading is quite certain, as this receipt is written with unusual distinctness. The graecized form is curious. Cf. no. 16 n.

## 19. Tax Receipt.

+ ⲉⲓⲥⲥⲟⲩⲛⲓϣⲉ ⲛϩⲟⲗ
ⲟⲕ/ ⲛ̣ⲁ̣ⲣⲓⲑⲙⲓⲁ ⲁϥⲉⲓ ⲉⲧⲟ
ⲟⲩ ϩⲓⲧⲟⲟⲧⲕ ⲛⲧⲟⲕ
ⲁ̣ⲃ̣ⲣⲁⲙ . . . . . . .
. . . . . . . . . . . . .

ϩⲓⲧⲛⲡⲣⲱ^ⲧ ⲕⲁⲧⲁ^ⲃ
ⲧ̣ⲉ̣ⲣⲟⲙⲡⲉ ⲧⲉ
ⲧⲁⲣⲧⲉ̣ⲓ̣ ⲓ̣ⲛ̣ⲁ̣ⲕ̣/ *γι*
*αρ ∫ θωθ ι ινδ/ ε*
ⲁⲛⲁⲛⲓⲁⲥ
ⲡⲁⲡⲏ̣ †̣
ⲥⲧⲟⲓⲭ

'Behold a half-solidus by reckoning has come to me from thee, Abram (?) . . . . . . . . . for the first payment of this fourth year (of the) indiction (?) = ½ sol. Thoth 10, indiction 5. I, Ananias[1], the headman, assent.'

[1] Known also from Crum, *Ostr.* no. 428, and *Berl. Kopt. Urk.* no. 87.

## 20. Tax Receipt.

[+ ⲉⲓ]ⲥ ⲟⲩⲧⲣⲓⲙⲓⲥ ⲁϥⲉⲓ
[ⲉⲧⲟⲟⲧ] ϩⲓⲧⲟⲟⲧⲕ ⲯⲁⲧⲉ ⲯⲏⲥ
[ϩ̣ⲁⲛⲥⲧⲓⲭ]ⲟⲥ ⲛⲧⲓⲣⲟⲙⲡⲉ ⲉⲛⲛⲁ
[ⲧⲏⲥ *γι ν^ο γ̄*] *τριτον π^χ ιζ ινδ/ ι*
. . . . . . †ⲥ]ⲧⲟⲓⲭⲉ ⲓⲱⲁⲛⲛⲏⲥ
ⲁⲓⲥⲙⲛⲧϥ +

On reverse: ⲡⲥⲁⲧⲉ ⲯ/
ⲛ^ο ⲃ

'[Behold] a tremision has come [to me] from thee, Psate (son of) Pses, [for the] taxes[1] of this ninth year [= ⅓ sol.] one-third, Pachons 17, indiction 10. I . . . . . assent. I, John, have drawn it up.'

On the back: 'Psate (son of) P(ses)—2 solidi.'

[1] Cf. Crum, *Ostr.* no. 421. 'Imposts' generally, Bell, *Brit. Mus. Cat.* iv, p. 9 n.

## 21. Tax Receipt.

+ ⲉⲓⲥ ⲟⲩⲧⲣ[ⲓⲙ/]
ⲁϥⲉⲓ ⲉⲧⲟⲟⲧ ϩⲓ
ⲧⲟⲟⲧⲕ ⲛ̄ⲧⲟⲕ ⲉ
ⲛⲱⲭ ⲥⲧⲉⲫⲁⲛⲟⲥ
ϩⲁⲧⲇⲓⲟⲓⲕ/ ⲛⲧⲓⲣⲟⲙ
ⲡⲉ ⲉⲛⲛⲁⲧⲏⲥ γι/ ρ̣ ν̣̊ γ
τριτον $\overset{\theta}{\alpha}$ θ ινδ/ ι
ⲯⲥⲙⲱ̣ͭ ⲥⲧⲟⲓⲭ/ ⲓⲱ
ⲁⲛⲛⲏⲥ ⲗⲁⲍⲁⲣⲟⲥ
ⲁⲓⲥⲙⲛⲧϥ +

'Behold a tremision has come to me from thee, Enoch (son of) Stephanus, for the *διοίκησις*[1] of this ninth year = ⅓ sol. by reckoning[2], one-third, Athyr 19, indiction 10. I, Psmotos[3], assent. I, John (son of) Lazarus, have drawn it up.'

[1] Lit. a district for taxation purposes, the word came to mean 'tax,' as the taxes at this time were levied in a lump sum on each district, the local officials determining the distribution of each tax among the individuals liable.

[2] These signs are uncertain.

[3] As the cursive ψ and the cross are often indistinguishable, it would be possible to take the first sign as a cross and read the name ⲥⲙⲱⲧ(ⲟⲥ). But ⲯⲥⲙⲱⲧⲟⲥ occurs in *Berl. Kopt. Urk.* no. 87 (where John Lazarus is also the scribe). Cf. also Crum, *Brit. Mus. Cat.*, p. 451 πσαμμοον, Id., *Copt. Mon.* no. 8293 ⲯⲁⲙⲱ, and perhaps Hall, *Texts*, p. 52 ⲥⲉⲙⲱⲑⲉ.

## 22. Tax Receipt.

+ ⲉⲓⲥ ⲟⲩⲧⲣⲓⲙͨ . . .
ⲧⲟⲟⲧⲕ ⲛⲧⲟⲕ . . .
ⲧⲱⲣ ϩⲁ̣ⲡⲉⲕⲇⲓ . . .
ⲇⲏⲙⲟ̣ⲥ̣ⲉ . . . . . .
ⲧⲣ . . . . .

'Behold a tremision [has come to me] from thee . . . . [Vic]tor for thy poll-tax [among the][1] public taxes [of this] third (?) [year] . . .'

[1] l. ⲇⲓⲁⲅⲣⲁⲫⲟⲛ ϩⲛⲡⲇⲏⲙⲟⲥⲓⲟⲛ. Cf. Crum, *Ostr.* no. 416.

## 23. Tax Receipt.

. . . . .
. . ./ ⲁⲣ̣ ⲁⲕⲧⲓⲩ ⲛⲁⲓ
ⲛⲧⲟⲕ ⲥ̣ⲁ̣ⲃⲓⲛⲉ ϩⲁⲡⲉⲕ
ⲧⲉⲙⲱⲥⲉ ϩⲁⲡⲉⲕⲧⲉⲙⲱ̣
ⲥⲉ ϩⲁⲧⲉⲣⲟⲙⲡⲉ . . . ⲫⲁⲙⲑ
ⲡⲁⲡⲛⲟⲩⲧⲉ ⲥ̣ . . ⲭⲉ

'. . . . . . by reckoning, thou hast given them to me, thou Sabinus for thy tax (*δημόσιον*) for thy tax (*sic*) for this year . . . Phamenoth. I, Papnoute, assent.'

## 24. Tax Receipt.

+ ⲉⲓⲥ ⲣⲑ (/ ⲓⲁ ⲁⲕⲧⲁⲁⲩ
ⲛⲧⲟⲕ ⲡⲁϩⲁⲙ ⲡⲁⲩ
ⲗⲟⲥ ϩⲁⲡⲉⲕⲇⲓⲁⲅⲣⲁ
ⲫ ϩⲁⲇⲉⲕⲁⲧⲏⲥ ⲡⲁ
ⲭⲱⲛ ⲕⲑ ⲙⲁⲉⲛⲕⲛ
ⲟⲩ ⲧⲥⲧⲟⲓⲭⲉⲓ +
ⲇⲁⲇ̅ ⲥⲧⲟⲓⲭⲉ +

'Behold 11 carats[1] by reckoning, thou Paham (son of) Paulos hast paid them for thy poll-tax for the tenth (year), Pachons 29. I, Maenknou, assent. I, David, assent.'

[1] This is not quite the usual symbol for *κεράτιον* which is in one piece and of a reverse form, ϥ; it cannot however be anything else here. It approximates to a form occurring in *Cat. Gk. Pap. Brit. Mus.* iii, p. 59.

## 25. Tax Receipt.

+ ⲉⲓⲥ $\overset{θ}{ρ}$ \/ ⲓ̈ⲁ [ⲁ]ⲕⲧⲁⲁⲩ
ⲛⲧⲟⲕ ⲓⲥⲁⲕ ⲙⲱⲥⲏⲥ
ϩⲁⲡⲇⲓⲁⲅⲣⲁⲫ/ ⲉⲛⲇⲉⲕⲁ
ⲧⲏⲥ $\overset{χ/}{π}$ ⲑ ϯ ⲓⲁ ⲇ̄ⲁ̄ⲇ̄ ⲥⲧⲟⲓⲭⲉ
ⲭⲣⲓ$\overset{α}{ω}$

'Behold 11 carats by reckoning, thou Isaac (son of) Moses hast paid them for the poll-tax of the eleventh (year), Pachons 9, indiction (?) 11. I, David, assent . . . . .'

## 26. Tax Receipt (Pl. XI).

+ ⲉⲓⲥ ⲁ$\overset{θ}{ρ}$ $\overset{?}{α}$/ ⲕⲃ ⲁⲕ
ⲧⲁⲁϥ ⲛⲁⲓ ⲛ̄ⲧⲟⲕ
ⲁⲛⲇⲣⲉⲁⲥ ϩⲁⲡⲉⲕ
ⲇⲓⲁⲅⲣ/ ϩⲁⲧⲣⲓⲥⲕⲁⲓⲇⲉ
ⲕⲁⲧⲏⲥ ⲓⲛⲇ/ $\overset{υ}{τ}$ ⲉⲓ̇ⲥⲁⲕ
ⲥⲧⲟⲓⲭⲉ ⲙⲟⲓ +

'Behold 22 carats (?)[1] by reckoning, thou hast paid it me, thou Andrew for thy poll-tax for the thirteenth indiction, Tybi. I, Isaac, assent for myself (?).'

[1] The symbol, which looks like ⲁ and a diagonal abbreviation mark, can hardly, in view of the number 22 following, stand for anything but carats. The poll-tax was always paid in money. The same symbol occurs in *Berl. Kopt. Urk.* no. 89, where a tax receipt begins ⲉⲓⲥ ⲁ$\overset{θ}{ρ}$ ⲁ/ ⲕⲃ ϛ, &c., and probably in Hall, *Texts*, p. 128, no. 29684, where I should read the first line + ⲉⲓⲥ $\overset{θ}{ρ}$ ⲁ/ ⲕⲃ . . In our ostracon there is a mark above the line after ⲕⲃ which I cannot read.

### 27. Letter (limestone).

*Recto*
[ϣⲟⲣⲡ] ⲙⲉⲛ ⲧ̣ⲛ̣ϣⲓⲛⲉ ⲉ
[ⲣⲟⲕ?] ⲙⲛⲥⲱ[ⲥ] . . . . . . ⲙ
ⲙ̣ⲟ̣ⲕ̣ ϫⲉ̣ . . . . ϣ . . . . ⲧⲉⲓⲃⲗ
ϫⲉ ⲉⲕⲛⲁⲃⲱⲕ . . . . ϣⲁⲥⲁϥ̅ⲧ̅
ⲛ̅ⲡⲡⲣⲉⲥⲃ/ ⲁⲛⲇⲣⲉⲁⲥ ⲁ̣ⲛ̣ⲡⲁⲣⲁⲕ/
ⲙ̅ⲙⲟⲟⲩ ⲛ̅ⲅ̅ϫⲓⲟⲩϫ̣ . . ⲛ . . ⲧϥ
ⲉϩⲟⲩⲛ ⲛ̅ⲧⲟⲟⲧⲕ ⲙⲟⲉⲓⲛⲁϩ̣ ⲙⲛ̅
ⲡⲉⲓⲱ̅ ⲙ̅ⲡⲥⲁⲱⲟⲩ ϫⲉⲉⲛⲛⲁⲃⲱ̣[ⲕ]
ⲛ̅ⲧⲛϭⲛⲡϣⲓⲛⲉ ⲙⲡⲉⲛⲉⲓⲱⲧ
ⲁⲡⲁ ⲡⲉⲥⲩⲛⲑⲓⲟⲥ ⲡ̣ⲉ̣ⲡⲓⲥⲕ
. . . ⲉⲡⲇⲓⲁ̣

*Verso*
ⲙ̅ⲡⲣⲁⲙⲉⲗⲉⲓ ⲟⲩⲛ ⲛ
ⲉϣⲛ̅ⲉⲓⲙ̅ⲡⲉⲛϣϫⲉ · ⲧⲛ
ⲟⲩⲱϣ ⲉ̅ⲙⲟⲟ̅ϣⲉ ⲛ̅ⲣⲁⲥⲧⲉ ⲡϣⲟ̣
ⲣⲡ ⲛ̅ϩⲟⲟⲩ ⲛ̅ⲟⲩⲱϣ · ϣⲓⲛⲉ ⲟⲛ ⲛ
ⲥⲁⲥⲛⲧⲉ ⲛⲥⲁⲕⲓⲁ ⲉⲩⲁⲥⲉⲓⲱ̅ⲟⲩ
ⲛ̅ⲅ̅ⲛ̅ⲧⲟⲩ ⲉϩⲟⲩⲛ ⲛ̅ⲧⲟⲟⲧⲕ
+ ⲟⲩϫⲁⲓ̈ ⲧⲁⲁⲥ ⲙⲡⲉⲛⲥⲟⲛ
ⲁⲡⲁ ⲙⲓⲭⲁⲓ̈ⲁⲥ
ⲁⲛⲧⲱⲛⲓⲟⲥ ⲡⲉⲓⲉⲗⲁⲭ

(*Recto*). '[First of all] we greet [thee]; next [we instruct thee that on receipt of] this potsherd thou shalt go to the monastery (?)[1] of the priest Andrew. We begged them that thou mightest get a . . . and bear it in thy hand (as a) sign to them (?) with the father (?)[2] of the blessing, for we will go and visit our father Apa Pesynthius the bishop[3] . . . .

(*Verso*). 'Do not neglect then to read these (?) our words (?); we wish you to go to-morrow at daybreak . . . .; inquire further for two light sacks[4] and take them in thy hand. Salutation.

'To be given to our brother Apa Michaias (from) the humble Antonius.'

[1] ⲥⲁϥⲧ prob. = ⲥⲟⲃⲧ, 'wall,' also used for any enclosed place and of a monastery. Cf. Peyron, *s. v.*

[2] The meaning of this phrase is very uncertain.

[3] A bishop Pesynthius is named on a contemporary ostracon in Crum, *Ostr.* no. 25, and is identified by Crum with the well-known bishop of Coptos (ibid., p. 8, where references are given). The name however was common, and bishops were many in Egypt.

[4] Greek *σακκίον*; cf. ibid., no. 473, p. 44.

## 28. Letter.

. . . . . . . . . . . .
. ⲁⲩⲱ ⲙⲡⲉⲩⲗⲟ̣ ϣⲁⲩ . ⲗ . . ϯⲧⲁ
ⲙ̣ⲱ̣ ⲅⲁⲣ ⲛ̄ⲧⲉⲕⲙⲛ̄ⲧⲙⲁïϩⲏⲕⲉ
ⲉⲧⲃⲉϯⲭ̣ⲏⲣⲁ ϫⲉⲡ̣ⲁ̣ⲩ̣ⲗⲁ̣ ϫⲉϯ̣
ⲥⲟⲟⲩⲛ ⲧϣ . . . ⲙ̣ⲡ̣ⲉ̣ⲕ̣ϩⲏⲧ ϣⲱⲛ̣
ⲉ ⲙⲙⲟⲥ ⲙⲛ̄ⲛ[ⲉⲥ]ⲛⲉⲟⲣⲫⲁⲛⲟ̣
ⲥ ⲉⲡⲉϩ̣[ⲟⲩⲟ ⲁ]ⲥ̣ⲡⲁⲣⲁⲕⲁⲗⲉⲓ
ⲛ̄ⲧⲉⲕⲙⲛ̄ⲧⲉⲓⲱⲧ ϫⲉⲉϣⲱ
ⲡⲉ ⲟⲩⲏ̣ⲛⲟⲩ . . ⲣ̣̄ⲧⲕⲉⲡ ⲛ̄ⲧⲟⲟ
ⲧ̄ⲕ ⲛ̄ⲅ̄ϫⲓ ⲡⲙⲁⲃ ⲛ̄ϣⲉ ⲛ̄ϩ
ⲟⲙⲛ̄ⲧ ⲛ̄ⲧⲟⲟⲧⲟⲩ ⲛ̄ⲅ̄ⲧⲁⲁⲥ ⲛ
ⲁⲩ ϫⲉⲙⲡ̄ⲟⲩⲟⲉⲓⲛ ⲙ̄ⲙⲟⲟⲩ ⲉⲃ
ⲱⲕ ⲉⲕⲁⲉ ⲕⲁⲓⲅⲁⲣ ⲡⲛⲟⲩⲧⲉ ⲥⲟ
ⲟⲩⲛ ⲛ̄ⲧⲟⲥ ⲙⲛ̄ⲛⲉϣⲉⲣⲉ ⲉ̣ⲙ̄ⲛ̣
ⲧⲉⲟⲩⲟⲛ ⲙ̄ⲙⲟⲟⲩ ⲣ̄ϣⲱⲛⲉ
ⲧⲉⲩⲛⲁϩⲃ ⲕⲁⲓⲅⲁⲣ ϯⲥⲟⲟⲩ
ⲛ ϫⲉⲕⲙⲉⲉ ⲛ̄ⲛ̄ϩⲏⲕⲉ
ⲟⲩϫⲁï ϩⲙⲡϫⲟⲉⲓⲥ ⲧ̣
ⲁⲁⲥ ⲙ̄ⲡⲁⲙⲉⲣⲓⲧ

ⲡ̄ⲉⲓⲱⲧ ⲉⲧⲟⲩⲁⲁⲃ
ⲁⲡⲁ ⲓ̈ⲥⲁⲕ ϩⲓⲧⲛ̄
ⲓⲱⲁⲛⲛⲏⲥ ⲡ
ⲓⲉⲗⲁⲭ

'. . . . . . . . . for I give thy charitable (lordship) information concerning this widow, Paula (?)[1], as I know the . . . . of thy heart is in pain for her and her orphans. Besides she begged thy paternity that if . . . . . . . were assigned (ⲉⲛ ?) to thee, thou wouldest take three hundred pieces of copper therefrom and give it to them, as they have no light to go to Kae[2]. Indeed God knows that she and the children each one of them have pains in the neck, and I know that thou lovest the poor. Health in the Lord!

'To be given to my beloved holy father Apa Isaac from John the humble.'

[1] The name is very uncertain.
[2] Unknown place-name. What is meant by 'light' I do not know.

## 29. Letter.

ⲥⲡⲟⲩⲇⲁⲍⲉ ⲧⲛ̄ⲛⲟⲟⲩ ⲛ̄ⲕⲁⲙⲟⲩⲗ ⲛⲁⲓ̈ ⲛⲟ̣[ⲩ]
ϣⲏ ϭⲛ̄ⲧⲱⲛⲉ ⲧⲟⲩϣⲏ ⲛ̄ⲣⲟⲉⲓⲥ ⲁⲩ̣[ⲱ]
ⲧⲛ̄ⲛⲟⲟⲩ ⲟⲩⲕⲁⲙⲏⲗⲉ ⲛ̄ⲃⲱⲕ ⲧⲁⲣ . . .
ⲛⲁⲓ̈ ⲙ̄ⲡϣⲁⲩ ⲛⲥⲛⲁⲩ ⲛ̄ⲁⲅⲅⲏⲛ . . .
ⲁⲩⲱ ⲧⲛ̄ⲛⲟⲟⲩ ⲛ̄ϣⲟⲙ̄ⲧ ⲛ̄ⲑⲉⲛ[ⲉⲉⲧⲉ]
ϫⲉϯⲭⲣⲓⲁ ⲛⲁⲩ ⲥⲉϩⲓϩⲟⲩⲛ . . . . .
ϩⲓⲡⲗⲁⲕ ⲃⲁⲣⲱⲧ ⲟ̄ⲩ̄ⲛ̄ . . .
ⲧ̄ⲧⲃⲃⲉ ⲙⲏⲣ ⲉⲡⲟⲩ . . .
ⲙ̄ⲡⲥⲛⲁⲩ ⲟⲩϣⲟⲩ . .
ⲙ̄ⲡⲉⲛⲓⲡⲉ ⲛ̄ⲧ̣
ⲁⲩⲗⲕⲧ̣ⲧⲃ[ⲃⲉ ⲛ̄]
ⲟⲩⲕⲗ̄ⲗⲉ̣
. ⲁ̣ⲩ .

'Make haste to send me the camels by night. Find out where is the vigil[1] and send a draught (?)-camel[2] that I may get (? ⲧⲁⲣⲓϫⲓ) for myself the value of two jars . . . . . .[3], and send the keys of the monastery as I want them; they are inside . . . . . in (?) the brass vessel[4]. Open . . . . the box (which is) fastened on both [sides?] with iron; the box is closed (?) [with?] a bolt . . . .'

[1] i.e. of some church feast. [2] From ⲃⲱⲕ, 'servant'?

[3] Some short word, doubtless ⲏⲣⲡ, 'wine,' or ⲛⲉϩ, 'oil.'

[4] Cf. Crum, *Cat. Rylands Pap.*, p. 116 ⲟⲩⲕⲟⲩⲓ ⲗⲱⲕ ⲉⲛⲃⲁⲣⲟⲧ. Here perhaps ⲗⲁⲕ is rather short for ⲗⲁⲕⲟⲛ, for which see Crum, *Ostr.*, p. 41, note to no. 455.

## 30. Letter.

\+ ⲁⲛⲟⲕ ⲥⲁⲙⲟⲩⲏⲗ ⲛⲧ̓ⲗⲧ̣ⲁ ⲉⲓ
ⲥϩⲁⲓ̈ ⲙⲡⲓ̈ⲕⲱⲥ ⲡⲁⲣⲁ ϫⲉⲡⲓ
ϫⲓ ⲁⲓ̈ϫⲉ̣ⲟⲩⲃⲓⲗ ⲛϫⲉⲥⲭⲁⲣⲓ̣
ⲛⲏⲕ ⲉⲧⲃⲉⲛⲉⲓⲱⲧ ⲁⲕϫⲟⲟⲩ
ⲛⲁⲓ̈ ϫⲉⲡⲓ̈ϫⲏ ⲕⲟ̣ⲩⲁϣϥ ϫⲟⲟⲩ
ⲧⲓⲛⲟⲩ ϫⲟⲟⲩ ϫⲓⲟⲩ ⲛⲉⲣⲧⲁⲁⲃ ⲛ̣ⲁ̣ⲓ̣
ⲛⲧⲟⲟⲧϥ ⲛⲁⲃⲣⲁⲁⲙ ⲕⲁⲧⲉ . .
ϣⲁⲡⲁⲟⲩⲛⲓ̈ ⲛⲧⲁϯⲡϫⲓⲟⲩ ⲛⲣ
ⲧⲁⲁⲃ ⲛⲥⲟⲩⲟ ⲛⲏⲕ +
ⲟⲩϫⲁⲓ ϩⲙⲡϫⲟⲉⲓⲥ
ⲉⲡⲓⲡⲓ ⲁ

'I, Samuel of Telta (?), write to Pikos[1] Para (?) that when I sent (?) a basket[2] of *diskaria*[3] in return (?) for the barley (?)[4], thou didst send to me saying, "When thou wishest it, send." Now send five artabas (of wheat) to me (?) from Abraham . . . . until Payni and I will pay thee back the five artabas of wheat + Health in the Lord. Epiphi 1.'

[1] It is interesting to see this old name—derived from the worship of the bull-god Montu and very common in pagan times at Thebes—still surviving so late. I do not know of its occurrence elsewhere in Coptic times.

[2] ⲃⲓⲗ = ⲃⲓⲣ. It is a M.E. form. Cf. O. v. Lemm, *Apostelacten*, *Bull. Ac. Sci. St.-Pétersb.* x (1890), p. 103.

[3] The reading may have been ϫⲉⲥⲕⲁⲣⲓⲛ. Cf. Crum, *Cat. Rylands Pap.* pp. 82, 84 ϫⲓⲥⲕⲁⲣⲓⲛ, Krall, *Kopt. Texte*, ccxli. 44 ⲧ ⲥⲕⲁⲣⲓⲛ. Crum takes it = διϲκάριον, 'dish,' but it does not suit his context in either case, where it is named with wine, oil, and eatables; it must be something similar, perhaps a form of bread or biscuit so called from its circular shape.

[4] Translation uncertain. ⲉⲓⲱⲧ, 'barley,' is often used in the plural.

**31.** Letter (limestone).

*Recto* . . . ⲉⲡⲣⲟⲫⲁⲥⲓⲥ . . . . .
ⲡⲙⲉⲉⲩⲉ ⲉⲁⲓ̈ⲧⲛⲛⲟⲟ . . .
ⲛⲁⲡϩⲱⲥⲓⲱⲧⲁⲧⲟⲥ ⲛ̣
ⲙⲡⲧⲟϣ ⲛⲕⲏⲃⲧ ⲁⲡ[ⲁ
ⲃⲓⲕⲧⲱⲣ ⲉⲁϥⲡⲁⲣⲁⲥⲕ̣
ⲉⲩⲉ ⲙⲡⲉⲥⲉⲛⲧⲉ ⲉ
ⲧⲙⲙⲁⲩ ⲙⲡⲉⲕⲉⲡⲓⲧ
ⲣⲟⲡⲟⲥ ⲁⲩⲱ [ⲉⲁ]ϥ
ⲥϩⲁⲓ̈ ⲛⲟⲩⲉ̣[ⲡⲓⲥ]
ⲧⲟⲗⲏ ⲛ̣
ⲡⲉϩⲱⲃ ⲡ . .
ⲗⲉⲡⲟⲛ
. . . . . .

*Verso* . . . ϣ ⲧⲁⲣⲉⲧⲉⲧⲛ
. . . ⲧⲉⲧⲛⲉⲓⲙⲉ ⲉⲧ̣ⲥ̣ϭⲟⲙ
ⲛⲧⲉⲧⲛⲛⲟⲟⲩⲥ .
ⲁⲓ̈ ⲙⲡⲉⲣⲡⲟⲣⲕⲟⲩ ⲉ
ⲃⲟⲗ ϫⲉⲙⲁⲩϩⲧⲉⲓ ⲉⲛϩⲱ̣
ⲛⲥⲉϯⲉⲡⲧⲓⲙⲉ ⲙⲁⲗⲓ
ⲥⲧⲁ ⲁⲩⲡⲱⲗ̄ⲩ̄ ⲙⲛⲡⲉ
ϩⲱⲃ ⲡⲁⲓ̈ ⲡ̄ⲕⲟⲩⲥⲟⲛ
ϯⲁⲥⲡⲁⲍⲉ ⲙⲙⲱ̣
ⲧⲛ ⲟⲩϫⲁⲓ̈ ϩⲙ
ⲡϫⲟⲉⲓⲥ

The *recto* and *verso* seem to have no connexion, the former being addressed to a single person, the latter to more than one. Perhaps they are drafts of two letters.

*Recto.* '. . . . pretext . . . . remembrance. I sent . . . . the most holy[1] . . . . of the nome of Koptos, Apa Victor who had procured (?) (*παρασκευάζειν* ?) Pesynthius there to be thy guardian and [who had] written a letter to me (?) about (?) this matter; but (*λοιπόν*) . . .

*Verso.* 'that ye may . . . . and recognize its (fem.) validity and send it to me. Do not root them up (?), for they are not flourishing (?)[2] . . . . . . . They came to an agreement on this matter again. I greet you (pl.). Health in the Lord.'

[1] This is the usual epithet of a bishop ; the missing word—of about three letters —is probably ⲓⲱⲧ or ⲉ̅ⲡ̅ⲥ̅ (*ἐπίσκοπος*). If so, ⲧⲟϣ is probably 'diocese' here.
[2] For ⲙⲉⲩϩⲧⲁⲓ (?).

## 32. Letter (limestone).

ϣⲟⲣⲡ ⲙⲉ
ϯϣⲓⲛⲉⲣⲟⲕ ⲡϫⲟⲉⲓⲥ ⲉ
ⲥⲙⲟⲩ ⲉⲣⲟⲕ ⲙ̅ⲛ̅ⲡⲉⲧϣⲱ
ⲡⲉ ⲛⲏⲕ ⲧⲏⲣϥ ⲁⲣⲓ̈ⲧⲁⲅⲁ
ⲡⲏ ⲙⲡϩⲏⲕⲉ ⲁⲧⲣⲓ̈
ⲡϫⲟⲉⲓ̈ⲥ ⲥⲙⲟⲩ ⲉⲣⲟⲕ
ⲧⲁⲁⲥ ⲙ̅ⲡⲣⲉϥⲣ̅ϩⲟⲧⲉ
ⲁⲩⲱ ⲙⲁⲓ̈ⲛⲟⲩⲧⲉ

(Below, a rude drawing of a man begging.)
*Verso.* Drawings of trees, birds, and a vase, ⲛⲛⲓ ⲡϫⲟⲉⲓⲥ.

'In the first place I greet thee. May the Lord bless thee and all that belongs to thee. Be kind to the poor man Hatre (?). The Lord bless thee. To be given to the devout[1] and God-loving . . . .' (name omitted)[2].

[1] Cf. Crum, *Ostr.* no. 61 n.
[2] Apparently a pattern for a begging letter.

## 33. Letter.

. . ⲁⲥⲁ . . . .  
. . ⲉⲓ̈ⲛⲁⲓ . . .  
ⲁⲓϫⲛⲟⲩⲥ ϫⲉⲁⲗⲗⲁⲥⲉ ⲙ̄ⲡϩⲟⲗⲟⲕ/  
ⲛⲧⲟⲟⲧ ⲛⲧⲁⲧⲁⲗⲟ ⲙⲁϩⲉ ⲛⲁⲓ  
ⲉϣϫⲉⲡⲱⲕⲡⲉ ⲡϩⲟⲗⲟⲕ/ ⲉⲡⲟⲩ  
ϩⲟⲗⲟⲕ/ ⲉⲛⲁⲛⲟⲩϥ ⲛⲁⲓ ⲛⲧⲁ  
ϩⲛⲁⲕ ⲁⲥϫⲛⲟⲩⲓ ϫⲉϯⲡϩⲟⲗⲟⲕ  
ⲉϩⲣⲁⲓ ⲛⲧⲟⲟⲧ ⲛϥⲁⲗⲗⲁⲥⲉ  
. . . . ⲛϥⲧⲁⲁϥ ⲛⲁⲥ . ? .  
ⲕⲟⲩⲓ ⲙⲁϩⲉ ⲛⲁⲓ ⲛϩⲟⲩⲟ

An involved and obscure communication relating to a piece of money. The translation seems to be as follows:—

'. . . . I asked her, saying, Exchange (*ἀλλάσσειν*) the solidus for (?) me, that I may buy (?) me some flax. If the solidus is thine (masc.), credit a good solidus to me and I will please thee (l. ⲣ̄ϩⲛⲁⲕ). She asked me, saying, Give up the solidus to (?) me and let him exchange it (?) and let him give it to her. Give (?) a little flax to me besides.'

## 34. Letter or Memorandum.

ⲛⲉⲃ . . .  
ⲗⲁⲩ ϩⲛⲁϩ . . .  
ⲙⲁⲃ̄ ⲛⲣⲧⲁⲃ ⲡ̄ⲛ . . .  
ⲛⲁⲣϣⲓ̈ⲛ ⲟⲩϩⲟ ⲛⲁⲣϣ . . .  
ⲕⲁⲙⲟⲩⲗ ⲟⲩϩⲟ ⲛⲟⲣⲝ . .  
ⲛⲁⲣⲧⲁⲃ ⲛⲁⲛⲁⲣⲕⲁⲧⲏ[ⲥ] . . .  
ⲙⲡⲗⲟⲩ ϣⲏⲙ ⲉⲧⲣⲟⲉⲓⲥ . . . .  
ⲛⲁⲓ̈ ⲧⲏⲣⲟⲩ ⲥⲉⲉⲓ̈ⲣⲉ ⲙ . . . .  
ⲟⲩⲧⲁϩ ⲛⲁⲡⲉⲕⲱⲧ . . .  
ⲙⲡϩⲁⲓ̈

'. . . . . .[1], thirty artabas of . . . . . lentils, a *ho*-measure[2] of lentils . . . . camels (?)[3], a *ho*-measure of *orax*[4], . . . . artabas belonging to the workmen (ἐργάτης) . . . . . of the small boy (ⲁⲗⲟⲩ) who watches . . . . all these make . . . . . . . fruit belonging to the builder . . . . of the farm.'

[1] There are several possible restorations for the first two lines, but the result must be guess work.
[2] Cf. Crum, *Ostr.* no. 309 n.
[3] Or the proper name Kamoul.
[4] Probably a species of vetch.

## 35. Letter.

. . . . . . . . . . .
. . ⲛⲛⲧⲟⲩ ⲉⲡⲉⲩ
ⲙⲁ ⲙⲉⲧⲁ ⲕⲁⲗⲟⲩ
ϩⲓⲧⲛⲛⲉⲕϣⲗⲏⲗ
ⲧⲛ̄ⲛⲁⲕⲁⲧⲟⲧⲛ
ⲉⲃⲟⲗ ⲁⲛ ϣⲁⲛⲧⲛ
ⲉⲓ̈ ⲛ̄ⲧⲛⲡⲣⲟⲥⲕ/
ⲛⲁⲕ ⲧⲁⲁⲥ ⲙ̄ⲡⲉⲓ̈
ⲉⲓⲱⲧ ⲉⲧⲟⲩⲁⲃ
ϩⲓⲧⲛ ⲡϫⲟⲩ
ϫⲁⲓ̈ . . .

'. . . . . . if[1] they are brought to their home (lit. place) happily[2] through thy prayers, we will not cease until we come and salute (προσκυνεῖν) thee[3]. To be given to this holy father from Pjoujai . . . .'

[1] l. [ⲉⲩϣⲁ]ⲛⲛ̄ⲧⲟⲩ.
[2] μετὰ καλοῦ. Cf. *A. Z.* xxii (1884), p. 147, Krall, *Kopt. Texte*, p. 81, Crum, *Ostr.*, p. 107 n., and *Brit. Mus. Cat.*, p. 490.
[3] The meaning is, 'if they return home in safety through thy prayers, we will come and salute thee as soon as possible.'

## 36. Letter.

ⲡϫⲟⲓ̈ⲥ
ⲉϥⲉⲥⲙⲟⲩ
ⲉⲣⲟⲕ ⲙ̄ⲛ̄
ⲛⲉⲕⲧⲃⲛⲟⲟⲩⲉ
ⲁⲣⲓⲧⲁⲅⲁⲡⲏ ⲛ̄ⲅ̄
ⲣⲡⲛ̄ⲁ̄ ⲛ̄ⲅ̄ϫⲟⲟⲩ ⲧⲁ
ⲕⲟⲗⲧⲉ ⲛ̄ⲅ̄ϫⲟⲟⲥ ⲛ . . . .
ⲙ̄ⲡⲁϣⲉⲓⲟⲩ̣ⲛ . . . . .
. . ⲓ̈ⲕⲉⲁⲕⲁⲛⲧ . . .
. . . . ⲥⲙⲟⲩ ⲉ̣ⲣ . . . .

'The Lord shall bless thee and thy cattle. Kindly have pity and send the wagon and tell . . . .'

## 37. Letter.

+
ⲧⲁⲁⲥ ⲙ̄ⲡⲁⲥⲟⲛ
[ⲁⲡ]ⲁⲕⲩⲣⲓ ϩⲓⲧⲛⲁⲍ
[ϯⲟ]ⲩ̣ⲱϣ ⲛⲧⲉⲩⲛⲟⲩ ⲉⲧⲕ
[ϣⲡϯⲃ]ⲗϫⲉ ⲁⲡⲟⲗⲟⲅⲓⲍⲉ
[ⲙⲡⲁ]ⲡⲉ ⲉⲧⲛⲁϯⲃⲗϫⲉ ⲛⲁⲕ
[ⲛⲧⲉ]ⲡⲛⲟⲩⲧⲉ ⲥⲙⲟⲩ ⲛⲉⲕⲛ .
. . . . . ⲙⲡⲉⲕⲉ̣ . . . .

'Deliver this to Brother Apakyre from Az[1]. [I] wish as soon as thou [receivest this] potsherd, pay the headman (?), who will give thee a receipt (lit. potsherd), and may the Lord bless thy . . . . . .'

[1] Az must be an abbreviation, probably for Azarias, a name which is found in Hall, *Texts*, and Crum, *Ostr.*

## 38. Letter.

. . . . . . . . . . . . ⲣⲁⲉ
. . . . . . . . . . ⲛⲟⲩϭ ⲁⲣⲟⲓ
. . . . . . ⲁⲓⲟⲩⲁϩϥ ⲛⲉⲟⲩⲱ
. . . ⲁⲗⲁⲕⲱⲧⲥⲉ
. . . ⲟⲩϩⲁⲗⲁⲕ/ ⲛⲁï ⲛⲉϥ
. . . ⲧϥ ⲕⲉⲓ ⲧⲁϥⲉⲓ ⲁⲕⲏⲙⲏ
. . . ϣⲉ ⲁⲣⲟⲓ ✝

This is a fragment of a letter in the Achmimic dialect. It refers to money matters, as the word for 'solidus' occurs twice.

## 39. Letter.

✝ ⲡⲁⲡⲛⲟⲩⲧⲉ ⲉϥⲥϩⲁⲓ . . . .
ⲛⲉ ⲉⲡⲉϥⲙⲉⲣⲓⲧ ⲛ̄ⲥ[ⲟⲛ . . .
ⲉⲛⲱⲭ ϫⲉⲉⲓⲛⲓⲧⲉ . . . . . .
ⲟⲩⲁ ⲛⲧⲏⲓϩⲉ ⲛⲉⲧ . . . . . .
ⲡⲉ ⲁⲩⲁⲛ ⲙⲙⲁⲩ ϫⲁⲩ . . .
ⲛⲁ ⲉⲓⲥⲙⲛⲟⲩⲁⲁϥ ⲙⲙ̣ . . .
ⲕ̣ⲁⲓⲅⲁⲣ ⲕⲥⲟⲟⲩⲛ ϫⲉ . . . .
. . ⲣⲏⲥ ⲛ̣ⲁⲕ ⲛⲧⲟϥ ⲓⲉⲣ . . .
. . . . . . ⲥϩⲁⲓ ✝ ⲙⲏ
. . . . . . ⲛⲛ . . . .

A letter written by Papnoute to his dear brother Enoch. The missing ends of the lines render the meaning obscure.

## 40. Letter.

. . . . . .
ⲣⲱⲙⲉ . . .
ⲥⲙⲁ . . . .
ⲙⲡⲛⲟⲩ[ⲧⲉ . . . .
ⲧⲁⲁⲥ ⲙⲡⲁⲙⲉⲣⲓ[ⲧ]
ⲛⲥⲟⲛ̄ ⲡⲁⲩⲗⲟⲥ
ⲡⲗⲁϣⲁⲛⲉ
ϩⲓⲧⲛ ⲁⲁⲣ
ⲱⲛ
ⲡⲉⲓⲉ
[ⲗ]ⲁ[ⲭ]

End of a letter addressed by one Aaron to his dear brother Paul the *lashane* (of Jême), whom we know also from *Berl. Kopt. Urk.* no. 71, and Crum, *Ostr.* nos. 120, Ad. 26.

## 41. Letter.

. . . . . . ⲥ
. . . . . . . ⲁⲣⲓⲧⲁ
[ⲧ̄ⲁⲡⲏ ⲛⲧ̄]ⲃⲓⲕⲁⲙⲟⲩⲗ
[ϩⲁⲡⲉ]ⲕϩⲟⲧⲟⲣ ⲛ̄ⲧ̄ⲧⲁ
[ⲗ]ⲱⲟⲩ ⲧⲁⲣⲉⲡϫⲟⲓ̈ⲥ
ⲥⲙⲟⲩ ⲉⲣⲟⲕ ⲧⲁⲁⲥ
ⲙ̄ⲡⲁⲥⲟⲛ ⲡϫⲟⲩⲓ̈
ϩⲓⲧⲛⲁⲛⲁⲣⲉ
ⲁⲥ ⲡⲓⲉⲗⲁ
ⲭ, ⳨

‘. . . . . . kindly take camels according to thy judgement and load them[1]. May the Lord bless thee. To be given to my brother Pjoui from Andrew the humble.’

[1] i.e. some goods referred to in the lost portion of the letter.

## 42. Letter.

. . . . . . . . . . .
ⲟⲩⲛ . . . ⲡⲛⲟⲩⲧⲉ ⲥⲟⲟⲩⲛ ϯⲟ
ⲛϩⲉⲧⲉⲙⲟⲥ ⲛⲧⲁⲧⲓⲟⲩⲛⲁⲕ
. . ⲧⲁⲡⲟⲃⲁⲛϫⲉⲙⲛⲛ
ⲉ̣ⲩ̣ⲣⲏⲩ ⲧⲁⲧⲓ ⲟⲩⲃ̣ⲗ̣ϫⲉ
ⲙⲛⲛⲕⲏϣⲉⲛⲧ̣ⲁⲓ ϩⲓ
ϩⲱⲃ ⲛⲓⲙ ⲧⲉⲛⲟⲩ
ⲧⲉⲣⲩⲁⲕⲱϣ ⲉ̣
ⲧⲉⲃⲉⲗϫⲉ ⲥϩ
ⲁⲓ ⲛⲁⲓ ϩⲱⲧ
ⲛⲧⲉⲕϫⲓ
ϫ +

‘. . . . .[1] God knows I am ready to give (?) them (l. ⲧⲁⲁⲩ ?) to thee . . . . . and I will give a receipt (lit. potsherd) with the other . . . . in all things. Now when (?) thou hast read this potsherd, write to me also with thy hand.’

[1] A few letters only remain of the first five lines.

## 43. Accounts (limestone).

*Recto* ⲡⲗⲟⲅ/ ⲛⲛϣⲁϣⲟⲩ
ⲛⲧⲁⲛⲧⲁⲗⲟⲟⲩ ⲉⲃⲟⲗ
ⲉⲧⲣⲉⲛϫⲓⲧⲉⲩⲧⲩⲙⲏ ⲛⲏⲣⲡ
ϩⲓⲧⲛⲓ̈ⲥⲁⲕ ⲙⲡⲉⲓⲗⲟⲩ
ⲁϯ ⲁϯ ⲣ̅ ϩⲓⲧⲛⲕⲟⲗⲟϫⲉ
ⲁϯ ⲁϯ ⲣⲛ ϩⲓⲧⲛⲥⲁⲣⲁ
ⲡⲓⲱⲛ ⲫⲁⲙ ⲁϯ ⲁϯ ⲛ̅
ϩⲓⲧⲛⲁⲅⲛⲁⲧⲱ ⲫⲁⲙ̣
[ⲁϯ] ⲁϯ ⲗ̅ ϩⲓⲧⲛⲁⲡⲁ
ⲃⲓⲕⲧⲱⲣ ⲁϯ ⲁϯ ⲗ

*Verso* ϩⲟⲓⲧⲉ ⲛ . . . .
ⲣϣⲱⲱⲛ ⲇ̅ . .
ⲗⲟⲧⲓⲍ ⲛ̅ϭ̣ⲟ̣ⲓ̣ⲗⲉ . .
ⲙⲁϫⲕⲉ ⲇ̅ ⲙⲁⲡⲡⲁ .

(*Recto*). 'List of the jars which we have delivered, so that we may receive their price of the wine: from Isaac (son of) Peilou . .[1] 100; from Colluthus . . 150; from Sarapion the carpenter (?) . . 50; from Agnato[2] the carpenter (?) . . 30; from Apa Victor . . 30.

(*Verso*). Dresses . . .; 4 cloaks; guests' (?) blankets . .; 4 . . .[3], . . napkins.'

[1] The measure is represented by ⲁⲓ or ⲁⲣ followed by an abbreviation mark and always repeated, perhaps to mark the plural. What word it represents I do not know.

[2] Cf. Hall, *Texts*, pl. 15 ⲁⲕⲛⲁⲧⲱⲛ.

[3] Cf. ⲙⲓϫⲕⲉ Crum, *Ostr.* no. 465, meaning unknown.

## 44. List of Names.

. . . . . ⲫⲟⲣⲟⲥ . . .
. . ⲓⲉⲣⲉⲙⲓⲁⲥ . . .
ⲍ ⲥⲉⲩⲏⲣⲟⲥ ⲡ . . .
ⲏ ⲅⲉⲟⲣ$^{ⲥ}$ ⲗⲟⲩⲕ̣ . . .
ⲑ ⲓⲱ . . . .
. . ⲙⲏⲛⲁ ⲉⲕⲟⲛⲟ . .
. . ⲡⲁⲡⲛⲟⲩ$^{ⲑ}$ ⲉ . . .
. . . ⲁ
ⲓⲱⲗⲁ . . .

'. . . . phoros . .; [6] Jeremias . . .; 7 Severus the . . .; 8 George (son of) Luke; 9 Jo . . . .; . . Mena, oeconomus[1]; . . Papnoute . . .; . . .; Iola . . .'

[1] This suggests a list of monastery officials.

## 45. Biblical. 2 Sam. i. 1 (limestone).

ⲁⲥϣⲱⲡⲉ ⲇⲉ
[ⲙ]ⲛ̣ⲛⲥⲁⲧⲣⲉ
[ⲥⲁⲟ]ⲩⲗ ⲙⲟⲩ ⲇⲁ
[ⲩⲉⲓⲇ] ⲁϥⲕⲟⲧϥ
[ⲁϥϩ]ⲓⲟⲩⲉ ⲛ[ⲥⲁ
[ⲡ]ⲁⲡⲁⲗⲕ̣[
[ⲁⲩ]ⲱ ⲁ . . . .
. .]ϩ̣[

This ostracon is written in very rude uncials and is evidently a school exercise. In l. 6 I think there is no doubt ⲡ and not ⲙ was written. This verse has been printed by Maspero in *Miss. Arch. fr.* VI as above (except that David is contracted in the usual way) down to ϩⲓⲟⲩⲉ, after which he continues ⲛⲥⲁ ⲡⲁⲙⲁⲗⲉⲕ ⲁⲩⲱ ⲇⲁⲇ ⲁϥϩⲙⲟⲟⲥ ϩⲛⲥⲉⲕⲉⲗⲁⲕ ⲛϩⲟⲟⲩ ⲥⲛⲁⲩ.

### 46. Biblical. Acts ii. 9.

ⲓ̅ⲥ̅ ⲭ̅ⲥ̅ ⲙⲡⲁ[ⲣⲑⲟⲥ ⲙⲛⲙ]
ⲏⲇⲟⲥ. ⲙⲛⲁ[ⲓⲗⲁⲙⲓⲧⲏⲥ]
ⲁⲩⲱ ⲛⲉⲧⲟⲩ̣[ⲏϩ ϩⲛⲧⲙⲉⲥⲟ]
ⲡⲟⲧⲁⲙⲓⲁ ϯ[ⲟⲩⲇⲁⲓⲁ ⲙⲛⲧ]
ⲕⲁⲡ̣ⲡ̣ⲁⲇ̣[ⲟⲕⲓⲁ]

A school exercise in uncials.

Printed by Woide from two MSS., one the same as above, the other with the following variations in spelling, ⲙⲏⲧⲟⲥ, ⲏⲗⲁⲙⲓⲧⲏⲥ, ⲙⲉⲥⲟⲡⲟⲇⲁⲙⲓⲁ.

### 47. Religious (limestone).

+ ⲓ̅ⲥ̅ ⲭ̅ⲥ̅
ⲁⲗⲉⲓⲗⲟⲩⲓⲁ̣
ⲁⲗⲗⲉⲓⲗⲟⲩⲓⲁ
ⲁⲗⲗⲉⲓⲗⲟⲩϊⲁ
ⲡⲱⲛⲁϩ
[ϣ]ⲁⲉ[ⲛⲉϩ]

'Jesus Christ. Alleluia. O Eternal Life.'
A school exercise.

## 48. List of Words.

| | | | |
|---|---|---|---|
| *Recto* | ⲃⲟ ⲙⲟⲥ | *Verso* | ⲙⲁⲣⲕⲟⲥ |
| | ⲃⲁ ⲃ̣ⲁⲥ | | ⲙⲏⲛⲁ |
| | ⲃⲓ̈ ⲟⲥ | | ⲙⲏⲉ̣ⲟⲇⲟⲥ |
| | ⲅⲓ̈ⲅ ⲅⲁⲥ | | ⲙⲁⲧⲭⲟ |
| | ⲅⲁ ⲙⲟⲥ | | |
| | ⲅⲁ ⲧⲟⲥ | | |
| | ⲅⲉ ⲇⲱⲛ | | |
| | ⲇⲁ ⲩⲉⲓⲧ | | |
| | ⲇⲟ ⲣⲟⲛ | | |
| | ⲇ . ⲣ . . | | |
| | . ⲏ . . . | | |

A school exercise. On the *recto* each word is divided by a space into two syllables, and there are remains of a second column divided from the first by a line; there remain however only the initial letters of three words beginning with ϩ followed by two with ⲛ.

# INDEX OF NAMES

(The numbers are those of the Ostraca.)

## Persons.

## Officials, etc.



## Place Names.

Lightning Source UK Ltd.
Milton Keynes UK
UKHW010747311219
356164UK00002B/182/P

9 789353 952297